WOULD YOU LIKE MATHS WITH THAT?

Improving numeracy in the primary years

THELMA PERSO

© 2023 Thelma Perso

All rights reserved. No part of this book may be reproduced or transmitted in any form or by any means, electronic or mechanical, including photocopying, recording or by any information storage and retrieval system, without prior permission in writing from the publisher.

Published in 2023 by Amba Press, Melbourne, Australia.
www.ambapress.com.au

Previously published in 2021 by Hawker Brownlow Education.
This edition replaces all previous editions.

ISBN: 9781923116122 (pbk)
ISBN: 9781923116139 (ebk)

A catalogue record for this book is available from the National Library of Australia.

Dedication

Dedicated to my husband, Ross Prout, who has supported my career, travelling across the world and to many parts of Australia with me in this pursuit. Ross is also a great critic of my work.

Acknowledgements

Special thanks to all the people who have been influential throughout my career in mathematics and numeracy: Bob McCreddin, Alan Cadby, Ron Newberry, John Malone, Barry Bastow, Will Morony, Robyn Jorgensen, Denise Neal, Glenys Reid and the many other colleagues who inspired me to strive for excellence.

Thanks to Rod McNeill and the teachers at Mundaring Christian College who worked hard to learn and contribute as members of professional learning teams and helped their students to learn about concepts rather than merely calculations.

And finally, a word of gratitude to my editor, Jacinta Dietrich, for her patience, insight and expertise in reading and suggesting improvements to the text, and to Olivia Tolich from Hawker Brownlow Education for her support and encouragement in the early stages of development.

Table of contents

About the author xi
List of figures xiii
List of tables xv

Introduction 1
        About this book 2

Chapter 1 Numeracy defined 5
        Mathematical literacy 6
        Numeracy as a capability 6
        Numeracy as a twenty-first century competency 8
        The importance of numeracy 8
        Links to literacy 9
        Critical numeracy 12
        Numeracy and mathematics across the years of schooling 13
        Numeracy in school 16
        The reasoning and problem-solving dimension of numeracy 17
        Conclusion 26

Chapter 2 Numeracy in and across the Australian Curriculum F–6 27
        The functions and roles of numeracy in the Australian Curriculum . . . 27
        All teachers as teachers of numeracy 34
        Numeracy demands in non-mathematics learning areas 38
        Numeracy opportunities in non-mathematics learning areas 42
        Opportunities for numeracy in non-learning area contexts 46
        Conclusion 48

Chapter 3 Teaching mathematics for numeracy attainment 49
        Teaching mathematics 'well' 49
        Being a concept-focused teacher 59
        What teachers and educators of children need to know to
           teach mathematics well 60
        Conclusion 62

Chapter 4   **Numeracy intervention and extension in the classroom** 63
    Intervention defined 63
    Planning for mathematics learning. 63
    Intervention 67
    Turbocharged intervention 74
    Intervention and student psychology 75
    Extension 79
    Maximising learning and challenge for *all* students 82
    Data and intervention planning 86
    Conclusion. 86

Chapter 5   **Assessment of mathematics and numeracy** 89
    The need for quality data 89
    What is assessment? 89
    Characteristics of quality assessment 90
    Assessing mathematics concepts 93
    Assessing numeracy 96
    Conclusion. 110

Chapter 6   **Evidence-based whole-school approaches to numeracy improvement**. 113
    Professional learning communities and teams. 113
    Numeracy achievement data 115
    Whole-school improvement. .121
    Roles in a whole-school approach. 126
    Whole-school numeracy focus 130
    A model for whole-school intervention 134
    Whole-school numeracy planning. 136
    Case study: Mundaring Christian College 140
    Conclusion. 148

Chapter 7   **Professional and personal numeracy** 149
    Initial teacher education student testing 149
    Australian Professional Standards for Teachers 155
    Financial literacy 157
    Personal diagnosis of mathematics for numeracy 159
    Numeracy disposition diagnosis 163
    Conclusion. 166

Chapter 8   **Numeracy into the future** 167
    Educators affecting numeracy outcomes 167
    Society, policymakers and numeracy outcomes 168
    Finally 171

Table of contents

Appendix	**Numeracy across the curriculum**	173
	The arts	173
	Technologies	175
	Health and physical education	178
	Humanities and social sciences (HASS)	180
	Science	188
	English	192
References		193
Index		203

About the author

Thelma Perso's career spans a diverse range of roles making her an expert in mathematics, numeracy, school improvement and school leadership. For eighteen years Thelma was a classroom teacher of mathematics in large secondary schools in remote, rural and urban in Western Australia, and a head of department for eight of those years. During that time she completed a master's degree and PhD in mathematics education. Following this she became the senior curriculum officer (mathematics F–12) with the Department of Education in WA. She has held a series of positions in other Australian states, including executive director of curriculum in Queensland, executive director of education in Central Australia and executive director of a literacy and numeracy taskforce in the Northern Territory. Thelma is now the chief education officer at Swan Christian Education Association (SCEA), which includes seven schools in the Perth metropolitan area.

She has also taught in a range of universities including Edith Cowan University, the University of Notre Dame Australia and Curtin University, and was a senior research officer for several years at the Centre for Child Development and Education at the Menzies School of Health Research. She was awarded an Australian postgraduate research award, which she used to research students' misconceptions in algebra (her PhD research area), and a Churchill Fellowship to investigate Indigenous numeracy overseas. Thelma has also contributed in voluntary roles including as a past president of the Mathematical Association of Western Australia (MAWA) where she is also a life member, and a past president of the Australian Association of Mathematics Teachers (AAMT).

In 2008 she was selected as a member of the Prime Minister's panel and co-author of the *National numeracy review report*. She authored *Teaching Indigenous students* with Professor Colleen Hayward (Allen & Unwin, 2015), and wrote and edited over thirty books for teachers and a multitude of peer-reviewed papers.

List of figures

Figure 1.1: Dimensions of literacy 10

Figure 1.2: The literacy capability 10

Figure 1.3: Dimensions of numeracy 11

Figure 1.4: The numeracy capability 12

Figure 1.5: A model of mathematical literacy in practice 18

Figure 1.6: Increasing numerate behaviours result from successful applications 23

Figure 2.1: Six elements of numeracy 29

Figure 3.1: Bloom's taxonomy 56

Figure 4.1: Curriculum alignment 65

Figure 4.2: Differentiating instruction for individuals and small groups 68

Figure 4.3: Intervention to improve learning quality and quantity 85

Figure 5.1: Example Year 4 assessment task on area 94

Figure 5.2: NAPLAN Year 3 numeracy test 2010, question 24 103

Figure 5.3: NAPLAN Year 7 numeracy test 2008, question 30 103

Figure 5.4: NAPLAN Year 3 numeracy test 2010, question 25 109

Figure 6.1: NAPLAN numeracy results for a particular school year group over time . .116

Figure 6.2: NAPLAN numeracy results for a particular student cohort over time 117

Figure 6.3: NAPLAN numeracy results for a specific student over time 118

Figure 6.4: PLC and PLT approach for improving numeracy learning 131

Figure 6.5: Whole-school approach to intervention 134

Figure 6.6: College newsletter NAPLAN celebration 143

Figure 6.7: Mundaring Christian College NAPLAN cohort growth,
Year 3 to Year 5, 2015–2017 146

Figure 7.1: Examples of numeracy questions from the LANTITE 152

List of tables

Table 1.1: Australian Curriculum general capabilities 7

Table 1.2: Numeracy across the phases of schooling. 16

Table 2.1: Levels in the numeracy continuum and their alignment with the EYLF and Australian Curriculum: Mathematics year by year 30

Table 2.2: Numeracy elements and their relationship with the Australian Curriculum: Mathematics strands 31

Table 2.3: Numeracy demands in the Australian Curriculum summary 39

Table 2.4: Numeracy opportunities in the Australian Curriculum 43

Table 2.5: Numeracy opportunities in non-learning contexts 47

Table 3.1: Content-focused teaching versus concept-focused teaching in mathematics 55

Table 3.2: Content-focused and concept-focused teaching aligned with Bloom's taxonomy and SOLO model 57

Table 3.3: Content-focused and concept-focused pedagogies compared 58

Table 4.1: Australian Curriculum: F–6 'Fractions and decimals' sequence 69

Table 4.2: Relationship between some Australian Curriculum: Mathematics content descriptors, elaborations for 'Fractions and decimals' and NNLP indicators for interpteting fractions 72

Table 4.3: Learning quality and activities that require thinking and affective skills . . . 81

Table 4.4: Learning quality rubric to support learning and assessment of the concept of area and its relationship to the concept of perimeter 83

Table 5.1: Different types of questions and questioning to ascertain depth of student learning 96

Table 5.2: Example of assessment rubric for assessing student numeracy 99

Table 6.1: NAPLAN numeracy test achievement data extract 119

Table 6.2:	The three levels of the whole-school approach to intervention	135
Table 6.3:	Example of a school numeracy plan	138
Table 7.1:	Financial literacy as a general capability	158
Table 7.2:	Australian Curriculum: Mathematics content descriptors and numeracy continuum learning descriptions for money, Years 7–10	159
Table 7.3:	Year 6–7 maths standards with numeracy examples	160

Introduction

Some would say there are many books about numeracy for both pre-service and in-service teachers; however, the majority of these are about mathematics teaching and not numeracy. Therein lies the problem. As educators we must deeply understand the difference between mathematics and numeracy. In particular, we must recognise the relationship between the two and the implications for teaching and learning. Until we do, we will not address the ongoing issues pertaining to student numeracy standards in our country.

The critical issue is a failure to raise student numeracy capability across the nation, a trend that has increased over recent decades despite international and national testing programs that continue to measure the extent of the problem. Results from these programs continue to raise awareness, which in turn yields increased government funding directed at the issue. Schools and schooling sectors develop numeracy strategies aimed at improving outcomes, but many of these only target maths teaching in a misguided belief that a focus on improved maths learning will naturally improve numeracy standards. While some schools and teachers across Australia have success with these strategies, results are not improving on a scale or at a rate that will meet the needs of our global society or the demands of the current and future workforce.

With the worldwide demand for science, technology, engineering and mathematics (STEM) professionals outpacing supply, STEM is an increasingly essential element of the school curriculum, of which maths is the foundation (Education Council, 2015). It is the mathematical reasoning required by science, technology and engineering – decisions about whether maths will help and what maths to use, and reflecting on calculated solutions to problems including whether they make sense in context – that is most often missing in classrooms where maths is taught. This is numeracy; specifically, this is critical numeracy.

Over the last decade the Australian government has sought to address the issue by initially developing and implementing standards for teachers, and more recently a numeracy standard for prospective teachers implemented through a numeracy test. This on-entry test informs governments and the broader population of the numeracy standards of young people intending to enter the teaching workforce. Although data gathered from this process will provide a clearer picture of the possible causes of low numeracy standards in our country, and the extent to which teachers might be contributing to it, it will not address the problem.

It is my informed opinion that to address this issue, teachers and school leaders need to better understand what numeracy is – that it is more than maths, although maths is at its heart – and better understand the mathematical concepts as opposed to concentrating on teaching methods and procedures to 'get the sums right' – an attitude that currently exists in many schools, often driven by parents and communities. What is needed is reform based on a paradigm shift: an understanding of the place and quality of maths learning in the development of mathematical literacy in our young people. This book will support teachers and school leaders to make this paradigm shift a reality.

About this book

Chapter 1 defines numeracy. It uses the current understanding of literacy to scaffold the essential learning that underpins numeracy as a capability that depends on purpose and audience, rather than a subject. It presents numeracy as having three dimensions: mathematics, problem-solving and understanding context.

Chapter 2 outlines numeracy in and across the school curriculum. It defines and describes the roles and functions of numeracy in the Australian Curriculum: as a general capability, a continuum and a demand for learning in other subject areas. Opportunities for demonstrating the application of maths in other subject areas are also provided along with teacher strategies for alerting students to when they are applying maths.

Chapter 3 puts theory into practice. While Chapter 1 introduces the phrase *maths taught well* and Chapters 1 and 2 use the phrase *teaching maths well*, Chapter 3 discusses the meaning of these phrases. What does it mean to teach maths well and does this mean that it currently isn't being taught well? What needs to change in the teaching of maths to raise the numeracy standards of our children and young people?

Chapter 4 discusses extension for students who have learned and deeply understood their age cohort maths expectations and intervention for students who have not yet attained the learning they should have. Intervention is presented as pedagogy to ensure all students are learning what is expected for their age cohort (content standards), and what might be expected for each concerning being challenged and reaching their potential (through learning quality).

Chapter 5 focuses on the assessment of maths and numeracy. It describes the importance of validity in assessment, revealing the need for teachers to deeply understand the required learning before they can assess whether their students have attained it. It addresses the validity of national numeracy testing, discussing the quality of National Assessment Program – Literacy and Numeracy (NAPLAN) tests in judging student numeracy attainment. It also shows the link between the definition of numeracy presented in Chapter 1 and the content of national numeracy tests.

Chapter 6 presents a successful evidence-based whole-school approach to numeracy improvement, as designed and implemented by the author in her previous role as school leader and principal. The complexities of improving numeracy in an educational site are described, indicating the challenges that need to be overcome and the commitment to professional learning required by both school leaders and teachers. Far from providing a recipe for success, it draws on the previous chapters to show what focused improvement can look like. Appendices to this chapter include tools for school leaders in determining the effectiveness of their whole-school interventions.

Chapter 7 addresses professional and personal numeracy for teachers. It describes the numeracy required for everyday life which, for a teacher, includes the workplace numeracy articulated in the Australian Core Skills Framework (ACSF; Commonwealth of Australia, 2012). This standard of numeracy is used to underpin the questions developed by the Australian Council for Educational Research (ACER) to ascertain the numeracy standards of prospective teachers. It also highlights the dimensions of numeracy outlined in Chapter 1, including being able to read and comprehend context. Chapter 7 also includes some diagnostic tools that teachers might use to determine their own level of and capability with numeracy, enabling personal reflection on whether their numeracy is strong enough to support their teaching aspirations and, if not, what they might do about it.

Chapter 8 presents concluding remarks on the state of Australia's numeracy achievement from both international and national perspectives. As an educator in this field for almost forty years, and having worked at every level of education in a range of roles from school to university classrooms to state government policy, I sum up the issues and make recommendations for how they might be addressed, in classrooms and through national and state policy.

The appendix includes a comprehensive table of the numeracy demands and opportunities across the Australian Curriculum to better support teachers to identify and plan for numeracy moments.

In conclusion, this book provides teachers with a greater awareness of:

- how to deeply understand the maths they teach and model numeracy, particularly critical numeracy
- how their own personal numeracy capability contributes to the future numeracy capability of the nation
- the steps required to develop their own numeracy and ultimately that of their students
- the urgent need to address the misunderstandings about this issue in every primary classroom.

There are also three downloadable resources available to support numeracy improvement. The tools might be useful for schools as they plan their improvement journey for numeracy and other school elements that support numeracy improvement. These tools are not provided as models of exemplary practice, but rather to assist school leaders in leading implementation of new practices and managing change for numeracy (and other) improvement in their school. They also serve to support schools to understand the complexity of improving numeracy in a school; it is rare that a single area needs work, but likely that a combination of areas must be addressed through interconnected strategies.

Numeracy defined

In the Australian Curriculum, literacy and numeracy belong to the group of general capabilities, which 'encompass the knowledge, skills, behaviours and dispositions that will assist students to live and work successfully in the twenty-first century' (School Curriculum and Standards Authority, Government of Western Australia, 2014, para. 1). Literacy and numeracy are needed *in* every subject and *for* every subject; without literacy and numeracy, students cannot access learning.

Numeracy is a broadly misunderstood term. Some believe numeracy is a synonym for maths, while others believe it is a subset of maths – the maths of the early years of schooling or being able to do arithmetic. The Australian Curriculum, Assessment and Reporting Authority (ACARA; n.d.-a) states:

> *Numeracy encompasses the knowledge, skills, behaviours and dispositions that students need to use mathematics in a wide range of situations. It involves students recognising and understanding the role of mathematics in the world and having the dispositions and capacities to use mathematical knowledge and skills purposefully.* (para. 1)

The Australian Association of Mathematics Teachers (AAMT; 1997) adds a further dimension to this definition, describing numeracy as 'the disposition to use, in context, a combination of: underpinning mathematical concepts and skills from across the discipline (numerical, spatial, graphical, statistical and algebraic); mathematical thinking and strategies; general thinking skills; and grounded appreciation of context' (p. 15). These definitions clearly differentiate between numeracy and maths. While we need to know some maths to be numerate, and the maths knowledge must come first, knowing maths is not sufficient for numeracy. Neither can it be assumed that all people who know maths well will necessarily be numerate.

Numeracy is an attitude (or disposition) that stems from having confidence and capacity to choose and apply maths to a situation, and to reason about the solutions obtained. I propose the following working definition: numeracy is the ability, confidence and inclination to use maths successfully to meet the demands of all phases of learning, life and living in a society.

Mathematical literacy

Numeracy is not a term used in many countries. The Cockroft (1982) report *Mathematics counts* included one of the earliest attempts to highlight the confidence needed to use maths: 'Most important of all is the need to have sufficient confidence to make effective use of whatever mathematical skill and understanding is possessed' (p. 10).

In recent decades we have seen the term *literacy* attached to a number of capabilities (for example, financial literacy, data literacy, digital literacy) to describe facility and confidence with a concept or skill set. Hence the term *mathematical literacy* is used in many countries to describe a facility and confidence with maths, which in effect is what numeracy is. The Organization for Economic Cooperation and Development (OECD) Programme for International Student Assessment (PISA) definition of mathematical literacy, which was used to inform the ACARA numeracy definition, is still regarded as accurate and relevant. PISA defines mathematical literacy as:

> *An individual's capacity to identify and understand the role that mathematics plays in the world, to make well-founded judgements and to use and engage with mathematics in ways that meet the needs of that individual's life as a constructive, concerned and reflective citizen.*
> (OECD, 2009, p. 14)

Numeracy has also been understood as *mathematical competence*, meaning exactly what it says: competence in and with maths.

Numeracy as a capability

A capability is something that you are or are not capable of. In the Australian Curriculum, general capabilities are 'an integrated and interconnected set of knowledge, skills, behaviours and dispositions that students develop and use in their learning across the curriculum, in co-curricular programs and in their lives outside school' (ACARA, 2013, p. 5). In this sense they are needed by all as general or broad life skills. The seven general capabilities in the Australian Curriculum are:

- literacy
- numeracy
- information and communication technology (ICT)
- critical and creative thinking
- personal and social capability
- ethical understanding
- intercultural understanding.

Since the definitions of the general capabilities include three dimensions – knowledge and skills, behaviours, and attitudes and dispositions – it is helpful to consider each of these dimensions for the seven general capabilities. The following table presents an interpretation of the knowledge, skills, behaviours and attitudes that are included in each of the general capabilities.

Table 1.1: Australian Curriculum general capabilities

General capability	Knowledge and skills	Behaviours and attitudes
Literacy	Language (not necessarily English)	Confidence in choosing, using and applying language in different contexts
Numeracy	Mathematics	Confidence in choosing, using and applying mathematics in different contexts
Information and communication technology (ICT)	Information and communication technology	Confidence in choosing, using and applying ICT skills in different contexts
Critical and creative thinking	Higher-order thinking skills	Confidence in choosing, using and applying higher-order thinking skills in different contexts
Personal and social capability	How to behave in societal contexts	Confidence in choosing, using and applying personal and social skills in different contexts
Ethical understanding	Comprehension of right and wrong, both legally and morally	Confidence in choosing, using and applying what is right or wrong in different contexts
Intercultural understanding	Knowledge of cultural differences	Confidence in choosing, using and applying appropriate behaviours for different cultural contexts

SOURCE: Adapted from ACARA, n.d.-e

Numeracy as a twenty-first century competency

In recent years education systems, leaders and groups such as the OECD have begun defining the capabilities and skills that students need as twenty-first century competencies (Fullan & Scott, 2014; Griffin et al., 2012; Ontario Ministry of Education, 2016). The most prominent of these twenty-first century competencies – critical thinking, communication, collaboration, and creativity and innovation – include literacy and numeracy as foundational curriculum, particularly the first two.

Alberta Education's (2011) *Framework for student learning* positions literacy and numeracy as fundamental tools for student acquisition of all other competencies. The report states, 'Being literate and numerate means going beyond the basic skills of reading, writing and solving simple arithmetic problems to acquiring, creating, connecting and understanding information' (p. 3). Further, in outlining the competencies that students need in the twenty-first century, they state 'students review, analyze and assess information from a variety of sources and points of view. They use applications, analysis, evaluation and conceptualization as appropriate for the context' (p. 3). The capability and competency of numeracy requires higher-order thinking skills that are essential in application, analysis, evaluation and conceptualisation of contexts into the twenty-first century.

The importance of numeracy

The Australian Government recognises the importance of numeracy in its National Assessment Program (NAP). In judging the literacy and numeracy capabilities of every student through population testing, the government can determine the health of education in Australia. Note that samples of students are assessed in other subjects and capabilities in NAP, but only literacy and numeracy are assessed for the entire Australian student population at Years 3, 5, 7 and 9 through NAPLAN.

Just as many people equate literacy with reading and writing – these skills being essential literacy components or tools – many people also equate numeracy with maths. This is unfortunate since in Australia the importance of numeracy is frequently played down by parents who say things to their children like 'Don't worry if you can't do maths. I couldn't either.'

Despite this, parents in the community generally understand the link between maths and numeracy results and future employment, from their own personal experience or through media reports. For example, in Forgasz, et al.'s 2014 study, up to 80 per cent of respondents from ten countries believe that studying maths is important for getting a job. In addition, Marr and Hagston (2007) state 'Numeracy skills are vital in the workplace context and will become more so because of the increasing use of technology' (p. 6).

While numeracy is valued by society, it would seem that it isn't as valued as literacy, with more prominence placed on the need to be able to read and write to learn. However, because many people believe that numeracy and maths are the same thing (Council of Australian Governments (COAG), 2008) they don't necessarily appreciate that numeracy is needed tfor learning in every subject. This is because they cannot see the maths as obviously as they see reading and writing in every subject.

We are being told that the twenty-first century is the century of maths, due to importance being placed on technologies, robots and coding. As a nation, we need to raise the importance of maths and numeracy or we risk creating a dual society: those who are numerate and those who are not.

Links to literacy

Literacy and numeracy are first in the list of ACARA general capabilities. Their position is not accidental; they are the most important capabilities needed for success in life. Literacy, as with numeracy, is not a subject. Its knowledge base is a language – in schools this is the language of instruction, which in Australia is standard Australian English. But people can be literate in any language, so clearly literacy is not about the English language. In learning a second language, learners can draw on the literacy knowledge of their first language to support their understanding and use of their second. For example, they have already learned in their first language what words, structures, levels of familiarity, genres and tones to apply depending on purpose and audience. They are now learning different words, phrases and perhaps sentence structures depending on the language. While they might need to learn different cultural expectations governing the when and how of tone and familiarity, they can often use the literacy knowledge of their first language to decipher these expectations. By deconstructing these aspects of literacy, we can see that literacy is more about the attitudes and behaviours guiding decisions about appropriate communication than about the technicalities of the specific language used. Purpose, audience and overall context must be considered when making choices and decisions about what to say or write.

These dimensions of literacy are linked and can be represented as a set of intersecting circles, as shown in figure 1.1 (on page 10).

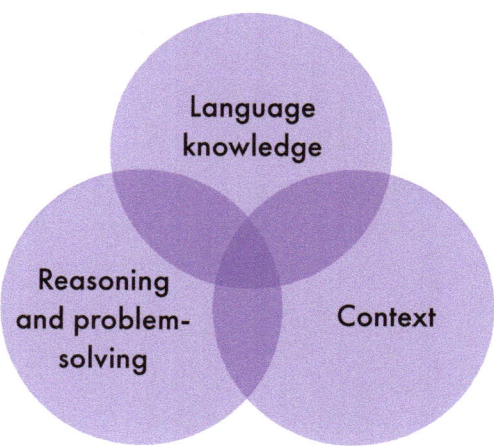

Figure 1.1: Dimensions of literacy

When confronted with a situation or context in which language application or literate behaviour is needed, a person has a knowledge base (language knowledge) to draw on. They must then understand the purpose and audience (context) and make decisions about which language tools they will use, apply them and then judge their effectiveness or correctness by the response. The decision-making process about what language tools are needed is effectively reasoning and problem-solving. The literacy capability can be drawn as a process, shown in figure 1.2.

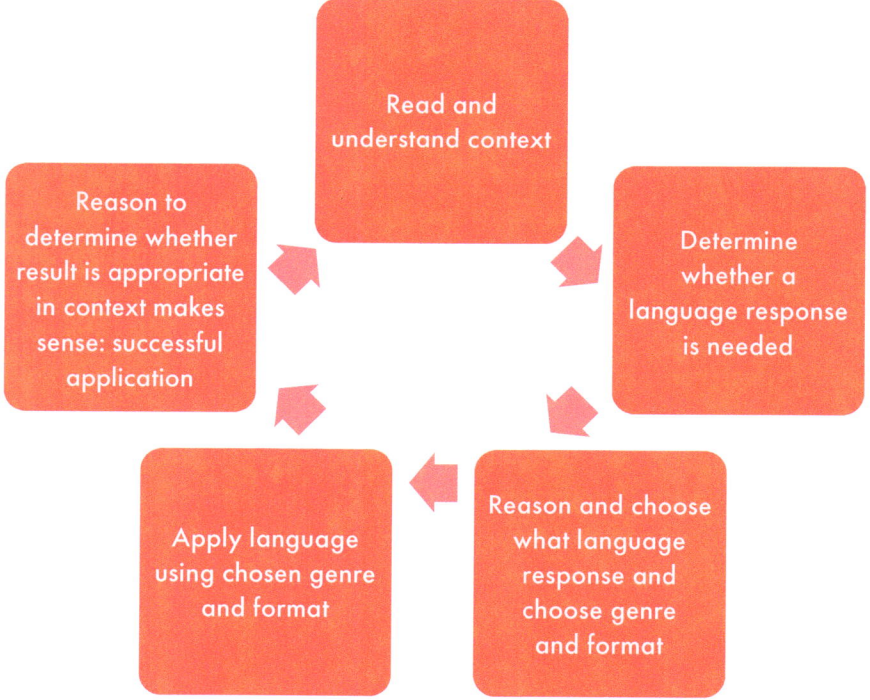

Figure 1.2: The literacy capability

Numeracy defined

The dimensions of numeracy include the maths knowledge base, the ability to read and understand context and the decision-making (or reasoning and problem-solving) needed to choose the appropriate maths and strategies. Similar to the dimensions of the literacy capability, the three dimensions of numeracy can equally be represented as a set of intersecting circles, shown in figure 1.3.

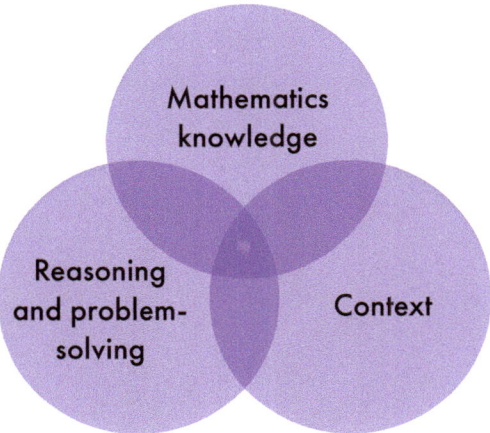

Figure 1.3: Dimensions of numeracy

It is clear that you first need to know some maths otherwise you will not recognise that it is needed. Moreover, the maths knowledge needs to include deep understandings if connections are to be made with situations and contexts (Anderson, 2009; Stacey, 2005). However, the maths knowledge on its own is insufficient: you need the confidence and disposition to think and reason about what maths is required. Willis (1998) states:

> *numeracy is regarded largely as the capacity to bridge the gap between 'mathematics' and 'the real world', to use in-school mathematics out-of-school. . . . Thus students are considered to be more or less numerate – not according to how much mathematics they know or what situations they can deal with – but according to how well they choose and use the mathematical skills they have in the service of things other than mathematics. (p. 37)*

For example, consider someone planning a barbeque for thirty-six people. They might decide that each person will eat three sausages and need to calculate how many sausages to buy. They recognise that some maths will help and consider what maths to use. They might then decide they need three lots of thirty-six sausages and choose a means to calculate this. They could use the multiplication method they learned at school or they might simply add thirty-six to thirty-six and thirty-six. They add rather than multiply since they reason that they are more likely to get the answer correct and they are not in any hurry. They might make this calculation in their head and get 108 in total. They could reason that this is roughly what they were expecting and don't check their answer since it is not imperative that they are right – one or two more or less will not matter, since some people at the barbeque will eat more or less than their allocated three sausages and the difference in cost is negligible. Note that it is the context that helps them decide the method they use and how much accuracy is needed in their calculation. The numeracy capability is shown as a process in figure 1.4.

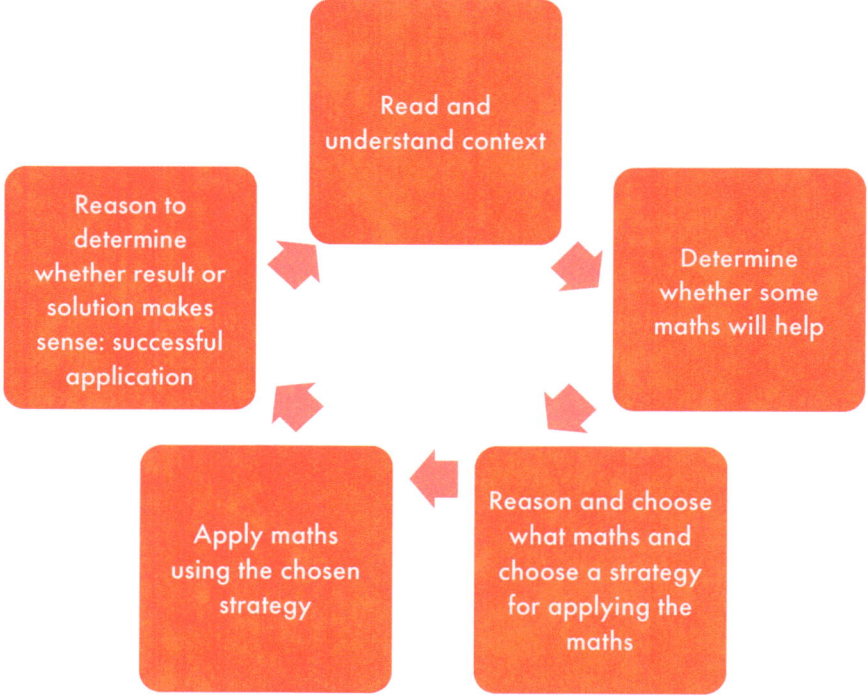

Figure 1.4: The numeracy capability

Critical numeracy

The person planning the barbeque in the previous example obtained an answer to the problem and then asked, 'Is 108 sausages what I was expecting?' At this point they were critiquing their numeracy, their maths choices and the strategies they had chosen and applied. This is a critical element to the problem-solving aspect of numeracy, otherwise known as *critical numeracy*. Having applied some maths, the

Numeracy defined

user must then consider whether their result or answer makes sense in the context; is it what they expected? If not, they might rethink their understanding of the context, of their choices of models or strategies, or of their application to determine what might have resulted in an unexpected result.

This critical numeracy can also be applied to someone else's results by considering the choices others have made in certain contexts and the appropriateness of their results and findings. This aspect of numeracy is essential in the modern world where we are surrounded by other people's results, for example, in the media, on the internet and in more personal everyday activities.

We might distinguish between *primary* critical numeracy (critiquing one's own numeracy choices) and *secondary* critical numeracy (critiquing someone else's numeracy choices). In the latter, choices might be made with the purpose of influencing an audience and hence could be intentionally incorrect or deliberately inappropriate.

For both literacy and numeracy, purpose and audience are critical. It is the purpose and audience – or context – that sets the parameters for the reasoning and decision-making and how much error can be tolerated. For example, consider what changes to the maths and strategy might occur if sausages cost $20 each. This would no doubt result in less tolerance for error and hence require a more accurate method of calculation. Similarly, if I were calculating how many 4-litre tins of paint I need to paint a room, how much error could I tolerate if I live 500 metres from the hardware store compared with if I live 300 kilometres from the hardware store?

Being able to make numerate decisions that minimise error requires deep learning of maths; to know whether an estimation or approximation will be sufficient, or if an exact answer is needed, depends on understanding the context and facility with, or availability of, the different calculation methods and tools required to generate a result. *Should I use mental calculation or a handheld calculator or other digital tool?*

Numeracy and mathematics across the years of schooling

To be numerate you need to know some maths. However, some of this maths does not need to be explicitly taught to be learned. For example, a child may learn elements of sharing before they start school without having had any formal (or mathematical) lessons. Similarly, a world-class chef may use their own specific numeracy developed in a commercial kitchen despite having never been to school or studied any maths. These numeracies might be described as *context-specific numeracies* and are often quite appropriate in many workplaces or common contexts. Applying these context-specific numeracies does not necessarily mean you are numerate in a general sense; you might merely be numerate in these specific contexts.

When students commence schooling, they formally learn maths as an explicit body of knowledge that they can then connect to other subject areas to enhance that learning and to deepen their understanding of maths. In the early years of schooling numeracy often has a focus on basic maths skills. This makes sense when we consider the fact that you need to know some maths before you can apply it in any context. As students learn more maths they have more options and strategies when faced with a situation that demands or is helped by it. In other words, explicit maths learning must come first.

Public commentary about whether numeracy standards are good enough generally focuses on whether students have learned maths skills by certain school year levels (COAG, 2008). The national numeracy learning progression (NNLP) certainly reflects this position (ACARA, 2018). As a tool, it supports teachers to identify and address individual student achievements and needs relating to their maths learning if they do not meet required numeracy benchmarks. This reflects national recognition of the fundamental importance of maths understanding underpinning numeracy development.

Maths across the school years

In Years F–2 the personal world of children is quite small. It consists mainly of their family network and their friends. They learn about numbers and how they work; they see shapes and patterns in their environment and can make patterns themselves in artwork, sounds and actions. They are able to draw on their emerging maths understandings to solve simple problems in familiar contexts, for example when counting or sharing out drinks at a party. They will learn more and more maths and see the connections between the maths learned at school and situations when they can use it or see it being used at home.

In Years 3–6, children's personal worlds are expanding. Children align themselves with their class peers, their cohort at school, and in other schools, as well as teams, clubs and groups in their community. They are more able to work collaboratively and to reason about what they hear others say. Problems requiring maths application should reflect this world so that students engage with them deeply and experience success in solving them.

In Years 7–10, students are moving towards adulthood. In the early adolescent years, students continue to align closely with their peer group, which can now include other early adolescents locally and from around the globe. Students use social media to engage with issues that are international, providing a plethora of contexts that typically engage this age group, including issues of social justice. Perspectives on issues of fairness, for example, will include opportunities for learning other general capabilities including intercultural understanding and ethical behaviour. While they can focus on the wider world, they might continue to be primarily concerned with how issues affect them personally.

The application of maths becomes increasingly subject (and hence context) specific through Years 7–10. This is often seen in the optional subjects that students in this age group generally study while at school. In design and technology subjects they might use measurement in learning to cut pieces of wood to size or to follow a recipe. These students may have learned skills in a general or abstract sense in their maths learning, but there is now a greater need for accuracy in these contexts since there may be less tolerance for error. Some students will be proficient in their maths learning, but many will experience less success when applying maths skills in these contexts because their understandings of maths are no longer sufficient.

In Years 11–12, students experience an even greater level of maths specificity in their areas of study. For example, physics, calculus and economics require levels of precision that demand different maths than that studied in Years F–10. These maths applications are best demonstrated and even retaught as needed in these contexts by subject experts since the maths applied goes beyond numeracy as a general capability. Students studying training courses in these senior years employ context-specific numeracies that have often been developed by each industry and have evolved over time with improved industry-specific technologies and efficiencies.

The scope of numeracy as a general capability – notwithstanding the increasing impact of digital technologies on expanding the size of children's worlds for those with access to them – is summarised in table 1.2 (on page 16).

The emphasis in the early years is on teaching the maths that children can draw on when confronted with a situation where some maths can help. However, teachers should also focus on supporting children to learn their maths in familiar contexts and to understand the contexts by visualising and paraphrasing. These skills are part of a problem-solving strategy that all children should be taught as part of their numeracy development, explored later in this chapter.

Table 1.2: Numeracy across the phases of schooling

Phase of school	Concerned with	Numeracy
Pre-school	Self and family	Commonly applied, not based on maths study
F–2	Self, family and friends	Emerging number and spatial sense; emphasis on early maths learning
3–6	Self, family, friends and peers	Emphasis on application in contexts concerning self, family, friends, peers and other school subjects
7–10	Self, family, friends, peers and issues	Emphasis on application in contexts concerning self, family, friends and peers, other school subjects with increasingly specific numeracies and global and social issues
11–12	Friends, peers, issues, the future, study and work	Numeracy as a general capability is used by all students in engaging with social and community contexts; for those studying school subjects including VET or workplace training, numeracy is context specific
Post-school	Workplace, community and wider society	Numeracy as a general capability is used by all adults in engaging with social and community contexts; for those in the workplace numeracy is context specific, each workplace having its own numeracy

Numeracy in school

Numeracy is not a subject. It cannot be taught as a body of knowledge. Some schools attempt to timetable numeracy but generally teach only maths during that timeslot, and in many schools the numeracy program and the maths program are the same. While this might be appropriate in the early years, maths learning alone will not result in students learning to be numerate.

It is my belief that the numeracy results of many schools plateau at Years 4 and 5 because schools continue to teach only maths and hope their students can apply it in a range of contexts and evaluate their results, despite having never been taught how. Thus, a numeracy program in a school needs to be balanced; it must focus on all three dimensions of numeracy (as shown in figure 1.3, page 11). It should focus on teaching maths well and on teaching children to reason, problem-solve and apply their maths in various contexts, including in maths learning. Children must be explicitly taught how to understand and read contexts and how to choose and apply their maths to these contexts. Application and problem-solving need to be taught and learned concurrently.

They must also have these skills modelled to them by confident and competent teachers. Without these skills being taught and modelled, only students who learn these skills in other subjects or have them modelled by parents and carers might develop numerate behaviours. Other students might simply go through schooling believing that maths is irrelevant to their lives and they will never really need it. These and other issues concerning why many students are not developing numerate behaviours in schools will be discussed in the next chapter.

Implications of the numeracy definition for schooling

As proposed earlier, I believe that numeracy is the ability, confidence and inclination to use maths successfully to meet the demands of all phases of learning, life and living in a society. An acceptance of this definition of numeracy is challenging for schools. It means that no longer can teachers assume that if their students are taught maths they will be numerate. Quite the contrary. This definition requires that to be numerate students must:

+ learn maths deeply
+ be taught maths in ways that develop their confidence to choose, use and apply maths independently when they aren't forced to do so
+ be taught to critically review their interpretation of context and to ask whether the result makes sense in the context.

In order for these three outcomes to result from schooling, teachers need to use powerful pedagogies that focus on the development of concepts rather than merely on rules and procedures which unfortunately still predominate in many maths classes across the nation and, indeed, the world.

The reasoning and problem-solving dimension of numeracy

Reasoning and problem-solving are two of the maths proficiencies that should be taught to students of maths (ACARA, n.d.-c). However, the question about whether or not maths will help in a certain context must be asked outside of maths lessons. Hence, reasoning and problem-solving as elements of numerate behaviour are far broader than those used in teaching and learning maths. They are connected to the critical and creative thinking general capabilities of the Australian Curriculum and include problem-solving in every context (including other school subjects), not just in maths classes.

Numeracy requires problem-solving to understand context and make choices about strategies; however, many people struggle with solving problems. It is helpful in schools to provide students with a model for step-by-step problem-solving that scaffolds the process and gives all students a starting point. The PISA 2015 mathematics framework (OECD, 2017) provides a model of mathematical literacy in practice, shown in figure 1.5 (page 18).

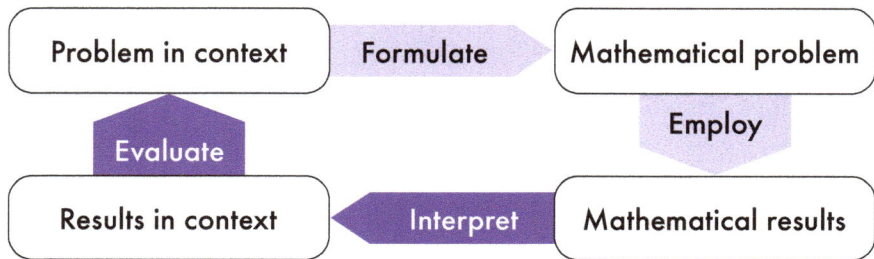

Figure 1.5: A model of mathematical literacy in practice
SOURCE: OECD, 2017, p. 68. Used with permission.

This process can be summarised as follows.

1. Problem in context: Read and understand the problem in context.

2. Formulate: Determine if some maths will help in the situation.

3. Mathematical problem: If some maths will be useful, reread or paraphrase the problem in context as a mathematical problem to choose the maths and strategies required.

4. Employ: Apply the maths and strategies chosen to the problem.

5. Mathematical results: Obtain results from the maths and strategies applied.

6. Interpret: Critique the mathematical result.

7. Results in context: Set the mathematical result in the context of the initial problem.

8. Evaluate: Assess if the result makes sense in the context of the problem. If the result does make sense in the context, then the result can be accepted. If it does not, then repeat the process from the beginning.

These steps also align closely with the elements of the critical and creative thinking general capability: inquiring, identifying, exploring and organising information and ideas; generating ideas, possibilities and actions; reflecting on thinking and processes; and analysing, synthesising and evaluating reasoning and procedures (ACARA, n.d.-e).

Numeracy situations also exist in text. A numerate person can draw out the maths from the context of a text. This involves problem-solving skills and higher-order thinking skills. The *National numeracy review report* indicates that numeracy has mathematical, strategic and contextual dimensions (COAG, 2008). As Goos and colleagues (2015) state:

> *a numerate person requires more than basic mathematical skills. They must also be disposed to using mathematical skills adaptively and strategically in order to deal with mathematically relevant situations across the range of non-mathematical contexts that can be encountered in private and public life.* (p. 2)

The importance of the contextual dimension cannot be overstated. People need to deeply understand a context before they can decide that some maths will help and then choose what maths and strategies are needed or demanded.

Teaching a problem-solving framework

There are many problem-solving frameworks used and taught in schools. The framework I prefer aligns closely with that shown in figure 1.5. It describes a five-step model that uses reasoning at every step and can be used in all phases of schooling.

The model is:

1. clarify
2. choose
3. use or apply
4. interpret
5. communicate. (Perso, 2013)

The words might seem too long or complex for students of particular ages. However, while there are many synonyms for these five steps, changing the word can remove the reasoning or change the meaning. For example, don't change *interpret* to *check*; interpreting is asking whether the answer makes sense in this context, whereas checking can just be making sure the procedure is correctly followed. Similarly, don't change *clarify* to *read*; clarifying involves understanding the context and comprehending the meaning, whereas reading might just mean the act of reading without requiring any understanding of what is being read.

While the framework can be successfully used by individuals, its power lies in its collaborative use. This is because collaboration allows for division of labour, inclusivity and the sharing of multiple worldviews, information sources, experiences and 'enhanced creativity and quality of solutions stimulated by the ideas of other group members' (OECD, 2017, p. 132).

Clarify

The first step in the suggested problem-solving framework is to clarify the situation or context. It is often difficult to teach students to clarify since many children want to jump in and get an answer. Coming up with an answer quickly is frequently a learned behaviour, both in school and at home. Teaching students to pause and think about the context before leaping into a strategy or finding an answer can be challenging, particularly for older students who might have been inadvertently conditioned to display answer-focused behaviours for many years.

The best way to explicitly teach students of any age to clarify is to teach them to ask questions about the situation and context. Organise mixed-ability groups and have them write down one or two questions about the question. This gives children permission to bring their own perspective and experience to their understanding, which can enrich this step. They might then report their shared questions back to the class and the class can decide which are relevant, which answers are embedded in the question and so on.

If answers to the students' questions aren't obvious, the class may agree to make some assumptions to proceed with solving the problem.

Suitable questions might be:

- What information can I get from reading the problem?
- What do the words tell me? What do I need to find out?
- What do all the words mean? How can I find out if I don't know?
- Will it help to highlight or underline the key words? What are the key words?
- Will some maths help here?
- How much time do I have to solve this?
- Who wants to know the answer? Who is my audience and how should I communicate or present my results?
- How much error can I tolerate? Is an estimate acceptable or do I need to calculate exactly?
- Will it be better to work with others or can I do this on my own?
- Should I find out more about this context – perhaps at the library or online? Maybe ask others?
- What can I assume? Are there any assumptions I can or should make?

✦ If I drew a sketch would it help to visualise what is happening? (This step is always helpful, especially for English as an additional language or dialect (EAL/D) learners).

In addition to asking questions about a context to better understand it, we need to teach students to visualise and paraphrase. That is, we need to teach them how to see in their mind's eye what the words are saying (for example, what does this situation look like?) and teach them how to talk about it in their own words.

Teaching very young children to visualise is done by describing something to them – it might be a short story, an object or a sentence – and then having them shut their eyes and picture what you've just told them. They then describe back to you, or their partner, in their own words what they saw, or draw a picture showing what they saw. For example, if you said, 'My dog had six puppies and we gave two of them to our neighbour', you would then get them to shut their eyes and picture or imagine that situation. They would then tell you or their partner what they saw. Older children can read these situations in words, imagine them and then paraphrase them or even write the symbolic representation.

Visualising and paraphrasing is the first step to solving a problem; it concerns reading and understanding or clarifying a situation. This helps people decide whether some maths will help here – the fundamental numeracy question.

Choose

By understanding a context and determining that some maths will help, students then make choices about:

✦ what maths will help

✦ the degree of accuracy needed for the context, or how much error can be tolerated

✦ what strategies, methods, technologies and tools they will use to apply the maths.

Most students need a great deal of practice choosing since teachers and carers frequently do this for them. Rarely are students given a problem, either in maths lessons or in other subject lessons, and allowed to choose how they will solve it. There is often an expectation that they use the models, methods, strategies and tools that their teachers have recently modelled or taught. Moreover, they often believe there is only one right way of solving a problem, which can result in a lack of confidence to invent intuitive strategies (Cai & Nie, 2007).

Students should work in pairs or groups to suggest and discuss methods, tools, technologies and strategies that would best suit the constraints considered in their clarification. They should be taught to justify or argue their choices in the context of the problem, for example, 'We need to add the numbers *because we want to know how many altogether*' or 'I think a pie graph is the best way to present this information *because we need to look at the proportions.*' These decisions can result from robust discussions coming out of a word problem confronting students. In arguing why a certain choice is made, higher-order thinking skills such as justification are required. Recommendation 3 of the *National numeracy review report* states:

> *That from the earliest years, greater emphasis be given to providing students with frequent exposure to higher-level mathematical problems rather than routine procedural tasks, in contexts of relevance to them, with increased opportunities for students to discuss alternative solutions and explain their thinking.* (COAG, 2008, p. 31)

It should be noted that students can't choose if they don't have a range to choose from. They will never be able to choose a mathematical model or a measuring instrument or unit, and justify their choice, if they do not first know when and how these might be used. Teachers need to teach this knowledge.

Use or apply

Having made their choices, students apply the maths and strategies to the problem. The speed of application will depend on the clarification of available time and the strategies they have chosen to use. The teacher might give these constraints, or students might determine them based on the audience or purpose. Students should always estimate first so that they have a rough idea of the magnitude and nature of their solution. Their estimate should act as a guide or benchmark to interpret their answer against; they should be expecting an answer or solution within a particular range.

Interpret

Students then make a judgement or interpretation on whether their solution makes sense in the context of the problem by comparing it with their estimate or expectations. They might ask questions such as:

- ✤ Do my answers seem reasonable? Do they make sense? Are they what I was expecting?
- ✤ Are my mathematical calculations correct and how do I know?
- ✤ If not, do my choices seem reasonable and rational or should I go back and re-choose?
- ✤ Are there any factors that I might not have considered that I should have?
- ✤ Are there any assumptions I made that might have been wrong?
- ✤ Can I make any conjectures or inferences from my results? What do my answers mean?

If the solution does make sense or is roughly what was expected, then students gain confidence in their application of maths and are more inclined to choose to use maths next time they identify a need. Continued success will mean they become more numerate in many different contexts. This can be shown diagrammatically as in figure 1.6.

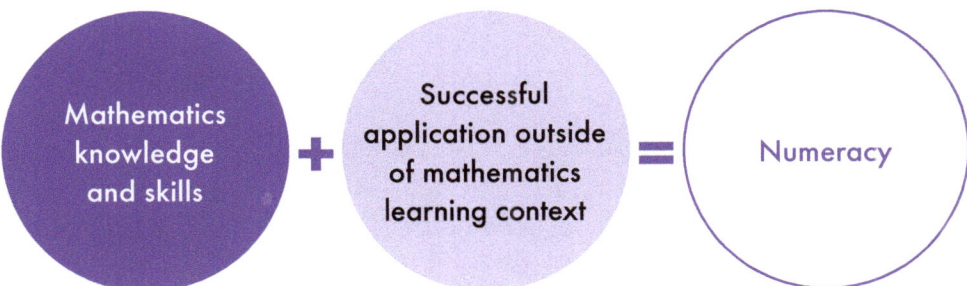

Figure 1.6: Increasing numerate behaviours result from successful applications
SOURCE: Perso, 2013, p. 7

Interpreting can also be making sense of the answer by placing it in a more familiar or relevant context. For example, Goos and colleagues (2012a) relate an incident where a student used a pedometer to record the number of steps taken in week. Having calculated this to be equivalent to 98.8 kilometres, the class were amazed 'with one student exclaiming "Wow – that's nearly all the way to Whyalla!" (a neighbouring town)' (p. 4334).

Communicate

This is the final step in the problem-solving framework. Although this step has not been included in the OECD model shown in figure 1.5 (page 18), I believe it should be included in classrooms since it requires that students demonstrate their mathematical thinking and use technical language appropriate for the context. This supports teachers in providing explicit feedback to students.

Communicating is much more than saying 'The answer is …' or 'Answer equals …' Communicating includes giving the answer, but more importantly it is being able to articulate and explain the thinking process of every step, beginning with the clarification. Students, including younger children, should be able to explain their reasoning verbally and critique their work. Communicating also involves evaluating their solution and the processes they used, explaining what they might do differently next time and what they learned from working on the problem. Children should be able to describe and explain:

- How did I clarify the task? What questions did I ask?
- What methods, tools and strategies did I choose and why?
- What results did I get when I applied them? Did they work?
- Did I have to re-clarify, re-choose or redo? Why?
- What would I do differently next time? Why?
- What conclusions can I make on the basis of my efforts?
- What did I learn from doing this task?

Each of the steps of the problem-solving framework are best learned through collaboration, 'through reflection in action and on action in order to become better at negotiating the messy, fuzzy, dilemma-ridden context of real-world life and work with positive impact' (Fullan & Scott, 2014, p. 4).

These steps in the framework are rarely used in a linear way. Problem solvers often need to go back to clarify again and again before and during the application – this is an iterative process. They might search for the best approach rather than choosing and using their first thought. They might decide the answer doesn't make sense in the context and decide to re-choose models, reread the problem or re-check their answers, and so on. Students should be given credit for this as it means they are reasoning as they progress.

Modelling problem-solving

Teachers will model this process to their students by asking themselves the appropriate questions in context and answering the questions after some verbal self-discussion. It is important that the modelling is visible to students; they need to speak aloud the questions and answers leading to the decision-making that occurs in their heads as they problem-solve and apply maths.

> ### Types of modelling and problem-solving with students
>
> **Modelled:** Teacher does the problem while sharing their in-the-head thinking with students by talking about the process as they work.
>
> **Shared:** Teacher and students do some of the problem together, both speaking aloud their in-the-head thinking.
>
> **Guided:** Students do the problem while speaking aloud their in-the-head thinking.

Teachers should speak aloud their thinking to show their students their cognitive struggle. Children need to hear their teacher struggle with the process, asking questions, changing their mind, having false starts, getting it wrong and choosing a different strategy to try again. This models to students that it's okay to not be able to do it automatically and you have to work at it; no one is born with the ability to solve problems. Speaking this process aloud teaches students that:

- Problem-solving is not innate; you are not born with the ability to solve problems.
- Problem-solving can be done in many ways; there is no one right way.
- Problem-solving can be hard work; it is not easy for most people.
- Problem-solving skills are learned; they must be improved with practice.

Clearly, students need favourable attitudes towards independently applying maths and being able to make strategic choices about what maths and methods to apply in which contexts. This has clear implications for the ways in which maths is taught in schools.

> ### Time to reflect
>
> Are you numerate?
>
> When you are confronted by a situation where you recognise that some maths will help, do you run a mile or do you think, 'Which maths?' and then choose and apply it?
>
> Have you always thought maths and numeracy are the same thing? Can you define their differences?

Conclusion

In this chapter numeracy has been described as a capability, or competency. Since numeracy includes problem-solving and the understanding of context, it is essential that numeracy remains at the forefront of learning in schools.

Teaching problem-solving has been presented in this chapter as a process that teachers can use to develop problem-solving skills. The process also addresses other twenty-first century competencies including collaboration, critical thinking and communication. This process develops and equips students with the twenty-first century skills identified globally and hence is useful on many levels in teaching (Harvard Advanced Leadership Initiative, 2014; Ontario Ministry of Education, 2016). As Fullan and Scott (2014) assert:

> *Learning is . . . not only the development of the fundamental competencies (skills and knowledge) necessary for the successful negotiation of an uncertain world. It is also about developing the personal, interpersonal and cognitive capabilities that allow one to diagnose what is going on in the complex, constantly shifting human and technical context of real world practice and then match an appropriate response.* (p. 4)

The following chapter includes a broader discussion of numeracy in the Australian Curriculum, including further unpacking its role in learning as a general capability.

Numeracy in and across the Australian Curriculum F–6

Having established the place of numeracy in learning and for learning it is essential to examine how numeracy is positioned in the documentation that outlines the Australian Curriculum.

The Alice Springs (Mparntwe) Education Declaration identifies two goals:

1. 'The Australian education system promotes excellence and equity.'
2. 'All young Australians become confident and creative individuals, successful lifelong learners, [and] active and informed members of the community' (Education Council, 2019, p. 4).

The second goal includes the desire that all young Australians become lifelong learners, who 'have the essential skills in literacy and numeracy as the foundation for learning' among other capabilities (Education Council, 2019, p. 7). These additional capabilities encompass the knowledge, skills, behaviours and dispositions that students need to live and work successfully in the twenty-first century and supplement the general capabilities of the Australian Curriculum outlined in Chapter 1 (ACARA, 2013).

The functions and roles of numeracy in the Australian Curriculum

Numeracy in the Australian Curriculum is presented as having interconnected functions and roles. These are:

1. numeracy as a general capability, needed by all people to fully engage in the demands of life
2. numeracy as a continuum across the years of schooling, which outlines what skills can reasonably be expected of students at biannual intervals for them to fully engage with learning

3. numeracy in and across the curriculum, needed to access and engage with discipline learning in all learning areas, with attention drawn to both demands (numeracy needed to access discipline content and concepts) and opportunities (numeracy needed across learning areas to practice the application of maths in real contexts).

Numeracy as a general capability

The Australian Curriculum presents numeracy as one of the seven general capabilities and states that:

> *students become numerate as they develop the knowledge and skills to use mathematics confidently across other learning areas at school and in their lives more broadly. Numeracy encompasses the knowledge, skills, behaviours and dispositions that students need to use mathematics in a wide range of situations. It involves students recognising and understanding the role of mathematics in the world and having the dispositions and capacities to use mathematical knowledge and skills purposefully.* (ACARA, n.d.-a, para. 1)

Table 1.1 (page 7) shows numeracy as the capability and confidence to apply maths to other contexts when and where it is needed. The connection between numeracy and maths has been discussed in Chapter 1; specifically, to be numerate you need to know some maths (see figure 1.3, page 11).

Numeracy as a continuum across the years of schooling

The Australian Curriculum is organised around eight learning areas of which maths is one. The Australian Curriculum presents numeracy as having six inter–related elements, shown in figure 2.1.

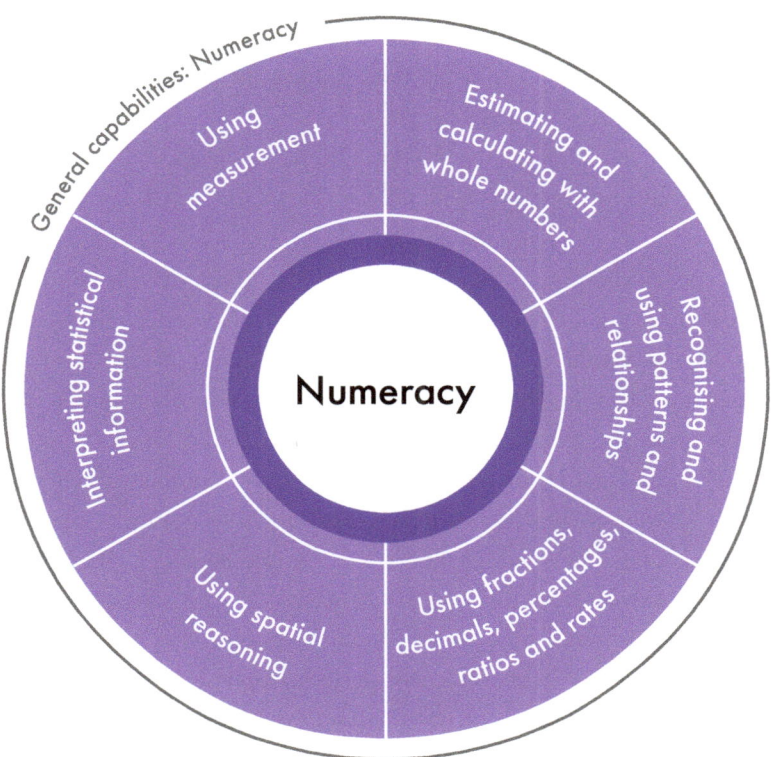

Figure 2.1: Six elements of numeracy
SOURCE: Adapted from ACARA, n.d.-a.

The key organising elements for numeracy are drawn from the strands of the Australian Curriculum: Mathematics. These are:

+ estimating and calculating with whole numbers
+ recognising and using patterns and relationships
+ using fractions, decimals, percentages, ratios and rates
+ using spatial reasoning
+ interpreting statistical information
+ using measurement. (ACARA, n.d.-a)

Note the higher-order cognitive functions captured in the verbs used in these elements; words such as *estimate* and *interpret* are at a higher level than others used in the Australian Curriculum: Mathematics content descriptors, such as *recall*, *investigate*, *count* and *develop*. These words reinforce to teachers the depth of maths learning needed to choose to apply maths to contexts outside the maths classroom.

> *To be useful for the student, numeracy needs to be learned and used in multiple contexts — in history and geography, in economics and biology, in agriculture and culinary arts. Numeracy is not just one among many subjects but an integral part of all subjects.* (Steen, 2001, p. 6)

The six elements of numeracy are drawn from the maths strands of the Australian Curriculum and are used to organise and describe numeracy across six levels. The six levels in the Australian Curriculum F–10 indicate that the numeracy scope aligns roughly with the eleven years of maths learning described in the mathematics scope and sequence (ACARA, n.d.-b). Level 1 is separated into two parts — 1a and 1b — indicating the close connection with the Early Years Learning Framework (EYLF), which refers primarily to early childhood development rather than the standards described in the Australian Curriculum (see table 2.1). The general capabilities complement the learning outcomes of the EYLF: 'children have a strong sense of identity; children are connected with and contribute to their world; children have a strong sense of wellbeing; children are confident and involved learners; [and] children are effective communicators' (Department of Education, Employment and Workplace Relations, 2009, p. 8).

This separation in Level 1 also clearly indicates that it is a transitional level where students transition from early childhood education to formal schooling during Foundation. An intentional overlap occurs in this level where educators working in early childhood settings and schools are expected to work with both the EYLF and the Australian Curriculum.

Table 2.1: Levels in the numeracy continuum and their alignment with the EYLF and Australian Curriculum: Mathematics year by year

Numeracy continuum levels	Level 1a (prior to formal schooling)	Level 1b Typically, by the end of Foundation	Level 2 Typically, by the end of Year 2	Level 3 Typically, by the end of Year 4	Level 4 Typically, by the end of Year 6	Level 5 Typically, by the end of Year 8	Level 6 Typically, by the end of Year 10
		EYLF	Australian Curriculum				
EYLF and Australian Curriculum	Pre-school and prior to pre-school	Foundation	Years 1 and 2	Years 3 and 4	Years 5 and 6	Years 7 and 8	Year 9 and 10

SOURCE: Adapted from DEEWR (2009) and ACARA (n.d.-d)

Similarly, the strands of the maths curriculum align with the six numeracy elements as shown in table 2.2.

Table 2.2: Numeracy elements and their relationship with the Australian Curriculum: Mathematics strands

Numeracy elements	Australian Curriculum: Mathematics strands
Estimating and calculating with whole numbers (in earlier versions) ♦ understand and use numbers in context ♦ estimate and calculate ♦ use money	Number and algebra
Recognising and using patterns and relationships	Number and algebra (and other strands to a lesser extent)
Using fractions, decimals, percentages, ratios and rates ♦ interpret proportional reasoning ♦ apply proportional reasoning	Number and algebra
Using spatial reasoning ♦ visualise 2D shapes and 3D objects ♦ interpret maps and diagrams	Measurement and geometry
Interpreting statistical information ♦ interpret data displays ♦ interpret chance events	Statistics and probability
Using measurement ♦ estimate and measure with metric units ♦ operate with clocks, calendars and timetables	Measurement and geometry

SOURCE: Adapted from ACARA (n.d.-a) and ACARA (n.d.-d)

The relationship shown in table 2.2 indicates the maths knowledge that students require to apply maths in contexts where it is needed. It is important to note that the numeracy continuum was designed to support the broad application of numeracy across the learning areas and to ensure the coherent inclusion of numeracy as a general capability in all learning area contexts. As a result, very little detail is provided.

The relationship shown in table 2.1, however, describes the expected numeracy development of students. The numeracy continuum describes numerate behaviours as outcomes and the words *Typically, by the end of year . . .* preceding these indicate student standards expected every two years. The continuum assumes that students have not only been taught the maths that the descriptors align to, but also that students have been taught:

+ to read and make sense of contexts and determine whether some maths will help
+ how to solve problems, including how to choose the appropriate maths and strategies.

These behaviours will only be typical if students have been taught how to do them and have also gained the confidence to make the choices described. These connections have not been made explicit in the continuum and may leave the user with the impression that children can be taught numeracy. Although the Australian Curriculum provides examples of where maths is needed for discipline-specific concepts, the skills needed to develop numerate behaviours are neither identified nor stated as being the responsibility of teachers. Numeracy, defined as a general capability, helps to minimise this possible misconception.

One thing is clear: students need to know some maths and need to know it *well* to have the confidence to choose and use it in situations where it is needed or where it can help. Children who learn maths in a superficial way – lacking deep understandings – are unlikely to have the confidence to choose and use maths when they don't have to. They are unlikely to become numerate or to demonstrate numerate behaviours. This discussion about the learning quality needed to develop deep mathematical understandings is discussed further in Chapter 3.

National numeracy learning progression

In 2017, a national numeracy learning progression project was undertaken by ACARA. This resulted in a numeracy learning progression, which provides a sequence of numeracy development skills. This progression is not part of the Australian Curriculum and does not replace any part of it. Rather, it amplifies numeracy in the Australian Curriculum.

The progression provides advice on the numeracy demands of each learning area in the Australian Curriculum and links to the levels and expectations in the Australian Curriculum: Mathematics (ACARA, 2018). The progression provides a tool to assist teachers to identify and address individual student needs – to determine where each student is currently at and what they need to learn next in their numeracy development to progress to where they should be (ACARA, 2018). In this sense, it is a diagnostic map – a tool to support teacher intervention in student numeracy development. Due to its application in intervention for students requiring additional support, the progression will be described in greater detail in Chapter 4.

> **Time to reflect**
>
> Would it be helpful to have clearer connections between numeracy and maths and what teachers and schools need to do to develop the general capabilities in students? Why or why not?
>
> When you read the student outcomes of the Australian Curriculum numeracy continuum and compare them with the content descriptors of the mathematics learning area scope and sequence, do you think they look the same? Should they? Why or why not?

Numeracy across the curriculum

Numeracy demands

The *Shape of the Australian Curriculum: Mathematics* (National Curriculum Board, 2009) defines numeracy as 'the capacity, confidence and disposition to use mathematics to meet the demands of learning, school, home, work, community and civic life' (p. 5). This definition recognises that maths is needed to meet the demands of learning; that is, many learning areas require maths to understand the concepts from the host learning area. In the Australian Curriculum, a specific icon (the four main operator symbols in a two-by-two table) is used to indicate where numeracy has been identified as a demand in learning area content descriptions (see Appendix: Numeracy across the curriculum).

> *While much of the explicit teaching of literacy and numeracy occurs in the learning areas of English and Mathematics, literacy and numeracy skills are strengthened, made specific and extended in other learning areas.*
> (ACARA, 2018, p. 5)

For example, students studying science need to organise their investigation data in tables and sometimes graph the data to identify changes over time. Without the maths knowledge relating to data collection, organisation and display, and interpretation, students are unable to learn what is required in the science learning area outcomes. Not only are maths skills essential, they enhance or enrich the understanding of science.

Similarly, students studying timelines in history would find it very difficult – if not impossible – to indicate changes and events over time if they were not able to show these on a timeline, or number line as it is called in maths. This demands knowledge and comprehension of using a mathematical representation to display time on a continuum. The understanding of the progression of historical events is enhanced by the mathematical tool.

Numeracy opportunities

The second function of numeracy in learning is the opportunity identified by the teacher to demonstrate to students the possible uses for maths. Numeracy opportunities, if harnessed by teachers, help students to understand that maths is everywhere and that applying maths can be useful. For example, in an English lesson a Year 6 teacher asked his class to make an envelope for a card they had made. They didn't need to make the envelope as part of the lesson, but the teacher saw it as an opportunity for students to apply their measurement skills to a real situation. The application of some maths would integrate the learning of the English, art and technology learning areas and extend numeracy skills.

In addition, students themselves have opportunities to choose to apply their maths in real situations where they decide it is useful. Seeing maths applied to real contexts can also be helpful for students in gaining confidence with their maths, particularly when they see it used successfully, or even unsuccessfully, by others who are prepared to try again after making modifications to their choices. In general, while demands indicate where maths is required by a concept or unit of work, opportunities are more likely to occur at points in time during lessons.

All teachers as teachers of numeracy

All teachers are teachers of numeracy. This role can be deliberate or circumstantial, but it cannot be discretionary; it is not an option but a responsibility.

The difficulty for teachers of maths to provide their students with every possible learning situation that may require maths has already been discussed. This is no more possible than an English (or other language) teacher giving students an example of every single time they might need to use a particular sentence type, grammatical tool or word.

In a classroom situation, teachers of maths must be able to give some examples of possible contexts where students might need maths – if they can't, they should reconsider why they are teaching particular skills. It is inappropriate to respond to the typical student question 'When will we ever have to use this?' with 'Now' or 'On the next test'. While these responses might sound glib and humorous, they are used by some teachers who really do not know the purpose of some of the maths skills they teach. Is it any wonder that many students cannot understand the purpose of, let alone the need for, the maths they are taught?

Marr and Hagston (2007) have undertaken considerable research of numeracy in the workplace and state:

> *Even when they had learned new numeracy skills in the workplace, such as complex tallying strategies and calculating freight costs, there was a tendency for the less confident to regard them as merely part of the job or 'common sense', perhaps because they no longer resembled mathematics learned at school.* (p. 9)

What contributes to the misunderstanding highlighted by Marr and Hagston is the gap between the teaching and learning of maths and its application in real-life situations. Many people do not recognise the application of maths when they see it, largely because it doesn't look like the maths they learned in classrooms. Most people, especially students, need the maths explicitly pointed out to them.

This is where the responsibility of all teachers comes in. If teachers explicitly draw students' attention to the times when maths might be helpful, or to when they are using maths in their teaching, students would more than likely become aware of the fact that their lives are full of numeracy moments or times when maths is needed or has been applied.

Numeracy moments

A *numeracy moment* is a point in time when a teacher recognises that maths can be helpful. The teacher uses this moment to ask students 'Will some maths help here?' Because teachers do not necessarily recognise numeracy moments until they are using and applying maths, a teacher might simply point out to their students that 'We are using some maths here'. Both these responses might be circumstantial (or serendipitous); teachers might find themselves in these numeracy moments without recognising that they are pending or without planning for them. Gcos et al. (2012a) state that:

> *although it is possible to plan for numeracy learning, teachers also need to be alive to serendipitous moments for promoting numeracy as opportunities occurring during lessons, for example, by 'seeing' the numeracy embedded in current events or students' personal experiences.* (p. 4335)

Either way, teachers need to engage with one of the two numeracy moment responses to meet their responsibilities as teachers of numeracy. The following vignette is an example of a Year 6 teacher addressing numeracy in a class:

> *Students in Year 6 science were engaging with the topic of the solar system. They read that the distance between Earth and the sun was 149.6 million kilometres. The teacher recognised this as both a demand and an opportunity since students needed to understand what a large distance this was in order to appreciate the concept of the sun's rays reaching and heating the Earth's surface, and similarly for light from the sun reaching the Earth's surface.*
>
> *To understand the distance, the teacher had students work together in small groups to determine how many times around the Earth this distance would be. Students googled the circumference of the Earth (400,075 kilometres) and then chose to divide that into the distance between the sun and the Earth. This involved students choosing a range of methods and tools; some students struggled to know how to enter 149.6 million into their calculator and this provided an opportunity for the teacher to intervene using probing questions to promote the learning.*
>
> *The enormity of the total distance became real to the students as they worked through this task and as they understood the mathematics and what the numbers actually meant in the context. As a result, the numeracy enhanced the learning of the science being studied.*

Teachers who deeply understand maths are more likely to deliberately plan numeracy moments and see it as their professional responsibility to plan for as many of them as possible in their lessons, no matter what learning area they are teaching. The Department of Education, Science and Training (DEST) publication *Numeracy across the curriculum* (2004) states, 'Teaching students what being numerate involves is important, and being aware of the possible numeracy demands in the curriculum when planning helps teachers identify possible numeracy moments' (p. xi). Numerate teachers should seek strategic inclusion of numeracy in their planning, understanding how the numeracy demands of new subject matter will enhance the concepts being taught. At the very least, they should scaffold the maths required for the new learning. They should also continually seek opportunities to use maths in every lesson to demonstrate the application of the maths and show the importance of maths and numeracy for learning and for life.

Some teachers might consider this an 'add-on'. However, its importance cannot be overstated. For example, in Goos et al. (2012a), Catherine, a teacher of English, health and physical education, and Year 8 mathematics, states, 'I'm still learning to address the numeracy as it arises, not to be so driven by content and getting things finished' (p. 4335). Moreover, by understanding that students in school are frequently not having access to this input, we can see that the teaching of maths is impoverished by the lack of recognition and modelling of maths application in schools. It is not surprising that the value of maths and its application is a serious issue for society.

> ### Time to reflect
>
> Do you recognise and appreciate the importance of maths in daily situations?
>
> Are you intimidated by numeracy moments in daily life?

Numeracy across the curriculum (DEST, 2004) provides a range of strategies for educators teaching for numeracy. These strategies, some of which are paraphrased here, adresss the core ideas around developing numerate teaching practices and improving student understanding.

1. Notice and identify possible numeracy moments when planning.

2. Pay attention to and understand students' own personal numeracy issues by:
   - listening purposefully
   - helping students see the purpose of learning
   - supporting them to work collaboratively
   - asking other teachers to help you understand.

3. Give time to numeracy across the curriculum in the classroom by:
   - asking students questions about the numeracy requirements of tasks, the link between numeracy tasks and the contexts
   - asking students to explain their thinking
   - giving students the chance to work on numeracy issues
   - finding another context to practice numeracy skills learned in one situation.

4. Reflect on the way maths is being taught (in acknowledgement of the fact that this impacts students' confidence to apply maths when they haven't been told to do so).

Inquiry-based approach

Teachers do well to allow students to work laterally and enable inquiry approaches in contexts where maths application is useful, rather than directing students to apply their maths. Modelling to students that it is okay to problem-solve in whichever way they choose and then critically assess the solution demonstrates numerate behaviour, a powerful way of developing students' confidence to apply their maths. This approach removes the constraint of doing it the right way, which students often believe is the way they were taught in their maths class.

Catherine, the teacher cited earlier by Goos et al. (2012a) was motivated to improve her students' dispositions and confidence to use maths in different contexts. Catherine knew that to do this, her pedagogical style needed to be less directive and more inquiry-oriented. Catherine found that once she let go of giving directions, her students became more creative in the ways they solved problems, using spreadsheets and other unfamiliar tools. By not having one right way of working on problems, Catherine was inadvertently modelling the attitude and dispositions she wanted her students to develop.

Numeracy demands in non-mathematics learning areas

We have previously discussed how Australian Curriculum learning areas have many contexts that demand the application of maths. The demands for each content descriptor are included in the appendix. They are explicitly explained so that teachers might determine what the demands are and consider them in their planning by asking questions such as:

- Should I assume that my students have these mathematical understandings before I teach the science, humanities and social sciences (HASS), or arts concept?
- Will I need to teach or reteach the maths concept before or during the lesson?
- Do I deeply understand the connection between the maths and the host subject myself or should I revise it before proceeding?

Teachers should be aware that if these numeracy demands are not explicitly attended to in planning and during the teaching of other learning area concepts, it is likely that students will not grasp the new learning. A summary of the numeracy demands in the learning areas is provided in table 2.3.

Table 2.3: Numeracy demands in the Australian Curriculum summary

Learning area	Numeracy demands — Teachers should ensure students understand that these mathematics concepts enable access to the required learning	
	Years F–2	**Years 3–6**
Science	• Students need to understand measurement concepts and skills to record precise measurements when performing scientific investigations. • Students need to understand what patterns are to learn that there are daily and seasonal changes in our environment that affect daily life. • Students need to use informal measurements (such as hand-spans, leaves) to collect and record observations for which they use data handling methods. • Students need to use provided tables to sort information.	• Students need to use their knowledge of number and data to calculate averages (such as mean, median and mode) to appropriate accuracy. They also need to understand possible causes of bias in the way they collect the data. • Students need to understand statistical concepts when collecting and organising data. They need to undertake measurement and be given opportunities to choose and use measuring tools and appropriate units of measurement. • Students need to understand measurement and numerical concepts to be able to convert between units, for example, grams to milligrams, and to estimate lengths and capacities. • Students need to understand and compare measures relating to the planet and solar system, for example, the relative size of planets and the distances between them.
English	• Students need to understand the concept of time and elapsed time to demonstrate the progression of time in a storyboard and to organise their writing in a planned sequence. • Students need to identify the sequence of a recount by understanding and using the correct vocabulary (for example, first, then, finally). • Students need to recognise that timelines and words of time are frequently used for cohesion and the drawing of a timeline can help (words include *once upon a time, yesterday, afterwards, before, and then, some time later, followed by* and *finally*). • Students need to understand patterns to learn about alliteration, rhythm, sounds in stories, rhymes, chants, songs and poems. • Students need to learn about counting to understand concepts of print and its organisation, for example, page numbering. • Students need to know that numbers represent quantity, for example, when deciding whether a word has one or two phonemes or syllables.	• Students need to understand the timeline of a narrative in order to understand the sequence of the story. • Students need to learn patterns in turn-taking and use words like first, second and third. • Students need to understand the concept of time when learning about tenses. • Students need to learn about vertical camera angle, scale and shot size when learning about the effect on audiences of techniques in texts types. • Students need to create imaginative texts using visual features such as perspective, distance and angle. • Students need to have a basic understanding of the concept of a rate (speaks fast, speaks slow, speaks slower) to learn about pace when speaking and listening. • Students need to learn words of time, including *firstly, in the beginning, and then, later* and *finally* when learning about text cohesion. • Students need to explore the effects of different placements of elements in an image. • Students need to understand how events can be placed on a number line in chronological order, for example, when reading texts about historical contexts.

SOURCE: Adapted from ACARA (n.d.-f)

(continued)

Learning area	Numeracy demands Teachers should ensure students understand that these mathematics concepts enable access to the required learning	
	Years F–2	**Years 3–6**
The arts	◆ Students need to understand measurement concepts and technical measurement language such as *length*, *size*, *mass*, *long* or *short*, *large* or *small*, *heavy* or *light* to make movements and heavy or light actions in dance; draw and paint long or short lines and small or large shapes in visual arts; and create long or short sounds in music. ◆ Students need to engage with technical maths language when creating visual artworks when working with textures and shapes. For example, words such as smooth, rough, pointy, straight and curved are all words with maths meanings and application.	◆ Students need to understand spatial concepts involving symmetry to create, present and respond to artworks. ◆ Students need to understand ratio and proportion when working with perspective. ◆ Students need to understand the concepts of reduction and enlargement when working with digital mediums. ◆ Students need to understand ordinal numbers when analysing dance movements and sequences, for example, first, second and third. ◆ Students need to understand pattern and ordinal numbers to understand rhythm. ◆ Students need to understand tempo to create, perform and record compositions. ◆ Students need to use media technologies and dramatic action to create a sense of time and space.
HASS	◆ Students need to learn about how to show and represent places and locations on simple maps. ◆ Students need to collect data and information from observations and identify information and data from sources provided. ◆ Students need to sort and record information and data in tables and on plans and labelled maps. ◆ Students need to sequence events as they occur, using the words *first*, *second* and *third*. ◆ Students need to understand and consider past and present times to compare the use of artifacts from past and present and how places have changed over time. ◆ Students need to read information displayed on maps and draw simple conclusions. ◆ Students need a basic understanding of scale to understand how places can be defined at a range of scales. ◆ Students need to have a sense of proximity to understand scale, for example, using words like *close*, *closer* and *further*.	◆ Students need to analyse and construct detailed comparative and multi-stranded timelines to show the sequence of key local, national and international events for a range of people for a given point of time to show change and continuity, progress and regression, and cause and consequence. ◆ Students need to use spatial, measurement or numerical concepts when calculating distances, describing directions and locating capital cities on a map. ◆ Students need to engage with concepts such as average, percentage and growth rates when engaging in discussions about social justice issues. ◆ Students need to use numerical and statistical data (including percentages, and mean, mode and median) when considering life expectancies, income distribution or population distribution to describe the demographics of their local community, Australia or the Asia-Pacific. ◆ Students need to use knowledge of graphical representations of quantitative data when constructing an economic model representing Australia's connections with its region or global community, including flows of trade, investment and tourism. ◆ Students need to understand measures of temperature and rainfall to understand climate types around the world. ◆ Students need to locate, collect and organise data from different sources and record, sort, organise and represent data from and in graphs, tables and maps. ◆ Students need to sequence information about people's lives and events using a variety of methods including timelines. ◆ Students need to interpret and analyse information and data, identify patterns and trends, compare distributions and draw conclusions or infer relationships.

(continued)

Numeracy in and across the Australian Curriculum F–6

Learning area	Numeracy demands Teachers should ensure students understand that these mathematics concepts enable access to the required learning	
	Years F–2	**Years 3–6**
Technologies	<ul><li>Students need to recognise and explore patterns in data and represent data in pictures, symbols and diagrams.</li><li>Students need to collect and sort data and use digital systems to present data creatively.</li><li>Students need to represent a sequence of steps needed to solve problems.</li><li>Students need to collect, create, organise and store information using applications such as databases and spreadsheets (this requires sorting based on given criteria).</li></ul>	<ul><li>Students need to examine how whole numbers are used to represent all data in digital systems.</li><li>Students need to acquire, store and validate different types of data and use a range of software to interpret and visualise data to create information.</li><li>Students need to use knowledge of spatial concepts and learning of measurement skills to generate and record design ideas for a 3D object (for example, a sun-safe hat or a space vehicle) using simple plans before they can produce the item from their design specifications.</li><li>Students need to use measurement skills to design and make products, including, for example, measuring lengths of timber, paper or metal, halving and doubling recipes, and determining fabric requirements and drafting patterns when working with leather or textiles.</li><li>Students need to understand the mathematical language, symbols and diagrams they encounter when comparing forms of news reports (for example, newspaper, television, radio) and examining purposes behind the news reports. These will need to be discussed explicitly so that the students can make sense of the information.</li><li>Students need to use knowledge of ratio (doubling or halving) or proportion when combining ingredients to bake or when moulding materials such as plaster of Paris.</li></ul>
Health and physical education	<ul><li>Students need to work with whole numbers, for example, to determine serves of food and count heartbeats per minute.</li><li>Students need to use simple collection tools and data displays, for example, paces, steps or pictographs.</li><li>Students need to describe how the body is growing, requiring the use of comparative words like *bigger*, *wider*, *taller* and other measurement words.</li><li>Students need to practise movement skills and movement sequences, requiring spatial language, including words of position such as *behind*, *in front* and *above*.</li><li>Students need to describe how their body moves in relation to people and hence need to know spatial words of position such as in *front*, *behind* and *beside*.</li><li>Students need to incorporate elements of space and time in performing simple movement sequences.</li></ul>	<ul><li>Students need to understand place value to engage with data comparisons, for example, comparing foods that contribute to the recommended intake of a nutrient.</li><li>Students need to understand percentage and chance, for example, when learning about health risks connected to smoking, obesity and drugs.</li><li>Students need to know how numbers work to apply basic rules and scoring systems to games and physical activities.</li><li>Students need to use sophisticated collection and display tools (for example, two-way tables or simple graphs) and use ICT to create displays when comparing exercise levels and types of physical activity.</li><li>Students need to produce sophisticated displays and analyses of data (for example, scatter plots, mean, median, range, stem and leaf plots), especially when representing football and netball scores.</li><li>Students need to be able to first access information when represented in charts and tables when discussing and interpreting health information in the media.</li><li>Students need to research data that connects physical activity to health and wellbeing when examining the benefits of these two variables.</li></ul>

Numeracy opportunities in non-mathematics learning areas

Numeracy opportunities are woven through the curriculum to encourage the application of maths across subjects and learning areas for students to see the value of maths. However, while an icon indicates the numeracy demands in the Australian Curriculum, it is expected that teachers will themselves recognise the opportunities in their planning and delivery. Unless teachers read the content descriptors of learning areas in the context of the numeracy definition, however, they are unlikely to engage with these opportunities. This fact has been acknowledged by Goos et al. (2012b), who observe that 'While the curriculum explicitly identifies numeracy demands via use of icons and online filters, additional opportunities for developing students' numeracy capabilities are invisible unless one knows how to "see" them' (p. 320). In other words, even if they do recognise an opportunity to apply some maths, they are unlikely to harness the opportunity unless they personally have the disposition or confidence to do so.

Consequently, the opportunities to demonstrate maths application and use maths in contexts other than maths lessons are not maximised in most classrooms, even if teachers do use the numeracy demands in their teaching. A sample of numeracy opportunities in the curriculum is provided in table 2.4.

Numeracy in and across the Australian Curriculum F–6

Table 2.4: Numeracy opportunities in the Australian Curriculum

Learning area	Numeracy opportunities: The teacher should use these and other identified opportunities to reinforce understanding of the mathematics learned by students through its application	
	Years F–2	**Years 3–6**
Science	◆ Teachers can take the opportunity to teach words of movement and transformation such as *forwards* and *backwards* when students are learning how objects move. ◆ Teachers can take the opportunity to teach students about patterns in time, words of time (for example, month names, season names) and how to read a calendar when learning about daily and seasonal changes.	◆ Teachers can take the opportunity to have students collect information that they might need to use statistical concepts and display and interpret their data. ◆ Teachers can take the opportunity to have students access numerical concepts related to estimation. ◆ Teachers can take the opportunity to have students collect data, for example, when sampling.
English	◆ Teachers can take the opportunity to teach students to describe spatial dimensions in a witness account of a television news item. ◆ Teachers can take the opportunity to teach students to gather or find data as evidence to support their case before writing a persuasive text. ◆ Teachers can take the opportunity to teach mathematical concepts arising from literary texts, for example, in *Gulliver's travels* Gulliver's waist is about half of his height, his neck is about half of his waist and the circumference of his thumb is about half of his wrist, or the 'nonsense maths' in *Alice in Wonderland*.	◆ Teachers can take the opportunity to have students describe the type of camera angle or spatial perspective to explain the point of view of the reader or viewer. ◆ Teachers can take the opportunity to have students to use the map or diagram provided in a fictional novel to help them understand the geographical location and dimensions of the setting (for example, the forest in *The hobbit*). ◆ Teachers can take the opportunity to have students gather or find data as evidence to support their case before writing a persuasive text. ◆ Teachers can take the opportunity to teach mathematical concepts arising from literary texts, for example in *Gulliver's travels* Gulliver's waist is about half of his height, his neck is about half of his waist and the circumference of his thumb is about half of his wrist, or the 'nonsense maths' in *Alice in Wonderland*. ◆ Teachers can take the opportunity to have students tally words themselves to determine which ones are used the most in speech and written texts (high frequency words). ◆ Teachers can take the opportunity to teach language devices such as personification, metaphor and simile by asking students to use numbers or shapes.

SOURCE: Adapted from ACARA (n.d.-f)

(continued)

WOULD YOU LIKE MATHS WITH THAT?

Learning area	Numeracy opportunities The teacher should use these and other identified opportunities to reinforce understanding of the mathematics learned by students through its application	
	Years F–2	**Years 3–6**
Languages other than English, EAL/D	◆ Teachers can take the opportunity to reinforce the concepts for counting as being one-to-one correspondence and 'adding on', when learning the words for numbers. ◆ Teachers can take the opportunity to reinforce the understandings of numerical order (first, second, third), matching these numbers to counting numbers when learning these words in another language. ◆ Teachers can take the opportunity to support students to understand when numbers are used as labels (for example, on football jumpers, buses or letter boxes) when seeing pictures of these in language texts. ◆ Teachers can take the opportunity when learning comparative language such as *big, bigger, biggest* and *tall, taller, tallest* to reinforce the language needed to engage in measurement concepts.	◆ Teachers can take the opportunity to reinforce the learnings essential for spatial concepts that children need in learning expressions for position or location such as 'it's under the chair', 'turn right', 'it's north of Brisbane' and in giving directions in another language. ◆ Teachers can take the opportunity to support students to apply measurement skills and skills of proportion in making and drawing flags belonging to other countries. ◆ Teachers can take the opportunity to reinforce the concept of likelihood in learning expressions of probability; for example in expressions such as 'he will definitely be there' there is an aspect of certainly meaning there is no doubt, whereas in the statement 'I don't think so' there is some doubt – these expressions lead to measurement of likelihood, which is fundamental to understanding mathematical probability and can be reinforced through questions such as 'Which is more likely?'. ◆ Teachers can take the opportunity to reinforce time concepts including the positions of the hands on a clock at various times, words for describing 'chunks of time' such as *months, decades* and *minutes* (teachers cannot assume students will know these) when learning to tell the time and expressions for time. ◆ Teachers can take the opportunity to reinforce the learnings that are offered (for example, that a minute is 60 seconds – 'Let's count up to sixty slowly in French and we can estimate how long a minute is') when learning to tell the time and expressions for time.
The arts	◆ Teachers can take the opportunity to draw attention to the repeating patterns students make when working with rhythm (for example, clap, stamp, click, clap, stamp, click). ◆ Teachers can take the opportunity to use proportional and fractional understandings and estimation when illustrating relationships between objects within artworks, for example, eyes are halfway up the head. ◆ Teachers can take the opportunity to use spatial concepts relating to location and movement when teaching students to follow and give oral and written instructions or directions in the context of drama or dance.	◆ Teachers can take the opportunity to use pattern and measurement concepts to create rhythmic patterns with music (including dance, performance, conducting) by manipulating the duration, beat, time values and metre. ◆ Teachers can take the opportunity to make connections between time signatures and fractional concepts when using timing in movement, music or performance sequences (for example, moving simple 2/4 and 4/4 time-signatures) and dancing (for example with 3/4 in a waltz time). ◆ Teachers can take the opportunity to have students use algebraic and spatial concepts to produce artworks that include counter change, repetition and tessellation, for example, in the style of Escher.

(continued)

Learning area	Numeracy opportunities — The teacher should use these and other identified opportunities to reinforce understanding of the mathematics learned by students through its application	
	Years F–2	**Years 3–6**
HASS	<ul><li>Teachers can take the opportunity to have students use simple mathematical language when describing the position of features on a map of a familiar place.</li><li>Teachers can take the opportunity to have students learn about data and particularly how it is generated by students having one data piece each.</li><li>Teachers can take the opportunity to have students explore different ways of organising their data in hard copy initially and then with technologies.</li></ul>	<ul><li>Teachers can take the opportunity to have students use mathematics to construct simple timelines or interpret data displays that sequence historical events or place people or artefacts within set time periods.</li><li>Teachers can take the opportunity to have students select and interpret statistical data that describes the representation of religious beliefs and cultures within Australian society at a particular time when investigating their local community.</li><li>Teachers can take the opportunity, when comparing the results of 'first past the post' and 'preferential' voting systems for a classroom ballot to select a leader or make a decision in response to an issue, to have students interpret results, including differences, and record the results in a simple table.</li></ul>
Technologies	<ul><li>Teachers can take the opportunity to teach students about data and particularly how it is generated by students having one data piece each.</li><li>Teachers can take the opportunity to have students explore different ways of organising their data in hard copy initially and then with technologies.</li></ul>	<ul><li>Teachers can take the opportunity to have students gather information about the desirable features of new playground equipment, use data displays to record survey information and make inferences from the numerical data.</li><li>Teachers can take the opportunity to have students also use estimation and measuring skills when considering the physical requirements of young students engaging with the equipment.</li><li>Teachers can take the opportunity to revisit with students a deeper understanding of measurement units relating to mass given students know that labels on food packaging are required to show the type and quantity of ingredients included.</li><li>Teachers can take the opportunity to have students use spatial and measurement skills in the planning, scale drawing and constructing phases when manipulating materials to produce a toy from recycled textiles.</li></ul>

> **Time to reflect**
>
> Did you realise that each of the learning areas demanded some maths?
>
> Did your own teachers draw attention to when you needed or were using maths in learning other subjects?

Opportunities for numeracy in non-learning area contexts

Teachers and school leaders should consider any event as an opportunity to model to students the numeracy capabilities learned. School leaders can even model these to teachers who in turn can use them with their classes to support the efficient management and operations of the school. The first recommendation of the *National numeracy review report* is:

> That all systems and schools recognise that, while mathematics can be taught in the context of mathematics lessons, the development of numeracy requires experience in the use of mathematics beyond the mathematics classroom, and hence requires an across the curriculum commitment. Both pre- and in-service teacher education should thus recognise and prepare all teachers as teachers of numeracy, acknowledging that this may in some cases be 'subject specific numeracy'. (COAG, 2008, p. 7)

This recommendation arose from a discussion based on two points:

1. For students to develop numerate behaviour they must practise it.
2. Mathematics can make a difference to whether and how well students learn the entire curriculum. (COAG, 2008)

With respect to the first point, successful application of maths to situations in contexts outside the maths lesson begins with recognition that some maths will help, as discussed in Chapter 1. It is apparent that this problem-solving process must occur outside the maths lesson. In a school, this can be either in other learning area contexts as discussed or in situations that arise outside formal lessons, such as school assemblies, the school canteen, drama productions, school excursions, budgeting for events, establishing a roster for lunchtime basketball equipment, creating a menu for camp meals, organising sports carnivals and so on.

Table 2.5 shows examples of possible opportunities that can be used to support the development of numeracy. They could be real or hypothetical opportunities; either way they demonstrate to students the power of each of these capabilities.

Table 2.5: Numeracy opportunities in non-learning contexts

Non-learning context	Numeracy opportunities in non-learning contexts The teacher should use identified opportunities to reinforce understanding of the mathematics learned by students through real-world application
School assembly	◆ Each fortnight one of the classes in the primary school has the job of organising and facilitating the school assembly. The class must present a program (including approximate times) to the deputy principal. The class needs to find out what the purpose of the assembly is and which year groups are required to attend, and decide when and where each year group sit and the order in which students will be brought out to take their places as well as the approximate times each participant on the program will appear. They should also consider whether parents need to be invited for any presentations (including advertising in the local paper if required) and how that should be done. Students must prepare a running sheet with approximate start times and elapsed times and have it ready for each class the day before as well as giving a draft to the deputy principal three days before.
In the classroom or playground	◆ The principal would like to know the area of the music room floor so that they can get some quotes for carpet. The Year 4 class is assigned this task. ◆ One of the students in the class has recently had a hip operation and will be in a wheelchair for the next five months. Their parents have phoned the teacher and want to know whether the school is wheelchair accessible. The principal also wants to know this so that they can make arrangements if necessary. The teachers decide to make this a class learning topic to support their measurement lessons over the next week. Students are to put their findings in a formal letter to the principal and the student's parents, including all measurements and recommendations. ◆ The school wants to create a map for visitors and newly enrolled students. The principal, in consultation with the teacher, asks the class to create a school map on a scale that would fit on an A4 sheet of paper. Students are requested to provide the map digitally so that it can be printed by office staff.
Food events or canteen	◆ The deputy principal has asked students from one of the classes to help him plan a sausage sizzle to raise funds for students at a school in Argentina which has recently been hit by a tornado. They set a goal of $2000 and have to decide how much to charge for a sausage, how many sausages they need to sell and how many sausages and bread rolls they need to buy, and estimate how much tomato sauce and mustard will be needed if they are to meet their goal.

Sports events	◆ The Year 6 teacher has been given the task of organising the school athletics carnival. She saw this as a real opportunity to enhance the numeracy learning of students in her class. She decided to assign tasks to pairs of students, each of which would work with another teacher on the school staff. The tasks are:
	  ○ determining a running sheet for the day, estimating event start and finish times and which events could occur at the same time
	  ○ measuring and recording the long jump lengths of each competitor
	  ○ measuring and recording the high jump heights of each competitor
	  ○ determining the winners up to third place
	  ○ measuring and recording the race speeds of competitors in each race
	  ○ measuring the distances of the racing tracks
	  ○ determining student points totals and the age-group champions.
	In order to prepare for their responsibilities, the teacher has students engage in measurement tasks in the weeks prior to the day so they can become familiar with their roles. They simulate the jumps and races so they can estimate lengths and times. This will enable them to critique actual measurements on the day, for example, by knowing what 1.2 metres looks like in their mind.

Other	◆ A plethora of other contexts can be added based on the nature of the school.

Conclusion

> *All teachers are responsible for contributing to their students' numeracy development. Teachers should have knowledge of the numeracy demands and opportunities inherent in their teaching, and be able to discern and respond to an individual student's numeracy learning needs, particularly for those students whose progress is at risk because of limited numeracy skills.* (AAMT, 1998, p. 3)

Numeracy, in and across the school curriculum, provides opportunities for students to practise applying their maths skills and concepts, and as a result they grow a deeper appreciation for the role that maths plays in their lives.

Since all teachers teach in these contexts – either in learning areas or in their school community – they should embrace the value of this learning and actively become aware of, and seek, the demands for both maths applications and opportunities in modelling the applications themselves. When arriving at a numeracy moment, teachers should deliberately pause and ask students 'Will some maths help here?' Whenever numeracy moments arise, be sure to use the problem-solving framework outlined in Chapter 1 (clarify, choose, use, interpret and communicate). At the very least, draw students' attention to the fact that maths is being used by saying, for example, 'We are using maths here'. In seeing someone using and applying maths outside their maths lesson, students develop their appreciation of the usefulness of maths.

However, as previously highlighted, students will often avoid applying their maths if they lack confidence. Teachers can help to ensure that their students are confident users of maths by teaching maths well: teaching for conceptual understanding rather than merely teaching mathematical methods, procedures and facts. The notion of teaching maths well will be explored in the following chapter.

3 Teaching mathematics for numeracy attainment

> *The teaching of mathematics has a key role to play – school mathematics must be taught well. . . . This means a focus on building knowledge of the concepts.* (AAMT, 1998, p. 3)

Teaching mathematics 'well'

Australia's performance in maths and numeracy has stalled or declined on national indicators such as NAPLAN and international assessments such as Trends in International Mathematics and Science Study (TIMSS) and PISA (Smith et al., 2018). PISA has been held every three years since 2002 and, for the first time in the assessment's history, Australia has failed to meet the OECD average in mathematics performance.

In previous chapters, I suggested that teachers need to teach maths well to address the slump in numeracy standards for children in Australia's schools. Teachers all around the country are teaching maths, but not always well enough for numerate behaviours to result. In no way is this statement a reflection of the effort being used to teach maths around the country; teachers are working very hard in often very difficult circumstances. In many cases it is the result of a lack of pedagogical content knowledge.

Clearly, teaching maths well requires both sound knowledge of the maths being taught and knowledge of the specific needs of students being taught. However, it is necessary to learn the maths and the pedagogies that work best to produce the learning required first so that decisions about the what and the how can be made to best support particular students and their needs.

In Chapter 1 we learned that numeracy is a disposition, an inclination, a can-do attitude. If children don't have that attitude – no matter how well they know maths – there is a risk they will not be, and possibly never will be, numerate.

To develop a favourable disposition towards choosing and using maths, children need to deeply understand the maths and what it is used for. It is this deep understanding that is needed if they are to make the connection between a context or situation and the maths they have learned in school maths lessons. The can-do attitude results from two things:

1. knowing the maths well
2. being taught the maths in ways that give them confidence to willingly 'have a go'.

Teaching for deep understanding

Some teachers themselves understand little of the maths they were taught in school. They likely learned the maths content at what Hattie (2012) calls 'surface level' (p. 60) or what Willis (1992) calls 'a plethora of de-contextualised mathematical facts and procedures' (p. 37). As a result, some of them teach it this way to their students, sadly perpetuating this type of learning. Many are unable to relate school maths to anything beyond the classroom where they learned it, let alone to connect it to other learning or make conjectures. As stated in *Numeracy across the curriculum*:

> the way mathematics is taught may impact on how students perceive mathematics, how they learn to use mathematics, how they see the usefulness of mathematics and their capacity to use mathematics in other contexts. It suggests that teacher demonstration and student practice of skills as the dominant pedagogy will limit students' capacity to use mathematics in other contexts. (DEST, 2004, p. xi)

Children in classrooms are often neither being taught nor learning maths concepts. Rather, they are learning only factual and procedural knowledge and methods, or surface content. What is meant by this distinction? The word *concept* implies the deep underpinning of an idea and the deep learning quality that goes with it. Factual content can be learned at a 'recall' (surface) level only, whereas if children really know and understand what they've learned they can then apply their learning to previously unseen or unfamiliar contexts, and they may be able to analyse and critique their own or another's use of it in a context.

Teaching students in ways that result in them having deep conceptual understandings instead of merely having low-level, surface or content knowledge requires teachers to comprehend the theoretical difference between these two to inform their planning and teaching.

> *By separating factual knowledge from conceptual knowledge, we highlight the need for educators to teach for deep understanding of conceptual knowledge, not just for remembering isolated and small bits of factual knowledge.* (Anderson & Krathwohl, 2001, p. 42)

Content-focused teaching is merely imparting knowledge of facts, information and procedures. It is teaching factual content as if having children learn it were the goal. Prior to the information age and the rise of digital technologies in schooling during the 1970s, a significant role of the classroom teacher was to impart as much knowledge of facts and procedural skills as possible while students were at school to maximise their success with calculations. The mainstream school maths curriculum was mainly surface or content focused. Now that this factual and procedural content knowledge is virtually available to anyone, anywhere and at any time through information and communication technologies, students need to know what to do with it and how to judge its authenticity in context.

Concept-focused teaching, on the other hand, is about teachers focusing on their students learning concepts or big ideas. This means that students are taught factual content and procedures as the important foundation for the concept and that the teacher understands this progression. The teacher focuses on the student learning the concept while teaching the factual content – teaching with a different focus, goal and purpose. This type of instruction leads students to:

- connect their learning to what they already know, their own situation and their prior experiences
- find relevance in what they are learning
- understand isolated mathematical facts and skills and their purpose more deeply
- think more critically about the purposes and goals of their learning.

Consider the following example. If children are taught the maths concept of addition as a set of low-level procedural skills only – how to add up – what results for most children is only the understanding that addition is adding up. Compare this with a class in which the teacher teaches children addition as a concept – an understanding about quantifying by bringing together or combining objects and groups of objects sometimes represented by numbers. Adding sugar to a recipe, for example, is a process of adding value, enhancing or increasing the quality of what is being made. What is important is the result, not whether you use a spoon, a cup or your hand, or do it standing on one leg!

The focus is on the outcome, not on the method used. While some methods might be more efficient, they are not essential to the outcome. This bringing together or combining can be undertaken in many ways depending on the number of objects or amounts and can occur and be helpful in a range of contexts situated in their own lives. The objects – sometimes represented by numbers and symbols to facilitate the quantification – are totalled, summed or brought together to show an increase in value, quantity or amount.

Addition is a deep relational understanding that results in children being able to determine whether the skill of adding using numbers to represent amounts or objects is useful, helpful or necessary in a particular context. Moreover, students' deep understanding of the concept of addition enables them to reflect on the reasonableness of the total they have calculated in the context. The method or procedure they might have been taught is almost irrelevant since the deep understanding means it can be applied in many different ways; the understanding of the purpose and application of the method itself results in children being able to determine whether their solution is or should be reasonable or not, not just whether the steps in the procedure were correctly used and in the right order. In the context of a maths lesson children might add amounts by touching and moving and counting on or skip-counting to determine how many there are altogether. Whether they can do it using an algorithm or not is often irrelevant if they can't interpret it in the context or judge the reasonableness of their solution.

Summarising, concept-based instruction – where the teacher teaches factual and procedural knowledge with a focus on student understanding of concepts – leads students to think about facts and procedures at a much deeper level (Schill & Howell, 2011). Hattie (2009) suggests that learning can be at three levels: surface, deep and conceptual. In *Visible learning for teachers*, Hattie (2012) states, 'So much of classroom instruction relates to the surface' (p. 86). Research by Mehta and Fine (2015) supports this. The reasons for this occurring in classrooms, it might be argued, is due to the increasing amount of knowledge that teachers are expected to teach. Many teachers would argue that to get through it all they must skim across the surface and don't have time to teach for understanding.

Research indicates that the process of teaching students through problems or at a big-idea level leads students to think about the context for their learning, thus enabling them to use their understanding of real world meaning of content knowledge. This results in them thinking about the knowledge at a deeper level (Erickson, 2017; Schill & Howell, 2011).

Concept-focused teachers must still teach surface-level factual and procedural skills and content and have students work with these. In fact, conceptual knowledge begins with knowledge and thinking about facts. Bransford et al. (2000) summarise the importance of conceptual understanding. They indicate that people connect and organise their knowledge around important concepts and that, to develop competence in an area of inquiry, students must:

+ have deep foundational factual knowledge
+ understand the facts and ideas of a conceptual framework
+ organise their knowledge in ways that facilitate their retrieval and application of it.

However, this content knowledge alone is insufficient to develop deep conceptual learnings and understandings. Erickson (2012) states that 'a cognitive interplay between the factual and conceptual levels of mental processing' (p. 8) is essential for intellectual development since thinking without this interaction can be shallow. Furthermore, conceptual understanding brings purpose and relevance to the factual content students are working with. So, it is not a case of either–or, (either surface content or concepts) but a case of both–and (both surface content and concepts).

Teachers of maths can support the deeper learning by focusing on the big ideas in the contexts of real-world problems. This is supported by Recommendation 3 of the *National numeracy review report*:

> That from the earliest years, greater emphasis be given to providing students with frequent exposure to higher-level mathematical problems rather than routine procedural tasks, in contexts of relevance to them, with increased opportunities for students to discuss alternative solutions and explain their thinking. (COAG, 2008, p. 31)

As we move further into the twenty-first century, deeper learning practices are needed for students to develop the competencies required (Fullan et al., 2017; National Research Council, 2012). Hattie (2012) states that there needs to be 'a major shift from an over-reliance on surface information . . . towards a balance of surface and deep learning' (p. 86).

Hattie (2012) explains that teachers need to consider three levels when they plan: the surface knowledge needed to understand the concepts; the deeper understandings of how ideas relate to each other and extend to other understandings; and the conceptual thinking that allows surface and deep knowledge to turn into conjectures and concepts on which to build new surface and deep understandings. Hattie (2012) uses the Biggs and Collis (1982) Structure of the Observed Learning Outcomes (SOLO) model for understanding these levels, explaining that the combination of surface learning and deep learning operating together result in (student) conceptual understanding.

Teaching with a focus on concept learning is supported and enabled through thinking frameworks such as the SOLO model and Bloom's (1956) taxonomy. If children aren't taught higher-order thinking skills, such as critical reasoning and interpretation alongside maths knowledge and facts, they will be unlikely to do anything with their learning. It is for this reason that many students on leaving school either do not identify when maths might be helpful or choose not to use their maths in contexts that demand it – they don't have the deep conceptual understandings of what they were taught in classrooms to connect it to real-life contexts. Instead, they have low-level ability to do sums when it is asked of them using mathematical procedures.

As a result of teachers understanding and using the levels of the SOLO model in their teaching, students are enabled to make connections and relate their ideas to other learning. For example, teachers who focus on their students learning maths factual content only tend to focus on recall of the what and the how of the content and procedural skills rather than on the big ideas or deep understandings of the concept that the factual content underpins. This is highlighted in table 3.1.

In comparing the columns of table 3.1, lower-order and higher-order (surface and deep) differences are highlighted. Content-focused teaching focuses mostly on students learning lower-order skills: memorisation, recall and rote learning with some application. On the other hand, concept-focused teaching focuses prominently on students using higher-order reasoning skills such as making choices, identifying connections, justifying reasonableness and decisions, and critiquing their own and others' work. This type of teaching understands the need for students to gain the foundational learning of facts and procedures *initially* but not as an end in themselves.

Table 3.1: Content-focused teaching versus concept-focused teaching in mathematics

Concept	Content-focused teaching	Concept-focused teaching
Addition	◆ Students learn to perform methods for adding but don't necessarily know how and when to apply addition in a real-life setting. ◆ Students define *addition* by explaining how to do it.	◆ Students understand that to add means to increase value or quantity, knowing that mathematical addition supports understanding of quantification to find totals and make comparisons. ◆ Students can choose and apply different addition skills in situations that demand it rather than simply when told to add up. ◆ Students judge their solution by its reasonableness in context.
Mean as average	◆ Students calculate the mean by adding numbers and dividing by how many numbers there are. ◆ Students define *the mean* by explaining how to find it rather than defining the concept of average.	◆ Students understand that the mean is a measure of centredness and that a number that can represent a group of numbers clustered around it. ◆ Students can estimate the mean by understanding the range and decide whether it is reasonable in a context.
Measurement	◆ Students know how to measure length, width and height. ◆ Students who only understand how to measure usually have to be told to do so, including what tool and unit to use. ◆ Students generally can't estimate or judge the reasonableness of their measure.	◆ Students understand that to measure means to find how much of a unit an attribute has (for example, how much length, how much height and so on) for a particular purpose, and that it is found by counting the number of repeats of the unit selected. ◆ Students can choose the unit themselves, justify it in context and estimate how many repeats of the unit there are, critiquing their own and others' measurements.

This difference becomes even more prominent when considering it in the light of Bloom's (1956) taxonomy. Bloom developed a hierarchy of levels of thinking, beginning with recall and culminating with evaluating or assessing what has been created. This hierarchy was later refined by Anderson and Krathwohl (2001).

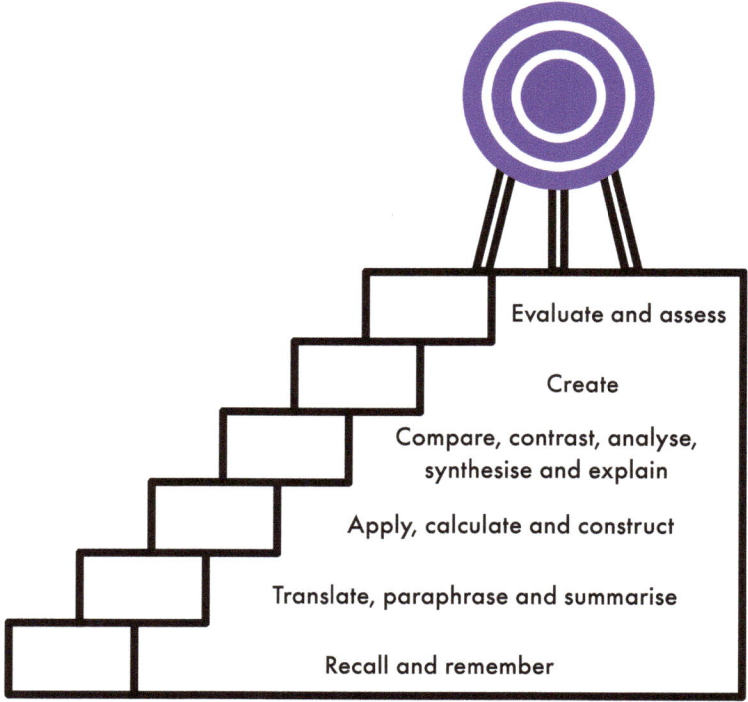

Figure 3.1: Bloom's taxonomy
SOURCE: Adapted from Anderson & Krathwohl, 2001

The lowest level of knowledge cognition is recall and remember. This describes learning that, however necessary for further learning, is superficial and lacking depth. Many mathematical algorithms demand this type of learning. The opposite end of the taxonomy describes learning that is deep; if a student has learned something deeply, they are more than able to apply it – they can evaluate it, assess its value and create new knowledge using their knowledge, thus transforming their learning and engaging it in something that is important to them and possibly even important globally (Fullan et al., 2017).

Since deep learning is required for students to be confident users of maths, teachers should be aiming for their students to be able to independently apply their learning of maths in a range of contexts and to reason about them. In other words, teaching strategies used, and tasks developed to assess the learning that occurs, should demand the use of students' cognitive skills beyond mere application.

Most representations of Bloom's taxonomy show it as a hierarchy indicating each level subsumes and assumes inclusion of the previous one. This also represents the gradual progression from lower-order to higher-order cognition. However, many previous school maths curriculums had very few higher-order conceptual understandings in them. Verbs in content descriptors tended to represent predominantly lower-order cognitive skills such as *recall, describe, recognise, use, apply, construct, calculate, add* and *divide*.

Recent versions of maths curriculums – including the Australian Curriculum – more frequently use higher-order verbs such as *represent, recognise, explore* and *investigate*. Unfortunately, some teachers do not really understand the difference between higher- and lower-order cognitive skills, let alone how to teach them. Teacher education programs should explicitly teach what these thinking skills are and support trainee teachers to understand their implications for both pedagogies and assessment.

Table 3.2: Content-focused and concept-focused teaching aligned with Bloom's taxnonony and SOLO model

Level 1	Level 2	Level 3	Level 4	Level 5	Level 6
Recall	Explain	Apply	Analyse	Evaluate	Transform
Remember	Understand		Connect		Create
Content-focused teaching			**Concept-focused teaching**		
Surface (uni- and multi-structural)			Deep (relational and extended abstract)		

SOURCE: Adapted from Anderson & Krathwhol (2001), Biggs & Collis (1982) and Hattie (2012)

Some maths teachers believe their responsibility is fundamentally to teach all children to apply the maths they have learned. Application requires some reasoning, but this is often limited by the familiarity of the context in which the application is required. Fewer teachers, either through explicit teaching or modelling, include or demonstrate higher-order requirements of the maths such as evaluation and transformation. This unfortunately further exacerbates the problem of students learning primarily factual content and skills, and limited conceptual understandings.

Teachers who are concept-focused think more deeply about how their students might best be taught the concepts, or the big ideas, of maths. Their goal is to increase the conceptual understanding (underpinned by factual content and skills) of what is being taught so that students make connections and can independently transfer their new learning from one context to another.

> *While curriculum is the most critical component for choice of subject matter, it is just as critical that we take account of challenge, commitment, confidence, and conceptual understanding.* (Hattie, 2012, p. 63)

While content-focused teachers tend to use mostly a pedagogy of 'teacher teaches the fact, method or procedure and then students practise it', concept-focused teachers are more likely to use an inquiry approach where learning experiences depend on concepts *and* facts to ensure that students make connections. Moreover, these teachers are more likely to explicitly teach and model higher-order cognitive skills using inquiry-based pedagogies.

Concept-focused teachers pose questions and make conjectures – often contentious – to engage students. These teachers know that creating cognitive dissonance (or 'struggle') is more likely to lead to students (especially those working collaboratively) having to construct their own knowledge based on their reasoning (Ahn & Class, 2011; Nottingham, 2017; Vygotsky, 1976). Their students choose to work collaboratively or independently to solve problems. They justify their results and can give well-reasoned arguments about their solutions based on understanding of context and what they are finding. These comparisons can be seen in the following table.

Table 3.3: Content-focused and concept-focused pedagogies compared

Content-focused pedagogies	Concept-focused pedagogies
Teacher uses and models lower-order skills, focusing on fluency and recall.	Teacher explicitly teaches and models higher-order skills to students.
Teacher uses predominantly didactic or lecture delivery style to disseminate knowledge.	Teacher uses inquiry and questioning to spark interest and engagement.
Students are passive recipients in learning.	Students are actively involved in their learning.
Students face the board, copy notes and answer questions when asked.	Students work collaboratively, often in groups or pairs, asking questions of themselves and others.
Teacher provides a summary of the lesson telling students what they *should* have learned.	Teacher asks students to reflect on their learning; students are encouraged to ask clarifying questions and to write down what they didn't understand.
Teacher considers conjectures or lateral thinking questions off-task.	Lateral thinking, making conjectures and hypothesising are encouraged in order for students to make connections between new content and pre-existing or newly learned concepts to encourage greater depth of learning.
Teacher develops assessments made up predominantly of factual recall and procedural questions, assessing memory rather than deep understandings.	Assessment draws out understanding across the whole range of Bloom's taxonomy levels, enabling students to demonstrate the full extent of their learning.
Teacher is driven by getting through the content of the course and students knowing the facts, definitions and procedures.	Teacher is focused on student understanding of deep knowledge and concepts, enabling connections between their learning.

Being a concept-focused teacher

To be a concept-focused teacher, teachers need to understand the concepts themselves and the content that underpins these and, as a result of this new-found understanding, make the pedagogical shifts indicated in table 3.3.

In their planning, they should initially consider the intended learning (learning intentions) as shown in their mandated curriculum (in the Australian Curriculum these are content descriptors). This means considering the entire content descriptor rather than merely parts or phrases of it. They should then ask: 'What are the concepts I want my students to know and be able to demonstrate at the end of this unit of work?' Then they need to design both appropriate ways of teaching these so that their students learn these big ideas and appropriate ways of assessing so that students have the opportunity to demonstrate their conceptual understandings rather than just their recall and application. They then need to provide appropriate feedback to their students aimed at developing the conceptual understandings they have been unable to demonstrate.

To understand the concepts themselves, teachers and prospective teachers need to examine their own mathematical position. The following reflective questions will help.

> ### Time to reflect
>
> Did you learn maths as a body of unconnected facts and procedures?
>
> Do you want your students to have deep conceptual knowledge or to merely be able to recall maths facts and skills?
>
> Do you understand the difference between higher-order thinking skills and lower-order thinking skills? Do you know the implications of these for teaching, learning and assessment?
>
> Do you plan and teach a balance of surface and deep, content and concept knowledge and understanding, and make the differences clear to students?
>
> Do you have the knowledge and skills you need to engage students in maths learning that is deep?

What teachers and educators of children need to know to teach mathematics well

Who their students are

It is important for educators of all year levels to know who their students are. What backgrounds (language, cultural, socioeconomic) do students come from? What are their individual needs for learning? Teachers should make no assumptions about children's backgrounds but should talk to parents or carers and previous teachers, educators and education assistants about behaviours they have seen demonstrated. This may include cultural and lingual background information, which may affect the pedagogies teachers use in their classrooms and be essential information when planning learning experiences. Talking to education assistants and support teachers who have long connections with the school can also provide invaluable information about students' families and backgrounds.

The mathematics knowledge and understandings children bring with them to the learning context

In particular, what numeracies have children been involved in through their families, their communities and any previous schooling? Teachers should make no assumptions about the maths applied (and hence modelled) in children's homes. This information can be accessed through a range of sources including Australian Early Development Census (AEDC) data and talking to other teachers, parents or carers and community workers or paraprofessionals. Assumptions should not be made by teachers based on their own personal experiences growing up. Do not assume parents have taught the number names in order. Do not assume parents have taught their children about shapes or sizes, used positional language such as *behind* or *above*, comparative language such as *bigger* or *smaller*, or language of chance such as *might* or *maybe*. If we assume these concepts have been taught and learned previously, we may gloss over them when teaching. This will have significant ramifications for children who have never heard them and don't know what they mean compared with those from homes or communities where parents use and model them on a daily basis (Perso & Hayward, 2015).

For children in Years 3–6, have a conference with the previous teacher about your students' mathematical learning. If that teacher has left the school, the students' school reports, log entries or other school data may inform their individual needs.

The mathematics and numeracy learning outcomes

Years F–2

Teachers should engage with the EYLF to get a sense of what children might be expected to know prior to commencing the Foundation year of schooling and then consider in their planning how they might collaboratively connect this learning to the Foundation and Years 1 and 2 mathematics curriculum and numeracy general capability.

Teachers need to know that children entering this phase of schooling might bring with them common understandings and experiences of maths application from their home. While they are unable to classify their knowledge yet, or give mathematical or technical names to it specifically, they will likely have some understandings gained through their learning of language. For example, they might see their dad read a map in their car and connect at some level with maps. Mum might cut a piece of bread in two pieces and say, 'Give your brother the biggest half.' Through these experiences they gain a sense of what mathematical concepts are but may not know explicitly the mathematical understandings. It is the explicit understandings that will ultimately result in appropriate and valid choices when applying their maths to contexts.

Years 3–6

Teachers of this age group need to be fully cognisant of the maths and numeracy skills their students should have been taught, but don't assume that they have. In particular, what maths, problem-solving and reasoning skills have they learned in their previous years of schooling? Have they learned what they were expected to learn? Have they been taught the maths of the F–2 Australian Curriculum and some application and problem-solving skills that enable them to choose and use this maths in contexts that demand it? Are they confident with their maths? The focus is on their deep knowledge of concepts, not whether they have been taught and have learned the factual content.

Since maths learning depends on the understanding of previous concepts and skills, it is essential that teachers know the building blocks to add new learning. There is no point trying to teach new material if children don't have the necessary learning to support it. It would be like trying to lay the fourth course of bricks in a wall if the first, second and third courses hadn't been laid! This doesn't mean that you can't teach new material if children haven't learned the necessary building blocks. What it means is that you should provide some revision of what all children should have learned. When children are given tasks to consolidate their new learning, you should help individual students one-on-one, or in small guided groups, to support the new learning while rebuilding or reteaching the missed building blocks. Knowing what the building blocks are is helpful, but you need to understand them yourself, understand the sequence of them and take the child or children back to their starting points to build up the wall – one block at a time. This intervention strategy is discussed more fully in Chapter 4.

> ### Time to reflect
>
> What do you know about your students? Do you know their likes and dislikes? Their interests? The languages they speak at home? The cultural backgrounds of their parents?
>
> If these are not the same as your own, are there any assumptions you believe you can make about the way their parents teach them? If not, how might you find out?
>
> Are there any assumptions you can make about what they have learned prior to being in your class? How might you find out, just to be sure?

Conclusion

Teaching maths 'well' is critical to developing students in ways that lead to them being effective numerate citizens. This requires a deep understanding of the maths to plan and present it to students in ways that build knowledge and deep understandings of mathematical concepts. This starts with students initially learning factual surface knowledge and skills that provide the foundation for deeper understanding of the concepts and connections between them. Ultimately a balance of surface and deep learning result in conceptual understandings.

Numeracy intervention and extension in the classroom

Individual teachers can make an outstanding difference to the numeracy outcomes of their students. However, the learning of numeracy skills occurs only when the classroom teacher creates the conditions for this to occur. This includes teachers having the pedagogical content knowledge as well as knowing what is needed for particular groups of students. Many students – for whatever reason – do not learn the curriculum that has been taught to them. As a result, they might come to the classroom with gaps in the foundational knowledge required for the next phase of learning. The content descriptors from year to year are consecutive and describe the standard expected for all children or what the average student working at the rate described can do by the end of the year. This chapter addresses this issue and takes the perspective that no student is an average student – all students need intervention of some kind to some degree.

Intervention defined

Intervention is the planned entry into a situation that is unacceptable or intolerable. In learning, if a student is unable to do what they should be able to do by a certain point in their schooling and development, intervention for improvement is required. On the other hand, a student who has already learned what they should be able to do by the same point in time requires intervention in the form of challenge and extension. These two forms of intervention will be discussed in detail later in this chapter.

Planning for mathematics learning

Teachers know that there is often a wide range between what each of their students are entitled to learn (as outlined in the Australian Curriculum for their age cohort) and what their students know. They might be ahead of or behind expectations. Teachers also know there will be students in their class who have not learned curriculum taught to them in previous years. They also know that some of this missing learning is foundational and essential to further progress. Hattie (2012) states that 'By Year 5, there is likely to be at least five years of spread in the capabilities of students in the class' (p. 109).

Gaps in student learning rarely extend across all the maths strands. Students may not have been taught certain topics for a range of reasons or may not have learned or struggled to learn others. This fact can be confronting for teachers. Some teachers avoid calls to differentiate the curriculum, believing it means prepareing different lessons for different students. However, supporting student learning is about recognising the different starting points of students, since students can be thought of as needing a lot of support, needing some support, mostly independent or needing extension. The primary goal of curriculum differentiation, as stated by Tomlinson and McTighe (2006), 'is ensuring that teachers focus on processes and procedures that ensure effective learning for varied individuals. . . . Differentiation is predominantly (although not solely) an instructional design model' (p. 3).

Smale-Jacobse and colleagues (2019) state, 'Differentiated instruction is a pedagogical-didactical approach that provides teachers with a starting point for meeting students' diverse learning needs' (p. 1). It is driven from a desire that all students thrive and develop their potential despite their varied starting points and differences.

To understand curriculum differentiation it is important to distinguish between teaching and learning. Students in a variety of contexts can be taught the same material. Some learn all of it and others do not. Why is this? To answer this question, we first consider the learning design process.

Curriculum alignment

In designing learning goals, activities and assessments, there are a number of considerations and steps through which teachers need to go. These steps must be aligned to ensure that the desired learning is in fact learned and that the student's report indicates this so parents can be assured their child is learning what they are supposed to be learning.

Designing learning is shown in the following diagram as a process (see figure 4.1). Curriculum alignment focuses on specific students and their strengths, needs and interests. Hence the design and planning of learning experiences must place students at the centre and consider them at every step in the process. Teacher planning is dynamic, certain to change every year or every term – even every day – depending on who the students are, what they already know

Numeracy intervention and extension in the classroom

and what they are learning. No teacher can write a detailed plan for more than a few weeks at a time (or a term, at most) without the flexibility to change in response to what students are learning. Any plan must be continually monitored and reviewed based on what student assessment information tells each teacher about their teaching effectiveness.

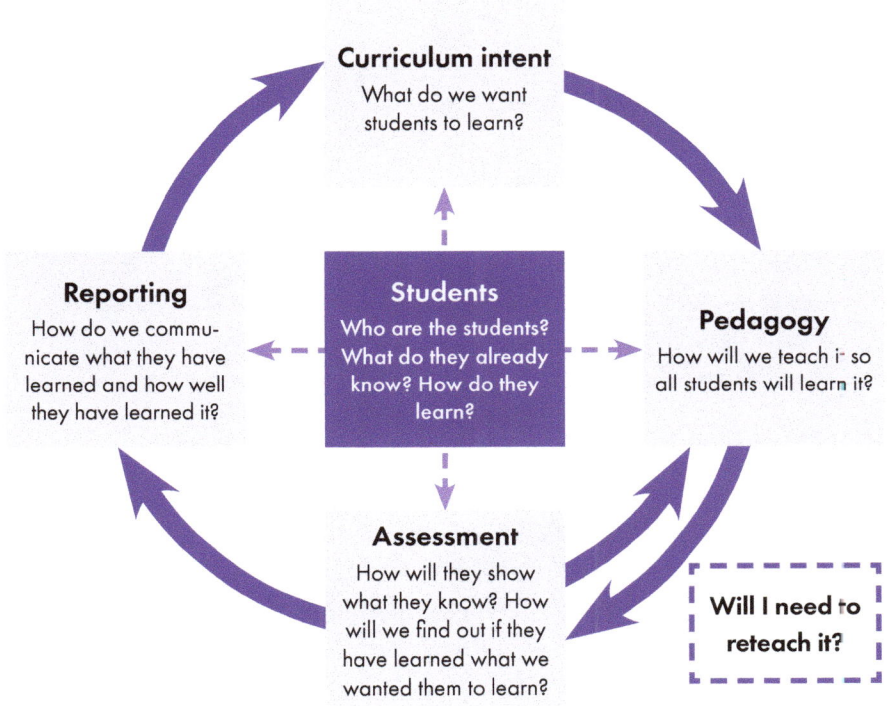

Figure 4.1: Curriculum alignment
SOURCE: Adapted from State of Queensland Department of Education, Training and The Arts, (2018)

> *School mission statements that promise 'learning for all' have become a cliché. But when a school staff takes that statement literally — when teachers view it as a pledge to ensure the success of each student rather than as politically correct hyperbole — profound changes begin to take place.* (DuFour, 2004, p. 8)

Teachers begin their design or plan with the big-picture view of the intended curriculum learning for students based on age expectations. This involves scrutiny of the intended curriculum document and age cohort requirements (for example, the Australian Curriculum) but also acknowledges the maths learning that underpins what is intended. The maths content descriptors are laid out like bricks or building blocks in a wall; the bricks describe the learning that underpins the next layer. Each of these bricks or blocks, and their placement in the overall structure, are informed by research into how children learn maths. Teachers planning to teach Year 5 maths concepts, for example, should consider the learning progressions that underpin these concepts prior to Year 5. This will assist them to understand the likely range of students' prior learning in their class. It will also remind them of the building blocks for what they plan to teach, which can be used as revision and scaffolding for the next layer.

> *In effective classrooms, teachers consistently attend to at least four elements: whom they teach (students), where they teach (learning environment), what they teach (content), and how they teach (instruction). If teachers lose sight of any of the elements and cease investing effort in it, the whole fabric of their work is damaged and the quality of learning is impaired.* (Tomlinson & McTighe, 2006, p. 2)

Teachers will then use some formal or informal diagnostic assessment to determine whether students have the knowledge of these building blocks. Most teachers use informal questioning in class, while others might give students a formal task question (which might be closed or open) to determine the extent to which students have the required foundational learning.

Having established who students are and what they need to learn, teachers then make decisions about what pedagogical strategy they will use to maximise learning for each student. It is the enactment or delivery of the intended curriculum that gives teaching its power. All teachers might use the same intended curriculum documents, but it is the strategies that they use that determine whether their students learn what is taught. Teaching is a sequence of pedagogical moments; the learning in a class depends on how these moments are structured, presented, sequenced and altered or differentiated to meet the needs of individual students.

As indicated in figure 4.1 (page 65), teachers will then choose an assessment strategy to determine the learning that has occurred. Analysing students' results will reveal whether teachers need to reteach some lessons, or aspects of lessons, using different pedagogies. This is often done with individuals or small groups of students who haven't learned what has been taught. It is this practice of teaching students at their point of need that is called *curriculum differentiation*.

Intervention

The key to differentiating curriculum (or providing differentiated curriculum) is deep knowledge of the intended learning and a recognition that all students in the class are different; they know different things, they have preferred ways of learning, they have preferred ways of demonstrating their learning and they have different starting points.

Having determined the support levels students require, teachers may subsequently structure the class by seating students with different needs in groups or pairs. They then teach new concepts to the whole class, continuing to gauge the acquisition of the building blocks that underpin the new concept and providing the support needed by each student or group to construct the new learning.

Differentiated instruction is not planning and providing individualised learning for each student. Rather, it occurs at a number of levels within a classroom. Initially this is at the level of the whole class, with the teacher using the curriculum documents to plan and teach what all students need to know. The next level is where the teacher interacts with individuals and small groups of students as they begin to apply (or not apply) their learning to tasks set by the teacher. By asking and answering questions and observing what the students are doing, teachers then determine where students currently are in relation to the expected learning: how far are they behind or in front of what is being taught? By providing point-in-time feedback and hence personalised (but not necessarily individualised) teaching strategies, or 'multiple learning pathways so that students can have access to the most appropriate learning opportunities commensurate with their capacity to learn' (Munro, 2012, p. 2), teachers ensure that each student moves forward in their understanding, albeit at different rates. Over time, teachers can bridge the gaps from what students know already to what they need to learn, using the process detailed in figure 4.2 (page 68).

It is this continual monitoring and support process that is the hallmark of a great teacher. Differentiation of curriculum, or providing differentiated instruction, is a powerful form of intervention – scaffolding students who are not learning and extending those who are. This support is freely and strategically offered based on the agentic thinking of the teacher and their belief that all their students can learn what is being taught.

There is no one way of intervening for a student who is behind where they need to be in their maths learning and numeracy attainment. The following sections provide the most effective evidence-informed strategies that might be needed during a child's schooling, often in concert with each other.

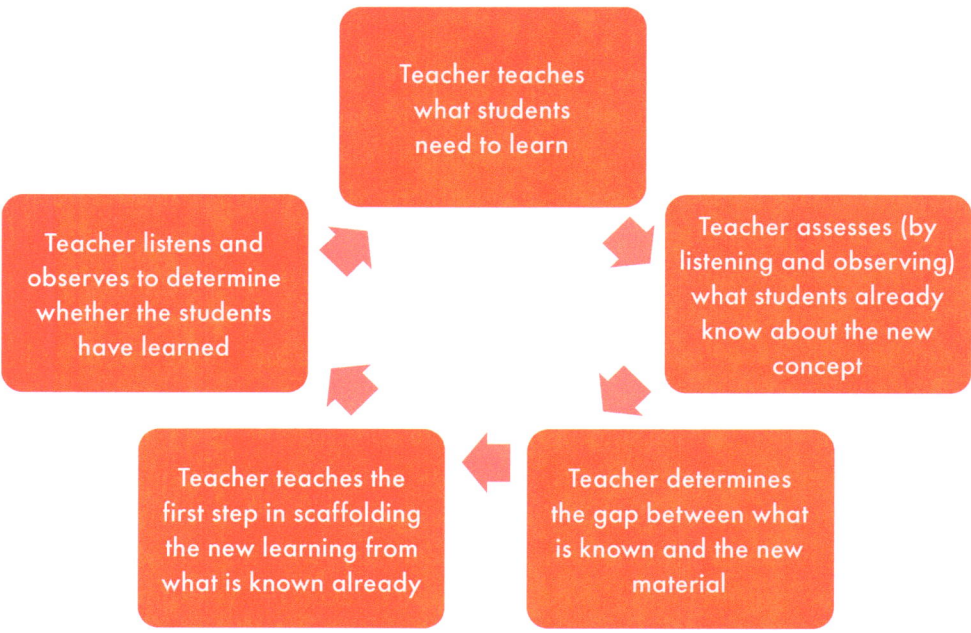

Figure 4.2: Differentiating instruction for individuals and small groups

Big conceptual steps

To differentiate maths curriculum successfully, teachers need to know the big conceptual steps, identified through research, that describe how students learn maths concepts. They may be surprised to know that they don't have to find these for themselves, since the content descriptors of the maths curriculum are written in such sequences already. (This is the case for most maths curriculums in the twenty-first century, drawing on a large research base in maths education compiled over recent decades.)

> *For classroom learning to be most effective, teaching and learning tasks should be ahead of students' abilities to complete alone, but within their ability to complete when scaffolding is provided.* (Hammond & Gibbons, 2005, p. 8)

Teachers move forwards and backwards along each maths sequence to determine what students already know, what they need to know next and how many of these big conceptual steps they need to learn to be able to learn the one described in the sequence for the particular stage in their year of study. For example, consider a sequence of content descriptors for fractions from the 'Number and algebra' strand of the Australian Curriculum.

Table 4.1: Australian Curriculum: F–6 'Fractions and decimals' sequence

Foundation	Year 1	Year 2	Year 3	Year 4	Year 5	Year 6
	Recognise and describe one-half as one of two equal parts of a whole. (ACMNA016)	Recognise and interpret common uses of halves, quarters and eighths of shapes and collections. (ACMNA033)	Model and represent unit fractions including $\frac{1}{2}$, $\frac{1}{4}$, $\frac{1}{3}$, $\frac{1}{5}$ and their multiples to a complete whole. (ACMNA058)	Investigate equivalent fractions used in contexts. (ACMNA077)	Compare and order common unit fractions and locate and represent them on a number line. (ACMNA102)	Compare fractions with related denominators and locate and represent them on a number line. (ACMNA125)

SOURCE: Adapted from ACARA (n.d.-d)

A teacher with a Year 3 class might, for example, begin planning by looking at the Year 3 fraction entry ACMNA058. They would then look back to the Year 2 entry ACMNA033 and think their students should be able to do this. They might decide to ask questions in the first lesson and make a mental note of who can't so that when teaching the next section of work – the Year 3 entry – they will have an idea of who to support individually or in pairs or small groups. If a large proportion of students are unable to do the new work, some new planning may be necessary. The teacher might decide to reteach all or some of last year's work, or even the previous year's work, and so on. This could begin with an open-ended task such as 'Tell me everything you know about fractions, giving examples' and perhaps some scaffold words or phrases.

This might sound simple, but it requires that teachers know deeply what students should already know and what they need to know, as indicated earlier. It requires that teachers have pedagogical content knowledge about the concept of fractions and how students learn it, their likely misconceptions and so on. Work with students (individuals, pairs or small groups) might be different depending on what students already know, the nature of the focus questions that the teacher uses to determine this and how much scaffolding students require. So, the classroom teacher needs to continue to move forward through the curriculum with the class as a whole, ensuring that all students are challenged and have access to the curriculum they are entitled to learn. At the same time, they need to meet the needs of all students in the class who have been left behind, by scaffolding the Year 1 or Year 2 understandings for fractions.

Determining where students are at in their maths learning and where they need to go next can be challenging for teachers. Moreover, the importance of being able to do this should not be underestimated in the context of numeracy development for all students.

Seeing the maths content descriptors as building blocks can support teachers to identify where students got left behind and to reach down and pull the student up using the learning progression described in the curriculum sequence. Teaching the fourth course of bricks will never result in learning if the first, second or third courses have not yet been laid down So, as indicated previously, the year-by-year content descriptors act as the necessary sequential courses of bricks needed to support the next learning. This metaphor is useful since it supports teachers in understanding:

+ the importance of prior learning in maths
+ the need to build up maths concept learning block by block
+ the consequences if they leave one out of the building blocks
+ the importance of teaching each content descriptor well
+ the need for intervention, particularly preventative intervention, but also turbocharged intervention
+ that children may not be able to understand new learning as they are missing previous building blocks.

If content descriptors are taught as new topics rather than as necessary parts of an integrated, conceptual chain of big mathematical ideas, children will generally find it difficult to make connections between the elements of maths that they learn.

> *Successful teaching and learning to address student needs in relation to literacy and numeracy requires the teacher to have an understanding of where the student is now and where the student needs to go next in their literacy and numeracy development.* (ACARA, 2018, p. 3)

National numeracy learning progression

The NNLP discussed earlier was designed 'to help teachers ascertain the stage of learning reached, identify any gaps in skills and knowledge, and plan for the next step to progress learning' (ACARA, 2020, p. 3). Teachers should use the NNLP indicators to diagnose individual student capabilities. This can not only inform their maths planning for students who are unable to show the maths learning expected, but also inform their intervention for students who are unable to learn concepts in other learning areas due to the numeracy demands.

The NNLP, while not being included in the Australian Curriculum, supplements and underpins the curriculum, providing a detailed sequence along which students might typically progress in particular aspects of the maths curriculum. This can help teachers diagnose current maths learning for students. Having done this, teachers can then use the NNLP to identify the numeracy needed to learn the content from other learning areas and then to identify the numeracy support needed to enable them to access this content. This means that teachers can use the NNLP to identify whether students are not learning material from other learning areas due to gaps in their maths learning or lack of adequate understanding to apply it in contexts outside maths lessons. This clarifies for teachers the connection between maths learning, numeracy demands and numeracy development.

The NNLP highlights the need for all teachers to take the numeracy demands across the curriculum seriously. When planning, teachers identify the numeracy demands of each unit of work and use the NNLP to assist them to ensure the learning is enabled by the numeracy capabilities that students bring to the learning context – or at least are not prohibited by the absence of the numeracy capabilities that students require to access the learning contexts.

Each sub-element of the NNLP contains sequences made up of levels that can be supported by research. The levels of each sequence describe student development as it increases in complexity and sophistication from preceding levels, in much the same ways as the content descriptors describe consecutive standards of required learning. The progressions recognise that all students develop numeracy knowledge and skills at different rates. Hence, the developmental levels are not linked to learning benchmarks such as time and are not evenly spaced (by time) as the annual content descriptors of the Australian Curriculum: Mathematics are. This means there are no standards or expectations set on student development levels. The alignment and relationship between the Australian Curriculum: Mathematics content descriptors and the levels of the NNLP sub-element 'Interpreting fractions' can be seen in table 4.2 (page 72). It is evident that the content descriptors of the Australian Curriculum: Mathematics do not align directly with the NNLP indicators. This is not surprising since the former represents expected standards of learning and the latter describes developmental levels. The entries connect only insofar as to show that the year-by-year standards relate directly to what research indicates that students learn developmentally and sequentially.

Table 4.2: Relationship between some Australian Curriculum: Mathematics content descriptors, elaborations for 'Fractions and decimals' and NNLP indicators for interpreting fractions

	Australian Curriculum: Mathematics content descriptors and elaborations Fractions and decimals					
	Year 1	Year 2	Year 3	Year 4	Year 5	Year 6
Content descriptors	Recognise and describe one-half as one of two equal parts of a whole. (ACMNA016)	Recognise and interpret common uses of halves, quarters and eighths of shapes and collections. (ACMNA033)	Model and represent unit fractions including ½, ¼, ⅓, ⅕ and their multiples to the complete whole. (ACMNA058)	Investigate equivalent fractions used in contexts. (ACMNA077)	Compare and order common unit fractions and locate and represent them on a number line. (ACMNA102)	Compare fractions with related denominators and locate and represent them on a number line. (ACMNA125)
Elaborations	Share a collection of readily available materials into two equal portions. Split an object into two equal pieces and describe how the pieces are equal.	Recognise that sets of objects can be partitioned in different ways to demonstrate fractions. Relate the number of parts to the size of a fraction.	Partition areas, lengths and collections to create halves, thirds, quarters and fifths, such as folding the same sized sheets of paper to illustrate different unit fractions and comparing the parts of numbers with their sizes. Locate unit fractions on a number line.	Explore the relationship between families of fractions (halves, quarters and eighths or thirds and sixths) by folding a series of paper strips to construct a fraction wall.	Recognise the connections between the order of unit fractions and their denominators.	Demonstrate equivalence between fractions using drawings and models.

SOURCE: Adapted from ACARA (n.d.-d) and ACARA (2020)

(continued)

| \multicolumn{2}{c}{**National numeracy learning progression**} |
| \multicolumn{2}{c}{**Interpreting fractions**} |

Level	Indicator
Level 1: Creating halves	The student: ♦ demonstrates that dividing a whole into two parts can create equal or unequal parts ♦ identifies the part and the whole in representations of one-half (for example, joins two equal pieces back together to form the whole shape and can identify the pieces as equal parts of the whole shape) ♦ creates equal halves using all of the whole (for example, folds a paper strip in half to make equal pieces by aligning the edges; cuts a sandwich in half diagonally; partitions a collection into two equal groups to represent halving).
Level 2: Repeated halving	The student: ♦ makes quarters and eighths by repeated halving (for example, locates halfway then halves each half; eight counters halved and then halved again into four groups of two) ♦ identifies that part and the whole in representations of halves, quarters and eighths (for example, identifies the fractional parts that make up the whole using fraction puzzles) ♦ represents known fractions using various models (for example, discrete collections, continuous linear and continuous area).
Level 3: Repeating fractional parts	The student: ♦ accumulates fractional parts (for example, knows that two-quarters is inclusive of one-quarter and twice one-quarter, not just the second quarter ♦ checks the equality of parts by iterating one part to form the whole (for example, when given a representation of one-quarter of a length and asked, 'What fraction is this of the whole length?', uses the length as a counting unit to make the whole) ♦ identifies fractions in measurement situations and solves problems using halves, quarters and eighths (for example, identifies quarters in an AFL match; uses two ½-cup measures in place of a 1-cup measure) ♦ demonstrates that fractions can be written symbolically and interprets using part–whole knowledge (for example, interprets ¾ to mean three one-quarters or three lots of ¼).
Level 4: Reimaging the whole	The student: ♦ creates thirds by visualising or approximating and adjusting (for example, imagines a strip of paper in three parts, then adjusts and folds) ♦ identifies examples and non-examples of partitioned representations of fractions ♦ divides a whole into different fractional parts for different purposes (for example, exploring the problem of sharing a cake equally between guests) ♦ demonstrates that the more parts into which a whole is divided, the smaller the parts become.

Table 4.2 (page 72–3) indicates clearly that the purposes of each of the continuums are entirely different. The detail shown in the NNLP indicates the *diagnostic purpose* of the progression compared with the *standards-purpose* of the content descriptors (being 'By the end of Year X, students should be able to . . . '). The purpose of the indicators, by contrast, is to describe detailed learning that contributes to the building blocks of the curriculum.

The fact that the NNLP levels are hierarchical or graded based on sophistication or complexity should not be missed. It is this fact that makes the level indicators useful for diagnostic assessment and for determining what students should do next. Each indicator is a behaviour or an understanding, which teachers can identify in each student (through formal or informal assessment) to help them decide whether students can or cannot do or understand them. Teachers can then intervene to provide support to assist each student to be able to understand. What drives this support is the knowledge that if teachers don't provide the needed support, students won't meet the content descriptor standards. This means students will not have the required maths learning needed by the end of the year or have the numeracy capabilities demanded by other learning areas in the next and possibly subsequent years.

Teachers use the indicators to make these decisions based on the evidence they have of what each student can do.

Time to reflect

Have you ever thought you'd done a good job teaching a lesson or unit of work only to discover through assessment that students didn't learn what you'd intended?

What was your reaction to this? How did you change your pedagogy the next time? How might you alter your pedagogy next time to improve student learning?

Turbocharged intervention

Earlier in this chapter we defined *intervention* as the planned entry into a situation that is unacceptable or intolerable. This can be either intervention for improvement or intervention for extension, depending on whether students are behind or beyond where they need to be.

The approaches outlined above (planning, curriculum differentiation and the NNLP) are examples of intervention for improvement. Some students need what might be called *turbocharged intervention* based on them being well behind where they should be. These might be students who are more than one year behind their age cohort peers. Turbocharged intervention – while using the same methods – includes an element of urgency. If students are unable to bridge the gap quickly, they will be seriously at risk in their learning.

The identification of this urgency for turbocharged intervention can occur only if teachers – and their schools – view the year-by-year content descriptors as standards and expectations. Teachers should teach with a strong belief and conviction that students should take ownership of their learning and be able to learn what is presented for their age cohort. This agentic approach coupled with high expectations by teachers can inspire students to believe in themselves and in their ability to learn.

For students in the turbocharged category, intensive one-on-one support – ideally provided by their classroom teacher – would be the best solution. However, this is usually impossible in a school environment during the course of the day's lessons. Many of these students will need to re-engage with one or more layers of knowledge taught in previous years. The intensive teaching they need requires more support and time that may need to be discussed with parents in determining an individual education plan – particularly if the time required will exceed one school year. Teachers might use any of the discussed approaches with individuals, pairs and small groups for longer periods of time while a support teacher or education assistant manages the remainder of the class, if such support is available. If not, the classroom teacher must try to bridge these gaps using more time and additional support found through other means. This might include finding time from elsewhere such as during other lessons or after school. Many schools have been successful at finding this time to address the urgency of the situation (Chenoweth, 2009; DuFour, 2004). This intensive turbocharged support will be discussed in greater detail in Chapter 6.

Intervention and student psychology

Research by Hattie (2003, 2009) and Rowe (2003) reveals that teachers make the single biggest difference in student learning.

Some teachers believe that students are not able to learn what is expected because of who they are. Major studies by Bishop et al. (2007), Hattie (2009) and Timperley et al. (2007) suggest that many teachers identify factors from within a child's background (including their home and family) as having the greatest influence on students' educational achievement. Some of these factors include low-level aspirations by families, poor behaviour, minimal access to resources, lack of motivation, absenteeism, antisocial behaviours in the community, inadequate parental support or care, and lack of positive role models.

In the past educational reforms have tended to focus on what is taught (curriculum) and how it is taught (pedagogy). More recently, intervention research has focused instead on the psychology of the student (Blackwell et al., 2007; Cimpian et al., 2007; Dweck et al., 2014). Non-cognitive factors, such as habits of self-control, beliefs about themselves and feelings about school, have been shown to affect students' achievement.

Weiner (1972) found that successful students with high self-concept and a history of high achievement tend to identify factors such as ability, task difficulty, effort and luck as the most important factors that can be attributed to achievement success. On the other hand, students with a history of failure tend to believe that their lack of success with learning is attributable to poor cognitive ability that they believe they were born with. This belief and self-concept can result in low achievement by students. This is particularly important for students who have fallen behind in their learning and perhaps believe they are unable to catch up. These students need a growth mindset.

A *growth mindset* is a personal belief that learning ability is not fixed; your capacity to learn does not depend on your genetic predisposition but rather on your own belief that you have the ability and power to control your own unlimited learning (Dweck, 2012; Leaf, 2015). When discussing Dweck's research, Krakovsky (2017) states:

> *More than ten years later, Dweck's essential finding – that children who have a 'growth mindset' that intelligence can be developed are better able to overcome academic stumbling blocks than those who have a 'fixed mindset' that intelligence is predetermined – is as relevant as ever.* (para. 1)

Teacher expectations

Carol Dweck's research shows that students with a fixed mindset are more likely to avoid challenges and to quit when they are confronted with challenges. Ultimately, they have less success academically. On the other hand, students who believe their intelligence can be improved by greater effort and guidance are more likely to take on challenging tasks and to persevere by trying new strategies and increasing the amount of effort. They ultimately achieve greater academic success (Limeri et al., 2020).

Teachers who attribute student learning to factors outside of their own professional control will generally have low expectations of students. As a result, these teachers may put less effort into their preparation and also may tend to focus on keeping students engaged and having students under control, rather than focusing on their learning of age-appropriate standards. In turn, the deficit perceptions by teachers can be prophetic (Bishop et al., 2007; Brophy, 1983). This type of deficit thinking can often result in students being given 'busy work'. This might include activities like worksheets, copying from the board, watching videos and other activities that present little or no challenge to students. Students tend to perform in ways that their teachers expect them to, which means being given less-challenging work usually results in low-level learning outcomes (Ferguson, 2002).

Other messages of low expectations by schools and teachers can be given through poor school design and limited organisational structure. Schools that look and operate like they don't care express that students and their learning aren't valued. Messages of high expectations should be explicit as a means of both preventative and turbocharged intervention. Saying to students 'I know you can do this and I'm going to help you', 'You can do this and I will support and expect you to' or 'You can learn this; your ability to learn doesn't depend on anyone but you' has been shown to impact positively on student self-efficacy and the strategies they use (Brophy, 2008; Sarra, 2005). In 2004, the Southern Regional Education Board (SREB) in the United States identified ten strategies for creating a classroom culture of high expectations:

- 'Help all teachers develop, communicate and implement classroom motivation and management plans' (p. 1).
- 'Develop instructional plans that facilitate bell-to-bell teaching' (p. 2).
- 'Create classroom organization and arrangement that spurs productivity' (p. 3).
- 'Establish high expectations' (p. 4).
- 'Communicate expectations to student and parents' (p. 4).
- 'The student as worker – implement instructional activities that actively engage students' (p. 5).
- 'Keep students on target' (p. 6).
- 'Encourage frequent and relevant feedback that works' (p. 6).
- 'Establish grading practices that communicate high expectations and decrease frustration' (p. 7).
- 'Deal with severe behavior' (p. 8).

Students pick up on teachers' low expectations for them. This in turn, lowers their motivation to succeed and can often lead to truanting and absenteeism. Teachers having high expectations of students sets the tone for learning in the school environment. Teachers must convey the message that each student has potential, rather than conveying a message that students are born smart or talented. They should also convey the message that greater effort will result in better results. Having high expectations refers to the way teachers position their students and hence contributes to the environmental conditions created by the relationships teachers have with their students.

Research by Blackwell et al. (2007) found that students with a growth mindset tended to be more oriented toward learning goals, caring more about learning than their grades. They also showed a far stronger belief in the power of their own effort, which they believe promotes ability. These students take control of their learning which can result in greater self-concept and improved results.

Teaching a growth mindset

Students can be taught to have a growth mindset. In two separate studies, Blackwell et al. (2007) and Good et al. (2003) taught students in a workshop that the brain is like a muscle that grows stronger with use. The brain forms new connections when students stretch themselves and learn something new (Dweck, 2008). Good et al. (2003) also found that students who were explicitly taught a growth mindset showed significantly higher scores on their next maths test than those in the control group.

Praise and a growth mindset

All too often teachers praise and reward students for the final product of their learning. High marks on summative tasks are often positioned in classrooms as the goal. By giving these tasks significant weighting in final grades or alternatively, not indicating what the grades reflect in terms of what students can do, this may reinforce for many students that these grades are out of reach. Research has found that praising students for their intelligence rather than for their effort or strategy means students are more likely to:

- avoid challenging tasks where they might risk failure
- lose confidence and motivation, especially when a task became too hard
- have reduced performance during or after difficult problems
- lie about their scores afterwards (Cimpian et al., 2007; Kamins & Dweck, 1999; Mueller & Dweck, 1998).

In contrast, praise for effort or strategy leads students to seek and thrive on challenges (Dweck, 2008). For this reason, implementing grading systems that are based on the effort students exhibit and transparency about what the expectations are for earning each grade will greatly assist students to take control of their learning and believe that they *can* achieve high grades. This will be unpacked further in the following section about learning quality.

All the factors discussed can impact on student learning of maths and subsequent development of numeracy capability. It is essential that teachers consider the significance of their own role when students are not learning and try a range of proven strategies, such as those outlined, to remedy this. The power of teacher expectations should not be underestimated, as many of us can attest to.

> ### Time to reflect
>
> Do you think that teachers play a powerful role in either perpetuating or addressing inequities in our society? Why or why not?
>
> How might you – as an individual teacher – address this?
>
> Do you have high expectations of your students?
>
> How do you or could you communicate high expectations to your students?

Extension

Extension is a form of intervention. All students need to be extended in their learning. There is no such thing as a D student or an A student. A student who consistently achieves D grades must be extended through believing they can achieve a C or higher and by being shown how to strive to do so. No student – including gifted or talented students – should be allowed to become bored through lack of extension and challenge. Therefore, deliberate entry into the situation by teachers is necessary to prevent undesirable consequences such as antisocial behaviours and learning disengagement.

Many schools and teachers accelerate students who are identified as mathematically gifted by having them access maths curriculum material designed for students in higher grades. While this acceleration is legitimate in some cases and can have positive outcomes, it does not address all academic and social problems frequently encountered by gifted students. For example, Gross (2015) indicates that these students are likely to feel different and that they don't fit in. This might result in them pretending to misunderstand rather than drawing attention to themselves, or they might have difficulties creating and maintaining relationships.

Munro (2012) cites a range of research that reveals why gifted students in regular classes are not differentiated appropriately. These include lack of teacher content knowledge necessary to extend and differentiate the typical curriculum content, lack of teacher classroom management skills necessary to support differentiated learning, lack of teacher beliefs about different learning styles, lack of teacher planning time and lack of teaching skill. Munro (2010) contends that it is therefore easier, in this context, for teachers to use the regular curriculum to differentiate for gifted students, since it is familiar to them. To differentiate effectively for those students who quickly understand the learning or might even know the content before it is taught, 'teachers need to recognise and interpret their [gifted learner] higher-level understanding and to implement teaching that guides these students to analyse and evaluate their intuitive theories' (Munro, 2013b, p. 13). Munro's use of the verbs *analyse* and *evaluate* is interesting in the context of the discussion about Bloom's (1956) taxonomy earlier in Chapter 3.

Extension and learning quality

All learning has both a quantity and a quality dimension. In the past, student grades were awarded based on norm-referencing (for example, the top 20 per cent of students obtained an A, the next 30 per cent were given a B and so on), meaning parents did not necessarily gain a sense of how well their child had learned what was required, but rather how much learning they had attained or remembered.

> *The indispensable conditions for improvement are that the student comes to hold a concept of quality roughly similar to that held by the teacher, is able to monitor continuously the quality of what is being produced* during the act of production itself, *and has a repertoire of alternative moves or strategies from which to draw at any given point.* (emphasis in original; Sadler, 1989, p. 121)

The quality dimension of learning is best understood through the following questions:

+ What is the depth of the learning?
+ How broadly can the learning be independently applied in unfamiliar contexts?
+ What is the sophistication of skills (thinking and affective) learned?

Were this quality dimension lens to be placed over classrooms it would soon become apparent that often students are not being given the opportunity to learn or to demonstrate higher-order thinking skills in the context of maths.

Learning quality was discussed in Chapter 3 through concept-focused teaching and content-focused teaching and in connection to Bloom's (1956) taxonomy. Table 4.3 indicates some of the activities that demonstrate learning quality, aligned to Bloom's taxonomy.

Table 4.3: Learning quality and activities that require thinking and affective skills

Bloom's taxonomy; levels of cognition	Activities
Creation and evaluation	Critique, solve, summarise, make recommendations, assess, make connections, convince, make judgements, infer, make generalisations, identify errors
Analysis and synthesis	Distinguish, investigate, examine, make conjectures, role-play, design, organise, classify, compare, analyse, compare, contrast, prioritise
Application	Sort, create pictures, solve puzzles, draw images that connect to words, choose, apply, interpret, connect represent
Comprehension	Paraphrase, restate, illustrate, match, demonstrate, show, classify
Recall	Find, quote, remember, state, list, label, define

SOURCE: Adapted from Anderson & Krathwohl, 2001

Teachers are in a very powerful position to provide students with access to differentiated learning quality levels and the achievement grades these can give access to. In other words, if teachers have low expectations of students, as we've previously considered, not only do they teach with little emphasis on higher levels of learning cognition, but they also assess with little demand for these. As a result, their students are unlikely to demonstrate learning at levels they might be capable of as they are not given opportunities to do so. The teacher controls this through the curriculum they provide and the assessment tasks they develop and use.

All students, but particularly those who are gifted, must have opportunities to evaluate, create and transform their learning. This might mean posing and researching hypotheses or investigating and making inferences about questions related to their learning. They might then evaluate their solutions and research through critical analysis, making judgements and writing a report or a critique of their own and others' learning. Maker and Schiever (2005), and more recently Munro (2013a, 2013b), emphasise the importance of teachers designing curriculums that focus on creative problem-solving, decision-making, planning and forecasting. To extend students who require greater challenge, teachers must focus on giving students access to the higher-order skills (see table 4.3 – levels beyond

'Application'). This means explicitly teaching these skills and enabling students to apply them independently.

> *When students are presented only with work which they can do effortlessly, they may never develop skills of time-management, persistence or striving for success.* (Gross, 2004, p. 15)

Generally, these students would choose to engage in topics that are important to them and potentially important globally. Having all students engage in such tasks increases the potential for deep learning (Fullan et al., 2017). Munro (2013b) suggests that teachers should permit and encourage students to work with real-world problems and create their own solutions.

These higher-order skills will extend students without the common social pressures that can occur when they learn at a faster rate than their peers or are placed in a higher year of schooling. It also provides an appropriate framework for differentiating the curriculum without unnecessarily giving students work from higher years of schooling, which can be cognitively low-level (Munro, 2010).

Maximising learning and challenge for *all* students

In Chapter 3, we considered Bloom's (1956) taxonomy as a means for guiding teachers in ensuring learning quality and deep learning are included in their teaching of maths. Teachers need to ensure that their selected pedagogies give all students in the class the opportunity to be challenged and to learn at high levels, not just those who might be gifted. This allows all children to be challenged and to have agency in their learning. This means teachers must:

1. have a clear understanding of the learning goals and intended learning
2. develop assessments, learning tasks and rubrics that give all students the opportunity to access and demonstrate learning of at least one of the learning quality levels depicted in Bloom's taxonomy (see figure 3.1, page 56)
3. use a range of teaching strategies, scaffolding the learning over time with a balance between content-focused and concept-focused teaching.

This pedagogical work by teachers encourages deeper learning by *all* students. It is also more challenging and hence more beneficial for gifted students than learning a greater amount of material at a lower, more superficial level, which can occur when gifted students are accelerated through years of schooling.

The previous three steps are indicative of a backward design approach to planning (Byrne, 2016; McTighe & Wiggins, 2012). To ensure that learning is deep and connects to student's realities, teachers should also consider using the 'teaching for understanding' approach designed by the Harvard Graduate School where teachers begin by ensuring the topic connects in genuine and meaningful ways to the lives of their students (Unger, 1994). For example, they might turn a required learning content descriptor such as 'Calculate perimeter and area of rectangles using familiar metric units' (ACMMG109; ACARA, n.d.-d) into a generative topic such as 'Rectangular lawns with longer edges provide greater areas for playing on'. This can then lead teachers to develop a rubric that students can use to scaffold and investigate the statement. Teachers can then also use this rubric to assess students' levels of understanding of the maths concept being assessed. Table 4.4 provides an example rubric for the topic of area and its relationship to perimeter.

Table 4.4: Learning quality rubric to support learning and assessment of the concept of area and its relationship to the concept of perimeter

Required enduring understandings	Calculate perimeter and area of rectangles using metric units
Recall	The student knows what a rectangle is and can make comparative statements about length and width.
	The student knows formulas for area and perimeter of a rectangle.
Interpret	The student can explain and paraphrase the research question and draw different rectangles, having different lengths and widths of sides.
	The student knows the formulas for finding perimeter and area of a rectangle and correctly interprets which to use in which context.
Apply	The student finds areas and perimeters of a range of rectangles and makes embryonic statements of comparison between each after organising dimensional data into a table.
Analyse	The student analyses organised data and makes conjectures about the nature of the relationship between rectangle dimensions, areas and perimeter.
	The student provides further examples to test conjectures.
Synthesise	The student makes generalisations about relationships between dimensions, areas and perimeters of rectangles.
	The student answers the research question and presents the answer justifying decision-making and processes chosen.
Evaluate and critique	The student compares results or findings with those of others and critiques the methods used, suggesting refinements for their own work and that of others.
	The student considers, proposes and researches hypotheses concerning areas of combined rectangular shapes and makes recommendations of lawn shapes to prospective home owners, based on research.

Note that all students will have entry to and success with some part of the task. The teacher should teach all students the foundational skills and knowledges of the levels, starting with what is required for recall, then scaffolding and supporting students to move through as many levels as possible. Gifted students should also be part of this initial process and should not ignore earlier levels. Students should be given the rubric prior to commencing the task and provided with ongoing feedback by their teacher as they proceed. They can take control by choosing which level they want to demonstrate capability with. Finally, the teacher can use the rubric to determine the quality of the learning and depth of cognitive understanding displayed by each student. They might assign grades to the levels demonstrated; for example, students demonstrating recall only might be assigned an E while students demonstrating synthesis and evaluation might be assigned an A grade.

This strategy not only intervenes for all students but also ensures that gifted students are extended beyond what might be viewed as the average learning contained in the curriculum content descriptors for every year group. The descriptor used previously for example, 'Calculate perimeter and area of rectangles using familiar metric units' (ACMMG109; ACARA, n.d.-d), is pitched at the application level of Bloom's (1956) taxonomy, so a teacher might be tempted to believe they are teaching well if all their students can successfully calculate as required. However, a great teacher would ensure that all students are taught and have the opportunity to go beyond this requirement of application and transform their learning through the deep understanding of the concepts of area and perimeter and how they relate to each other as dimensions are altered. Teachers might also expect gifted students to undertake this research and communicate their findings in real-life contexts.

The quality and quantity dimensions of learning should be considered by teachers when they are planning maths learning experiences for all students. Their aim should be to both give all students access to the learning required for their year of study and at the same time challenge and stretch each student to higher levels of learning cognition. Visually, this relationship can be shown in figure 4.3. In this example, Student A should be at the Year 4 level. Student A requires turbocharged intervention (vertically along the quantity dimension or content descriptor scope and sequence) as they have only attained learning at Year 2 level. Student B, who already knows, understands, applies and analyses what is described in the Year 4 content descriptors requires extension intervention (horizontally along the quality dimension).

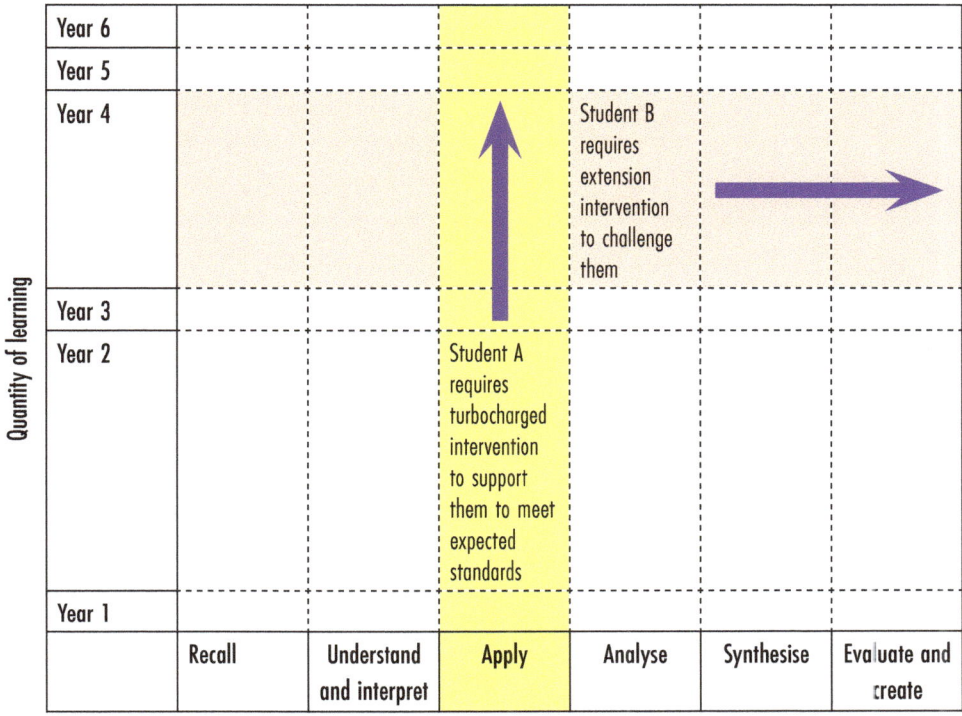

Figure 4.3: Intervention to improve learning quality and quantity

Rubrics that describe learning goals, such as in table 4.4 (page 83), assist teachers in planning for all students and encourage students to strive for improvement to be the very best they can be. Teachers might use the representation in figure 4.3 to teach students about growth mindsets and to help students set their own goals for improvement using feedback provided by the teacher.

Teachers should recognise that there is a heterogeneity of students in every mainstream maths class, generally with as many years of spread in their capabilities and cognition as the year of study (Hattie, 2012). The class will be comprised of:

+ students who are currently unable to access the intended maths learning curriculum for their year of study, all of whom require intervention of some form and may require turbocharged intervention
+ students who are currently equal to their maths year of study who require good teaching aimed at assisting them to continue learning and prevent the need for turbocharged intervention in the future
+ students who might be gifted and either already understand the maths being taught to them or who learn it quickly and require intervention in the form of extension.

Data and intervention planning

> *If we, as teachers, are to be effective across the broad range of students we encounter, we must know how to accurately and equitably assess the learning that goes on in our classrooms.* (Kusimo et al., 2000, p. 3)

Since curriculum differentiation is responding constructively to what students know (Munro, 2012), teachers need data (gathered formally and informally) to provide evidence of what each student knows and how well. Data is an invaluable tool for teachers in determining which students need intervention and which students require extension. Data can come in many forms. Informal data has already been alluded to earlier, gathered through teacher questioning and student responses as a way of determining what students already know about a concept. Data gathered through formal means, such as classroom-generated assessment data (from tests, assignments, extended projects and so on) and national testing data, can be analysed to determine both individual needs and subgroup needs. All such data can provide guidance for teachers to inform their planning for further intervention or extension. The use of data to inform teacher planning for intervention will be investigated further in Chapter 6.

Conclusion

In this chapter we have considered the intervention practices by individual teachers working with their own classes. This includes:

- differentiating learning design and delivery that meets the needs of individuals and small groups at their level
- helping student 'catch up' using the big conceptual steps of the curriculum
- using the psychology of high expectations and, in particular, teaching a growth mindset
- intervening to ensure all children are being challenged in their learning using qualities of learning as described in cognition models.

The role of the teacher in designing and providing intervention is complex and a very challenging part of their role. To effectively undertake this task they need to choose which form of intervention to use. This must be informed by valid data or information about what students know, understand and can do. Even tools such as the NNLP sequences and monitoring processes are useful only if informed by formal or informal assessment data that reveals what students have learned – or have not learned.

Chapter 5 will outline the nature of quality assessment of both maths and numeracy and how to develop tasks that generate valid data and information needed by teachers to determine whether and how well their students are learning.

Assessment of mathematics and numeracy

The need for quality data

To ensure that children and young people in schools learn to their full potential, teachers and schools need to regularly monitor and review the learning taking place in classrooms. Effective pedagogies rely strongly on analysis of data generated by class assessment tasks and national and international testing programs. The quality of this data is critical. This is captured in the Alice Springs (Mparntwe) Declaration which states, 'Good quality data allows teachers to evaluate the effectiveness of their classroom practice and supports educators to effectively identify learners' progress and growth, and design individualised and adaptive learning programs' (Education Council, 2019, p. 18). The role of data in underpinning and informing intervention strategies for numeracy means it must be rigorous and robust. To obtain such data, the assessment used to generate it must, in turn, be rigorous and robust.

What is assessment?

Assessment is a process of gathering evidence to determine what students know, understand and can do. Teachers and educators use it primarily to:

- understand what students already know and what they bring to the learning environment to inform planning
- discover which of their students are learning what is being taught and how well
- evaluate whether the pedagogical strategies they are using are effective and for which students
- inform students about what they are learning and how well, and how they can improve.

The third of these reasons may not be very palatable for teachers who might predominantly believe that if students are not learning, the fault lies with the student.

However, Hattie (2003, 2009) informs us that much of the reason for students not learning lies with the teacher. As Wiliam (2013) states, 'Our students do not learn what we teach. It is this simple and profound reality that means that assessment is perhaps the central process in effective instruction' (p. 15). Data generated through assessment, when analysed, can tell us a lot about our teaching practices and what we might do differently to improve student results. Quality assessment can, as a result, raise learning standards in classrooms (Black & Wiliam, 1998).

Types of assessment

If an assessment task is used to inform planning and self-reflection to promote student learning, it is called *assessment for learning* or *formative assessment*. If an assessment task is used only to generate a score or result, with no analysis of what or how the task was completed by students, it is called *assessment of learning* or *summative assessment*.

> *Is there evidence that improving formative assessment raises standards? The answer was an unequivocal yes, a conclusion based on a review of evidence published in over 250 articles by researchers from several countries.* (Black et al., 2004, p. 9)

Assessment is also either formal or informal. Formal assessment tasks usually occur in class and are often in written format. Such tasks generate quantitative information, which is frequently used to inform grades. Informal assessment is often spontaneous rather than planned. It provides teachers with qualitative information, which can sometimes be used to inform grades. Informal assessment occurs continually in most classrooms by teachers who gather assessment information through the learning environment. For example, answers given by students to their questions, and questions that their students ask in turn, provide information to teachers about what their students know or don't know. Other means of gathering informal assessment information include watching what students are doing and listening to their conversations when they are engaged in learning activities.

Characteristics of quality assessment

It is essential to ensure that the tasks used to generate information about students' learning are of good quality. Quality assessment tasks have the following characteristics.

Assessment of mathematics and numeracy

Quality assessment tasks are valid

Good assessment tasks assess what they claim to assess. The validity of a task will depend on whether a deliberate attempt is made by the teacher to ensure that tasks developed assess the intended learning goals described in the curriculum documentation. If teachers do not fully understand these goals, then their assessment tasks might assess only what they have taught their students instead of what the students were required to learn (sometimes these are not the same). Less experienced teachers should ask colleagues or school leaders to help them understand the intended curriculum goals if they are unsure.

For example, in Chapter 3 we considered the likelihood that students were primarily taught mathematical content rather than mathematical concepts. If a teacher teaches their students to add using one method, rather than to understand addition as a range of strategies to solve value or quantity problems, then it is likely that the assessment tasks will assess whether students can add using that one method. The Australian Curriculum in Year 1, for example, requires that students 'Represent and solve simple addition and subtraction problems using a range of strategies including counting on, partitioning and rearranging parts' (ACMNA015; ACARA, n.d.-d). Teachers must teach children a range of strategies (more than one or two ways) that they can use to solve addition and subtraction problems.

Note also the use of the word *problems* in the content descriptor meaning that students need to be able to be able to represent a situation before using a strategy to solve it. For example, 'Sylvia has three shells and her friend gives her two more. How many does she now have?' A student might represent this using shells or some other objects, or even represent it with a drawing or symbolically as $3 + 2$, before solving it by counting on. This assessment task is valid since it requires students to represent and solve. A task such as '$3 + 2 =$' assesses only one skill, meaning success would not indicate the student has met the requirements of the content descriptor. Understanding the content descriptors requires that teachers look closely at the important words and visualise their students doing what is described, then teach their students how to do what they have visualised.

An effective means of ensuring that an assessment task aligns with the intended learning is for teachers to develop an assessment task as soon as they are sure that they understand the learning goals. This backward design approach, described in Chapter 4, will minimise the risk of teachers merely assessing what they've taught, which they frequently do when they develop an assessment task after they've completed teaching a unit of work. An assessment task developed before teaching begins can become a planning reference point to ensure that the intended learning aligns with both the pedagogical strategies used and the assessment task.

Quality assessment tasks are comprehensive

An assessment program designed to cover a reporting period (for example, a term or semester) should be based on multiple and various kinds of evidence. Just as students have preferred learning styles, so too do they have preferred ways of demonstrating their learning and should consequently be given a range of ways to demonstrate this. These might include a written test, take-home assignment, skills test, group task, PowerPoint presentation, verbal presentation or writing task.

> **Time to reflect**
>
> What is your preferred way of demonstrating your learning?
>
> Which assessment type do you dislike the most? Why?

Assessment tasks should enable all students to demonstrate the full extent of their learning. This includes assessment tasks that provide opportunities for students to demonstrate higher-order thinking, depth of understanding, and an ability to apply their knowledge and skills in a range of contexts. Tasks that are low-level, such as those that only require recall, description or application in known contexts (see Chapters 3 and 4), do not give students the opportunity to demonstrate higher-order skills, such as the ability to analyse, create, critique, evaluate and transform their learning. A rich task will provide multiple entry points enabling students to access them at different levels. Each level might scaffold to the next, or students might enter at their ability level. A comprehensive set of assessment tasks should include higher-order tasks to challenge the full range of ability levels in the class, including those who are gifted.

> **Time to reflect**
>
> Have you ever been assessed through a task that you thought didn't allow you to show all that you had learned?
>
> How did it make you feel?
>
> What would have been a better way for you to demonstrate the full extent of your learning?

Assessment should be fair and equitable

The intention of assessment is to allow all students to show their learning. It is important that teachers assess the required knowledge and not skills that haven't been taught. It is also important that the assessment does not limit access to what is truly being assessed. For example, if a maths test uses words or phrases that students are unfamiliar with then students are limited in accessing the questions and showing their maths understanding. Consequently, this limitation results in data and information that does not accurately reflect their learning or knowledge of the maths. Other examples of tasks that lack fairness are those that require students to demonstrate higher-order thinking when students haven't been taught how.

Tasks should also contain questions and activities written in familiar and engaging contexts, not biased or discriminatory to a particular group. If tasks do this – particularly in terms of contexts in which questions are set – the other tasks used during the assessment period should be set in different contexts to balance any unintended biases. For example, a question about football in one task might be balanced by a question about netball in another task. This will avoid accusation of some students being advantaged due to their familiarity with a particular context.

Assessing mathematics concepts

The majority of maths tests and other assessment forms in schools assess maths skills, knowledge, methods and applications. They also assess the maths proficiencies, fluency, understanding and reasoning described in Chapter 1.

Maths assessment tasks do not assess numeracy. There is no requirement for students to decide 'Will some maths help?', since it obviously will. Maths assessment tasks can generate data that informs teachers of one dimension of numeracy – maths knowledge – but a maths test is insufficient to assess whether a student is numerate or not. Nevertheless, a maths test can provide valuable information about whether a student has the potential to be numerate, or is likely to be numerate. Both of these depend on the student's demonstrated understanding of maths concepts. Students who only know how to apply maths procedures but are unable to explain why they work are unlikely to have the depth of maths knowledge that will result in them using maths in context (see Chapter 2).

It is important, however, that maths assessment tasks generate data and information that informs teachers of their students' maths capability, both for maths learning and for numeracy potential. Consider the following example maths test developed for a group of Year 4 students having just completed a unit of work on area.

AREA TEST – YEAR 4

1. What is the area of this rectangle?   2 cm [rectangle] 6 cm

2. What is the area of a shape which is 3 m long and 7.1 m wide?

3. What is the area of carpet needed to carpet a room 2.6 m wide and 5.4 m long?

4. What is the area of a square with sides 5 m long?

5. If the length of a rectangle is 15 cm and the area is 30 cm², what is its width?

6. What is the cost of piece of plastic 2.3 m by 85 cm used as a tablecloth, if it costs $2.50 per m²?

Figure 5.1: Example Year 4 assessment task on area

The test purports to assess student learning of area, but not one of the six questions assesses student understanding of the concept of area. The only information it provides to the teacher is that the student, getting all answers correct, can perform area calculations. It is likely that this test assesses the content that the teacher has taught about area skills (low level), but it does not lead us to believe that students – even if they get all the questions correct – understand what area as a concept is. Because of this, the test is, in fact, invalid.

For these questions to be considered a valid assessment they would need to be part of a more comprehensive test. As discussed previously, assessment must be valid, comprehensive, and fair and equitable. The questions on the test (lower-order questions) should be combined with questions that include opportunities for higher-order cognitive skills and deep learning as indicated in Chapter 3. Higher-order questions might include:

✦ Use diagrams to show what it means if a rectangle has an area of 20 cm².

- A piece of A4 paper has an area of 560 cm². What does this mean?
- Estimate the area of your classroom floor and explain how you did it and what the estimate you obtain means.
- Could you use a piece of carpet 4.2 metres wide and 2 metres long to carpet a floor 3 metres wide and 2.5 metres wide? Explain your reasons.
- Draw three different shapes, each with an area of 4 cm².

These examples are all open-ended questions allowing for more than one possible answer. Teachers of maths frequently avoid using these types of questions since they are considered time-consuming to mark. However, one good open-ended question can take the place of many lower-order, closed-answer questions, meaning they potentially take no more time to mark because fewer questions are required.

You can see that one or two of these higher-order, open-ended questions added to the test in figure 5.1 will give richer and more meaningful information concerning a student's learning of the concept of area. The modified assessment task would give all students the opportunity to demonstrate the full extent of their knowledge.

Open-ended questions

Open-ended questions work extremely well to ascertain whether students understand concepts, as opposed to merely being able to apply and use methods and procedures they may have practised in class (Clarke & Sullivan, 1990, 1991; Sullivan, 2003). What follows is an example of the process of writing open-ended questions:

1. First, think of a closed, lower-order question pertaining to what students need to learn in class. For example, consider the concept of addition and the closed question '10 + 15 = ?'
2. Then flip that question by providing the answer and asking what the original question might have been. For example, two numbers added together total 25. What might those two numbers be?
3. To extend the question further, the open-ended question might then become the basis for an investigation or further inquiry work. For example, how many pairs of numbers can you find that add up to 25? Do they have to be whole numbers? Can you find any patterns in the pairs of numbers?

Note that open-ended questions can be used for both teaching and for learning. They are especially good for collaborative work where students justify, reason and explain their thinking to members of their group or class as well as to their teacher. They also help develop deeper conceptual understandings of maths concepts over teaching procedures only. Further examples of closed- and open-ended questions are shown in the following table.

Table 5.1: Different types of questions and questioning to ascertain depth of student learning

Concept	Closed question	Open-ended question	Investigation or inquiry
Perimeter	What is the perimeter of a rectangle that is 23 cm long and 14 cm wide?	The perimeter of a rectangle is 74 cm. What might the length and width of the rectangle be? Find three more rectangles that have this perimeter and draw them.	What other shapes have a perimeter of 74 cm? What lengths might their sides be?
Length	Measure the length of this line.	Find three lengths in the class that are more than 20 cms long. How long is each one? Put them in order from longest to shortest.	Investigate the lengths of shapes and objects in the classroom. The lengths may be straight lines or curved lines. Classify the shapes and objects based on what is the same and what is different.
Mean	What is the mean of 4, 6 and 8?	Three numbers have a mean of 6. What might they be? Can you think of two more sets of three numbers that have a mean of 6? What are they? Use your sets of numbers to explain what the mean is.	Investigate the sets of numbers that have a mean of 6.
Fractions	What fraction is halfway between ½ and ¾?	⅔ is halfway between two fractions; what might they be? Give two more pairs of fractions that have ⅔ as halfway between them. Show these pairs on a number line.	Investigate properties of pairs of numbers that ⅔ is halfway between.

The open-ended questions shown are quality maths assessment questions since they assess conceptual understandings. Gifted students in the class may be further challenged to research an aspect of area that might stem from one of the open-ended questions, shown in the investigation or inquiry column.

Assessing numeracy

Student numeracy achievement is used nationally as an indicator of learning. In Australia, school numeracy results are one of the few measures used by the government and by parents to determine the quality of the teaching and learning programs in a school. Why are numeracy results used in this way? In Chapter 1 it was shown

Assessment of mathematics and numeracy

that numeracy is a capability that all students (and people in general) need to successfully 'meet the demands of learning, school, home, work, community and civic life' (National Curriculum Board, 2009, p. 5). Numeracy is used in learning and for learning and hence numeracy attainment by students is an essential indicator of the effectiveness of a school. Schools are accountable for the numeracy achievement of their students: accountable to the government, their school system (if they are public or Catholic schools), and their school boards and communities.

The school level

Numeracy is rarely assessed by schools at a school or classroom level. Most teachers and schools only assess students' maths achievement, not their numeracy, against the Australian Curriculum: Mathematics. Some assess only their students' knowledge of procedures and methods. As we read in Chapter 1, this is not assessment of numeracy but merely assessment of some aspects of numeracy, or students' potential to be numerate. As the AAMT (1998) states, 'Assessment of progress in mathematics can also inform judgements and plans in relation to numeracy development. By their nature and focus, many assessments of mathematics – whether at the classroom, school or state level – can assess only some aspects of numeracy' (p. 5).

To assess a child's numeracy capability one would, in effect, need to follow each child around and watch:

+ when the child determined some maths would be useful
+ which maths they chose to use
+ how they applied the maths, taking into account the degree of accuracy or tolerance for error deemed acceptable
+ how they compared their calculation or method with their predetermined estimate to judge their response reasonable or not, and accept their answer as being appropriate, or not, given the context.

Clearly, this method is feasible given the constraints of teaching.

Assessing numeracy across the curriculum might be possible to some extent if teachers were to ensure that assessment in all learning areas contain questions or tasks that demand some numeracy and then observe whether their students choose to apply their maths skills. This would be challenging for most teachers, many of whom are unable to identify the numeracy demands in other learning areas, much less write assessment tasks that assess student application of numeracy.

Unfortunately, what is usually missing in numeracy assessment is the need for students to first decide whether maths will help and, if so, which maths. Students are not required to make decisions about whether maths will help (since they already know that it will, being a maths assessment), nor are they given the opportunity to choose which maths they will use (since this will be outlined by the unit of work being tested or by their teacher). For example, consider the following assessment item:

Gavin picks 400 lettuces to sell to the local supermarket. If he is paid $1.75 for each lettuce, how much does he receive? (Give your answer in dollars.)

The context for this question is that the students have been learning decimal multiplication for the past week and this question is on their test titled 'Multiplying decimals'. From this, the students already know some maths will help here, which type of maths and how to communicate their answer. As a result, what is being assessed is maths skill as opposed to numeracy, since most decisions have been made for the students already. If a student had experienced many questions like this in the classroom and for homework, then it is likely that only the student's recall is being assessed. Even if students had not experienced questions like this previously, it is likely they still would not be very challenged by it due to the lack of decision-making and reasoning required. This same comment might apply to the following questions if found on an assessment task:

$23 \times 4.8 =$

$5606 + 207 =$

$243 \div 7 =$

In fact, some teachers believe it to be unfair that more of these types of questions do not appear on national numeracy test papers, since class time often focuses on these skills. This is likely the result of them not clearly understanding the difference between maths and numeracy; they would prefer that what is assessed in a NAPLAN numeracy test is the maths that they teach in their classrooms.

By contrast, a student's numeracy capability could be assessed by observing their ability to determine independently how to apply the problem-solving framework discussed in Chapter 1. Students can be assessed against each of the five components of the framework, independently or in groups. The AAMT (1998) states, 'School numeracy should be assessed as performance, and in discourse and critical thinking in contexts across the curriculum' (p. 6). Assessment of numeracy should include the degree of autonomy and independence demonstrated in numerate behaviour as well as the level of confidence exhibited.

Assessment of mathematics and numeracy

A powerful way of supporting students to take control of their learning and their demonstration of learning is to have students involved in the writing of the assessment rubric. This can be done using samples of student work collected from previous similar tasks, where students identify features that distinguish higher-quality work from lower-quality work (Sadler, 1989; Wiliam, 2013). If this is to be included as part of students' formal assessment program then the rubric should be designed with grades or marks, indicating to students the achievement standards required for the specific task. For example, if students were required to develop a map of the school for visitors as discussed in table 2.5 (page 47), the following rubric could be given to students before they embark on the activity.

Table 5.2: Example of assessment rubric for assessing student numeracy

Developing a map of the school – task achievement criteria

	A	B	C	D	E
Clarify	Clearly states the desired outcome of the task. Identifies all considerations and risks	Clearly states the desired outcome of the task. Identifies most of the considerations and risks	States the correct outcome of the task. Identifies some of the considerations	Restates the task showing some understanding of what the task require. Does not identify considerations other than those given in the task	Shows little understanding of what is required
Choose	Chooses and justifies an appropriate format and size. Chooses to use a bird's-eye view layout to ensure best fit. Chooses and justifies an appropriate method to measure buildings and distances between them. Includes scale and legend for important features on the map	Chooses an appropriate format and size. Chooses a method to measure buildings and distances between them. Considers scale and some important features of a map	Chooses a format and scale using measurements of buildings and play areas. Chooses to undertake some measuring of buildings deemed important. Labels buildings	Chooses to informally provide a sketch of the school campus paying little attention to scale or fit of the campus on the page	Makes no connection between mathematics learned and the task

(continued)

	A	B	C	D	E
Use	Gathers and organises measurements appropriately and accurately makes calculations of scale Indicates all locations clearly on the map, with correct scale, legend and north point	Gathers selected measurements and makes some calculations without clearly explaining their purpose Includes important features on the map, but not necessarily in the correct locations	Takes some measurements, making some calculations without clearly explaining their purpose Positions and orients buildings and other features correctly	Provides not-to-scale sketch of school campus Positions some buildings and features correctly with respect to each other	Draws a sketch showing no understanding of location or scale
Interpret	Presents an accurate map analysed and presented with measurements, layout, positioning and orientation justified Assumptions made and risks managed by clearly labelling all features Student trials accuracy by asking a visitor to find their way to some point on campus and analysing feedback provided	Presents a map of campus presented with correct scale and some justification of measurements taken and reference to calculations Some key features drawn to scale and oriented correctly	Presents a map of campus, with some accurate measurements, provided Limited reference to calculations and some justification for positioning of buildings and features	Presents a bird's-eye view map of campus provided with some attention given to the arrangement of buildings and features Student at times not able to point to specific locations on their map	No interpretation provided
Communicate	Provides a neat, legible and accurate map with accompanying description of method and processes used to obtain the finished product, including refinements made following review of their trial with a visitor, resulting from reflection and evaluation of effectiveness	Provides a neat, legible map with accompanying description of methods and processes used for its development	Provides an attempt to summarise the method used in map development, activity undertaken and resulting map	Provides an attempt to describe activity undertaken and resulting map	Provides answers to questions when prompted only

Note that this rubric is a rating scale or continuum used to describe the learning quality, increasing in depth of learning, complexity of skill and sophistication of understanding of concepts as it progresses toward the left.

Education providers and researchers worldwide continue to investigate procedures, processes and validity of assessment and measurement of capabilities (OECD, 2017; Soland et al., 2013). This is likely due to the fact that the capabilities involve students making choices of what skills (including critical thinking, creative thinking and collaboration, often applied simultaneously) to apply (Scoular et al., 2020). Since critical and creative thinking are higher-order skills and many teachers are still learning how to teach these, it is understandable that capabilities are often difficult to measure.

The national level

One of the fundamental principles of good assessment listed earlier, is that children should not be assessed on what they have not been taught or not had the opportunity to learn.

This explains the mismatch between the maths taught in many classrooms around Australia and the material included in the numeracy tests of NAPLAN. While educators across Australia are teaching children maths, they are often not teaching the other two aspects of numeracy: problem-solving and making sense of contexts. Children are not being taught how to make choices about what maths to use in different contexts when there are no hints provided (such as what maths they have been learning recently). They are being assessed on three aspects of numeracy after only being taught one.

To demonstrate their numeracy development, children need to be placed in situations where they have no clues or prompts about which maths to apply and how to apply it to achieve sufficient accuracy for a given context. In school, they should regularly be given problems to solve – preferably not during their maths lesson time. There should be no clues about the maths or the strategies they might use to solve it. Collaborating is the ideal way to have students work on these problems using the problem-solving framework described in detail in Chapter 1. As they gain confidence, they can attempt these tasks independently. (This can also be used as a deliberate strategy for teaching children the genre of NAPLAN tests, as presented later in this chapter.)

Numeracy assessment questions

With the definition of numeracy in mind – numeracy is the ability, confidence and inclination to use maths successfully to meet the demands of all phases of learning, life and living in a society – we can see that a maths test is not sufficient to assess the capability of numeracy.

Generally, questions and tasks that deliberately and explicitly assess numeracy:

- contain no hints or clues about which operations or strategies to use
- don't necessarily indicate that 'some maths will help here'
- are situated in any context or learning area
- relate to students' everyday lives, written in real-life contexts
- use real-life language rather than technical mathematics terminology (you won't see words like *multiply*, *subtract*, *divide* and so on)
- require students to read, clarify and comprehend context through language
- usually try to test application and reasoning, rather than mathematics skills, while those testing skills only are concerned with fluency needed in numeracy.

These criteria hold for most questions used in the NAPLAN numeracy tests. Each question on a past Year 3 and Year 5 NAPLAN numeracy test paper can be mapped directly onto the Australian Curriculum: Mathematics from Year 1 to Year 7, and hence can be used for students in Year 1 to Year 6. Past papers are an excellent source of numeracy assessment questions and can be used as tasks for students to work on collaboratively to develop their numeracy skills.

While NAPLAN tests might not be the perfect way to assess numeracy (given that students already know that some maths will help), the questions nevertheless function well in assessing numeracy. This is because students have to bring all prior maths learning, from every year of study, to each question and choose the appropriate maths for the context.

Examples of NAPLAN-style questions include the following:

1. Freya has twelve nuts, which is seven nuts more than Susy. How many nuts does Susy have?
2. Jo has fifteen five-cent coins in her purse. How much money does she have altogether?

While these might seem very simple, it is the words and problem-type situations and contexts that are important. Reading these questions indicates to teachers the power of their students being able to visualise the situation. Working in small groups to clarify, choose and use strategies, interpret their answer and then communicate their thinking processes in context will help students to become familiar with how to apply their maths learning in numeracy situations.

Assessment of mathematics and numeracy

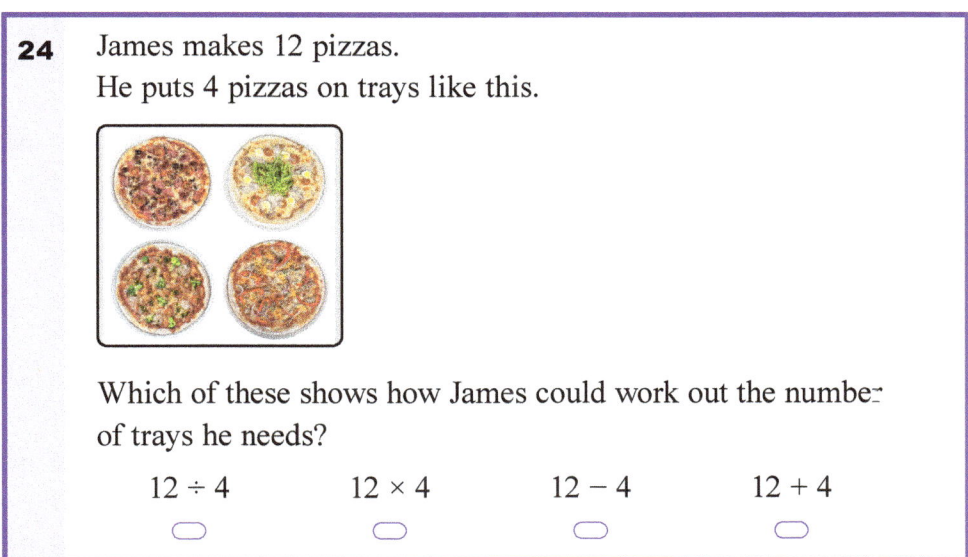

Figure 5.2: NAPLAN Year 3 numeracy test 2010, question 24
SOURCE: ACARA (2010). Used with permission.

Teachers in a professional learning team (PLT – discussed in Chapter 6) considering the question shown in figure 5.2 would first ask 'What is this question assessing?' or 'What is the intended learning being assessed here?' The intended learning being assessed is that a student must *choose* the operation to use that is best for the context. Nationally in 2010, 44 per cent of students chose the correct answer (division), 25 per cent chose multiplication, 14 per cent chose subtraction and 15 per cent chose addition (all percentages rounded).

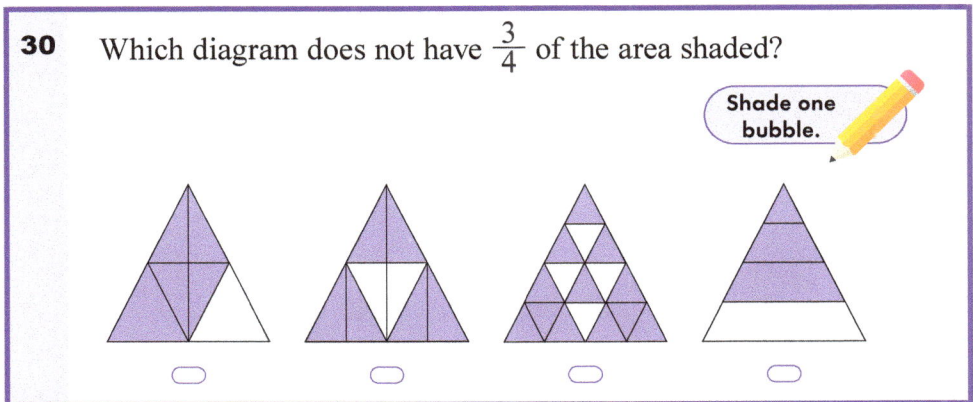

Figure 5.3: NAPLAN Year 7 numeracy test 2008, question 30
SOURCE: ACARA (2008). Used with permission.

The question shown in figure 5.3 (page 103) assesses whether students deeply understand what fractions are, rather than whether they can operate with them. If students had learned that ¾ is 'three out of every four equal parts' they would be able to do this question correctly, at a glance. The first diagram shows three out of every four equal parts shaded, the second does the same, the third does the same, so by elimination the answer must be that shown in the fourth diagram. Students not attempting by elimination would know that the word *equal* indicates that the fourth diagram cannot be correct since the four parts shown are *not* equal, despite only one of them being unshaded. Note the deep understandings of fraction concepts required. Results nationally in that year revealed that 10 per cent of Year 7 students chose the first answer, 20 per cent chose the second, 44 per cent chose the third and 24 per cent chose the fourth. This is alarming and serves to remind teachers of the importance of teaching children to understand concepts before calculations, since no calculations are required here. The implications for intervention are equally alarming, given students – at the time the results were released – were learning ratios and proportion, which require deep fractional understandings.

Being confronted by numeracy questions such as these and having to draw on 3–6 years of maths learning can be extremely daunting for students – even those who are good at maths. Some children freeze without their teacher to prompt them about how to start. Moreover, as suggested earlier, many children have been conditioned to expect questions that assess the maths they have been studying recently. Consequently, many don't consider the maths they have learned over many years and don't know where to start.

Children need a strategy. The problem-solving framework prepares students for numeracy assessments including NAPLAN tests; it gives them confidence. It will also help them throughout their entire learning, including when they leave school and are faced with numeracy situations in real life.

Genre of NAPLAN numeracy tests

NAPLAN numeracy tests have a particular genre – text format and style – that students need to be familiar with if they are to feel safe in the testing environment. Most numeracy questions are multiple-choice and can often be done by first estimating the solution and then looking for the answer closest to their estimation. However, students need to deeply understand mathematical concepts if they are to estimate solutions, as discussed in earlier chapters. Since many students don't have this capability and deep knowledge, this strategy is often avoided or not even considered. Instead, students choose to attempt to calculate the exact answer, which usually requires a lot more time than estimation. Moreover, research has shown that in real-life situations, more calculations require estimation than exact answers, and more than 85 per cent of these calculations are done mentally (Northcote & McIntosh, 1999).

NAPLAN numeracy tests also assess mathematical fluency, one of the maths proficiency strands, since students are required to complete the test in a given time frame. When students choose to calculate exactly instead of estimate, they usually need to work more quickly to complete the test. As a result, many students may have increased levels of anxiety and their risk of error is greater. However, if they have been taught to estimate using mental calculation and visualisation skills, then they will be well placed to choose their method of calculation. If they have not been taught these skills, they may only have one method in their repertoire – exact calculation using an algorithm.

NAPLAN numeracy results

Schooling does not revolve around NAPLAN and student results on the tests. However, the tests provide important information at all levels – national, state or territory and, most importantly, classroom. NAPLAN results are, despite some limitations, valid and reliable. When used effectively, they provide data to inform:

+ school and teacher planning
+ whole-class and student intervention
+ pedagogies
+ judgements about individual student progress.

When NAPLAN results are used for these purposes, the tests can be considered assessment for learning rather than assessment of learning. Assessment for learning (formative assessment) is assessment that informs school and teacher practice; results generated by assessment tasks are used by schools and teachers to help them evaluate the quality of the teaching and learning programs provided. Assessment for learning is responsible for the feedback loop between pedagogy and assessment indicated in figure 4.1 (page 65). Both the assessment task and the results generated provide a foundation for professional learning discussions about what is working and what isn't, which will be discussed in Chapter 6. Analysis of the resulting data focuses on questions such as:

+ Are our students learning what we're teaching? How do we know?
+ Are we teaching our students what they are expected to learn?
+ Which type of questions are students getting wrong? Why might that be?

- Are all students answering all questions? Why or why not?
- Do our students understand the genre used in the test? Can they *access* the questions?
- What proportion of students are selecting each answer? Why or why not?

Assessment of learning (summative assessment) by contrast, is assessment that generates final information about whether learning has occurred or not. The data generated is, in general, neither rigorously nor publicly analysed and results are used primarily to rank or compare schools, validate judgements and provide evidence about the quality of education being offered. Results are summative rather than formative. While the government and media might use NAPLAN results in this way, smart schools will use the results for learning.

> ### Time to reflect
>
> Do you use all results generated from assessment tasks you write formatively (to inform your own learning about the effectiveness of your teaching?)
>
> Which organisations are you aware of that use NAPLAN results summatively (as assessment of learning)? Is this a valid use of these results? Why or why not? And for whom?

Preparing for NAPLAN numeracy tests

The following strategy supports teachers in preparing their students for national numeracy tests, held in May each year. Teachers can prepare students to sit the tests not only technically but also academically and cognitively.

Using past papers, students can learn technically about the format and structure of the test. They can learn how to read the questions, how and where to indicate their chosen answer, how to understand the genre used and how to use the genre for their advantage.

Academically, teachers can better understand what numeracy is and teach in ways that support numeracy development. They must understand that the test developers expect students to comprehend the context of each question, make choices about what maths to apply and interpret their result in the given context by determining whether it makes sense. The test attempts to assess the holistic nature of numeracy – all three aspects as opposed to just the maths knowledge.

The evidence-based strategy that follows provides a structure that teachers can use with students to determine what their students know and how their students think about particular concepts and word structures and, importantly, how they comprehend or make meaning of each question or task. When used as suggested, this strategy supports students in their learning, with many schools throughout Australia gaining improved test scores after successful implementation.

Ideally, the strategy should be used once a day using questions from previous NAPLAN tests or similar. The time spent will vary depending on the class. Fifteen minutes a day as part of a numeracy block is recommended for each of the test types (the same strategy can be used for preparing students for the literacy portions), depending on the specific needs of students. This preparation should continue for at least Term 1 and the weeks of Term 2 prior to the formal test. However, the procedure can be continually used by all teachers (not just those of Years 3, 5 and 7) at intervals throughout the year.

It is the metacognitive higher-order functions (including clarification, justification, analysis and evaluation) that support deep learning. Hence this type of preparation is not teaching to the test, but rather a valuable teaching strategy for all aspects of numeracy considered critical by educators, the community and the nation. The chief benefit of this strategy, apart from students learning how to access the test questions and technically work with them, is that teachers can listen to their students talking about their understandings and as a result learn about their students' learning and understanding. This serves to inform their future planning and pedagogy and any required intervention. Another benefit is that students are forced to think about their own learning and consolidate or re-adjust their understanding when they listen to other students using different ways to explain what is written and justifying their position.

Students can use the process to prepare cognitively in that by practising the act of thinking about the questions and what they mean, and what choices they need to make to do what is being asked of them, they learn that this is part of the test activity. They learn not to 'rush in and do', but instead to use the problem-solving strategy (clarify, choose, use, interpret and communicate). They will then know to interpret their chosen result – does it make sense? If not, they will know to go back and rethink.

STEPS FOR QUESTION DECONSTRUCTION

1. Read the question aloud together.

2. Ask students 'Who doesn't know what the words mean?' If they don't know, pause and explicitly teach them.

3. If the question is situated in a context, ask two students to explain or further describe it.

4. If a context isn't given, ask students to give a real-life situation or context where they might need to use the skill being tested. For example, for '31 + 42' students may explain that buying something worth 31 cents and something that costs 42 cents requires adding them together to find the final cost.

5. Ask at least two students to paraphrase what they are being asked to do by telling another student what the question requires.

6. Ask students to estimate the answer and to justify their choice, explaining why they think their answer is correct.

7. Ask other students who agrees, who disagrees and why. Don't use any body language that will give students clues about the answer.

8. If multiple-choice answers are given, ask students to consider which individual answers could be right.

9. Ask students to think carefully and put their hand up if they would have chosen the first, second, third or fourth answer – they can only choose one. Choose a student from each group and ask them to justify their choice.

10. Facilitate a healthy discussion between the four students, allowing other students to join in after a few moments. You may need to initially teach students how to have this debate, modelling this yourself with students. The student discussion is likely to reveal misunderstandings or areas that you will need to reteach to ensure deep, correct understanding.

11. To conclude the discussion, ask all students again which of the choices they would choose. Many will have changed their minds by hearing the justifications and reasons of others and adjusted their thinking. They may have interpreted their result differently in the context of more deeply understanding the question from hearing the clarifications of others.

12. Finally, tell students the answer and justify it with your reasons. Students should be given the opportunity to write down the correct answer with the correct reason.

What follows is an example of this strategy.

Assessment of mathematics and numeracy

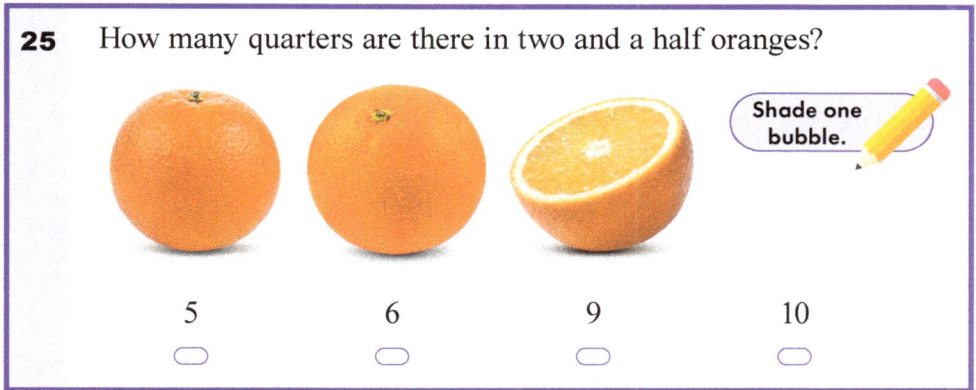

Figure 5.4: NAPLAN Year 3 numeracy test 2010, question 25
SOURCE: ACARA (2010). Used with permission.

The question could be projected on the board in a Year 2, 3 or 4 class. Students would read the question aloud with their teacher who would then ask: 'Does everyone understand the words in the question?'

Note that the teacher would gauge from the student responses which students can't read or understand words like *quarter* and *half*, and which students may have frequently heard their teacher use these words but not have seen them written before – explicitly teach these students the technical language of mathematics, including how to read and write words spoken in class.

The teacher might then ask some students to repeat the question in their own words while all students listen. They might then ask, 'Who thinks that something else is being asked?' and continue in this way until there is agreement between the whole class.

The teacher might continue by asking students 'When might we want to know this? Can anyone give me an example?'

The teacher would then ask students to look carefully at the four choices and decide which is the correct answer – but not call out their answer choice, rather keeping it to themselves. The teacher might ask students 'Has everyone chosen one of the answers?' Any student who has not should be asked again whether they understand the question and asked to paraphrase it.

The teacher would then ask: 'Raise your hand if you think that there are 5 quarters.'

'Raise your hand if you think that there are 6 quarters.'

'Raise your hand if you think that there are 9 quarters.'

'Raise your hand if you think that there are 10 quarters.'

The teacher might then ask one or two of the children who put their hands up for '5' to explain why.

They would then ask one or two of the children who put their hand up for '6' to explain why.

They would then ask one or two of the children who put their hand up for '9' to explain why.

They would then ask one or two of the children who put their hand up for '10' to explain why.

The teacher might then ask other children to explain why they chose their answer; for example, 'Why do *you* think there are 10 quarters?' or 'Why do *you* think there are 6 quarters?' and so on, continuing in this way and playing devil's advocate until all students' misconceptions and incorrect understandings have been revealed.

If a healthy argument or discussion occurs the teacher should facilitate this knowing that cognitive conflict is likely to be occurring and students may be reconstructing their own learning as a result of hearing different perspectives and beliefs.

Following this student discussion, the teacher would again ask the children to raise their hands for what they believe to be the correct answer and may also ask, 'Who changed their mind and why?'

The teacher would then finally tell the students what the answer is and explain the correct reasoning.

During this process, the teacher will have learned a great deal about the students' learning, misconceptions and reasons that underpin any of their incorrect beliefs or understandings. This can greatly inform teacher planning for the future, both in a general sense, as in the need to teach the technical words of mathematics concepts, and also in a conceptual sense regarding the teaching and learning of fractional understandings. It also reveals which students still require intervention.

Conclusion

The importance of numeracy for learning requires us to attempt to measure student development of this capability. However, assessing all aspects of numeracy is challenging. Australia uses a national test to generate data that can be reported to the nation. However, schools can use the information in ways that help their teachers and students improve.

In this chapter the difficulties of assessing numeracy as a general capability have been outlined and attention has been drawn to the limitations of a test that is not able to determine students' understanding of the three dimensions of numeracy. However, assessment of numeracy is an important requirement for parents and the nation as a whole – given the importance of the numeracy capability to learning and living in society. A strategy was provided to support classroom teachers to prepare their students to demonstrate the full extent of their numeracy understanding on an annual 'snapshot' test undertaken by ACARA on the federal Government's behalf: NAPLAN. Use of this strategy will serve to maximise the validity of students' results and broaden the use of NAPLAN numeracy tests as formative rather than merely summative assessment.

Much has been written about the successes of whole-school approaches to improvements in developing numeracy led by strategic leaders. These leaders work with teachers collaboratively in professional learning teams. Together, they analyse student achievement data and teachers reflect on their practice and how it might be improved to increase numeracy learning by students. Such an approach is explored in the following chapter.

Evidence-based whole-school approaches to numeracy improvement

Professional learning communities and teams

What is a professional learning community?

A professional learning community (PLC) is a group of school leaders and teachers who share a strong commitment to student learning. They work together and learn collaboratively, making collective decisions about how to improve learning in their school. DuFour (2004) in his article 'What is a "Professional Learning Community"?' describes a community of professional learners who assume that the core mission of formal education is not simply to ensure that students are taught but to ensure that they learn. Colleagues work collaboratively to focus on learning rather than teaching and hold themselves accountable for the results.

Sergiovanni (1992) believes that for schools to succeed they need to adopt the metaphor of 'school as community' rather than 'school as organisation'. He observed that schools that are learning communities have a connectedness among staff that is similar to what is found in a family. Similarly, Kruse and Louis (1993) describe PLCs as being characterised by teachers with shared norms and values collaborating and collectively focusing on student learning while engaging in reflective dialogue about their practice in uninhibited ways. The collective mindset of an effective PLC is one of 'How do we know if students are learning what we are teaching? Are they all learning or just some? What can we do about those who aren't?' This approach has proven effective in schools where staff have a commitment to the learning of all students and to their work and learning in a PLC (Chenoweth, 2009; DuFour, 2004; DuFour et al., 2004; Dufour & Marzano, 2011; Hord, 1997, 2009). There are four core PLC questions that help guide discussion, planning and teaching in a collaborative school community. They are:

1. 'What is it we want our students to learn?

2. 'How will we know if each student has learned it?

3. 'How will we respond when some students do not learn it?

4. 'How can we extend and enrich the learning for students who have demonstrated proficiency?' (DuFour et al., 2010, p. 119)

The desire to address these questions and improve student learning leads teachers and school leaders alike to engage with and analyse multiple sources of student data. The purpose of this is to find out where their students are performing well so they can celebrate and build on successes, and to intervene where students are not performing well. When a school is or has a PLC, all staff are engaged regularly and collaboratively in this practice.

What is a professional learning team?

Professional learning teams (PLTs) are groups of educators undertaking these activities within a whole-school PLC. Each team focuses on maximising learning for every student. While large schools may have many PLTs, smaller schools may have only one – the PLC is their PLT. PLTs acknowledge that if students are not learning to their full potential, this is a challenge for the whole school. They collaboratively develop strategic approaches to planning and resource deployment, using student demographic and achievement data as the basis for decision-making.

PLTs work collaboratively using a specific process closely aligned to that used by individual classroom teachers, described in Chapter 4. They:

1. analyse student data

2. generate hypotheses about what students require to further their learning

3. gather more data to test their hypotheses

4. develop and implement strategies to improve student learning, while consolidating and learning from areas of strength

5. closely monitor and evaluate the strategies used, discarding those that do not result in improved student learning and then generate new ones

6. celebrate successes, however small, and use them as the basis for further improvement.

This last point is very important for the health of a PLT. School leaders need to ensure that they, and the whole school community, appreciate what is being done well. It is current and learned practice, done well, that feeds the desire to improve further and fulfils the need that all educators have to feel valued and appreciated (Bandura, 1995).

The process put in place to deal with these questions is fundamentally the same at all levels, whether enacted by a PLT or a PLC. The difference is whether the process is collaboratively applied and monitored through the collective power of a team, for the former, or that of a community, for the latter.

Numeracy achievement data

Central to the work of a PLT is quality data. To determine whether students are learning what they should be learning and being taught, achievement data needs to be evaluated to connect what is taught to what is learned for every student. Snapshot data or data from one assessment task is insufficient for this purpose. Longitudinal data, such as NAPLAN data generated biannually, is preferred since it provides a point from which growth and additional value can be determined. Data provided from other schools on the same assessment tasks is also useful so that schools can compare the growth in achievement with benchmarked averages from similar schools. Teachers can analyse the data to determine what proportion of their students need help and which individual students need help. They can then target resources at these students and design and implement an improvement plan. Increasing accountability for learning, and particularly for literacy and numeracy attainment, requires that resources be used in ways that have maximum positive impact on students' learning outcomes.

Data literacy

School improvement through improving students' results in achievement data (including NAPLAN numeracy data) relies on the data literacy of staff; that is, staff being able to interrogate data to make decisions about what is working and what isn't working. Data literacy is part of every teacher's professional skill set and should be learned on the job. The Australian Institute for Teaching and School Leadership (AITSL; 2018) Australian Professional Standards for Teachers (APST) states that proficient teachers should be able to 'Use student assessment data to analyse and evaluate student understanding of subject/content, identifying interventions and modifying teaching practice' (p. 19). For teachers, their ability to meet this sub-standard is a question of their own personal numeracy capability.

While school leaders tend to work more with class and year-group averages and trends from data, classroom teachers need to recognise each data point as representative of an individual child and their learning.

NAPLAN data

All state and territory curriculum authorities in Australia deliver annual school NAPLAN data using various formats. Most formats can be used to inform the school about how they compare with previous years and how well particular cohorts of students are progressing.

Consider figure 6.1 showing the NAPLAN numeracy results for a school from 2010 to 2016. The most important thing to keep in mind here is that the data for each year shows the average results for a different cohort of students. It is therefore not the same students that are improving or going backwards in their understandings. To interpret this chart a school PLT needs to look for a trend. Here, the trend – judged by eye and superimposed using an arrow – is definitely upwards, showing school improvement over time but not individual student improvement for every student. It is rare that successive cohorts are stronger than those before them – more often their average scores vary up or down from year to year.

The variation in the results year by year indicates variation in the results of student cohorts in different years. However, the trendline shows that the results, in general, are improving over time and this can be attributed to the work of the school leaders and teachers.

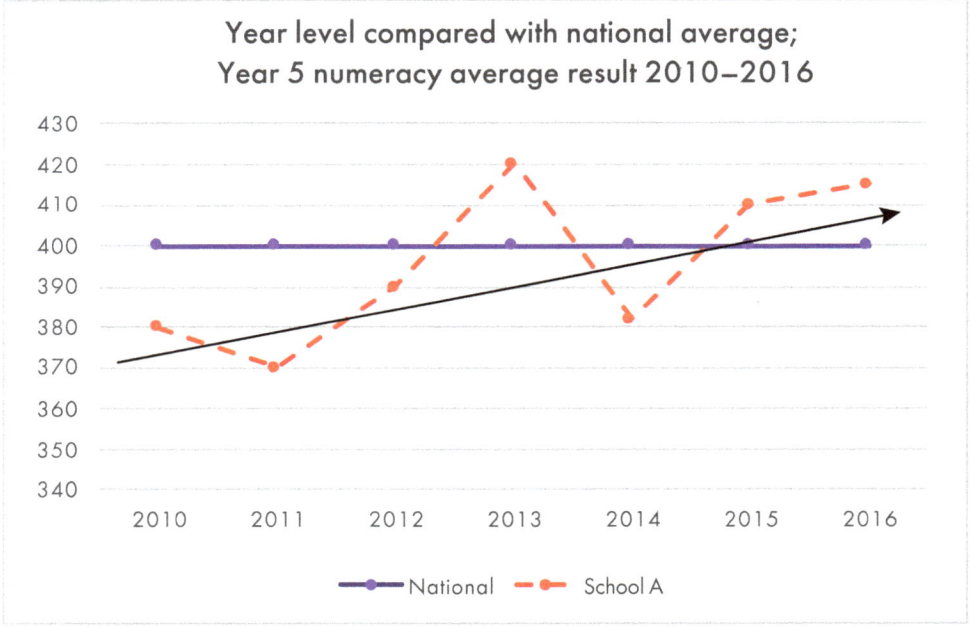

Figure 6.1: NAPLAN numeracy results for a particular school year group over time
SOURCE: Association of Independent Schools Western Australia (2018)

Evidence-based whole-school approaches to numeracy improvement

This result can be verified by observing the data and chart that displays results of a cohort over time. Figure 6.2 shows data for the same school in the same test (Numeracy, Year 5, 2016) and reveals the numeracy learning growth of these same students since their last NAPLAN numeracy test in Year 3.

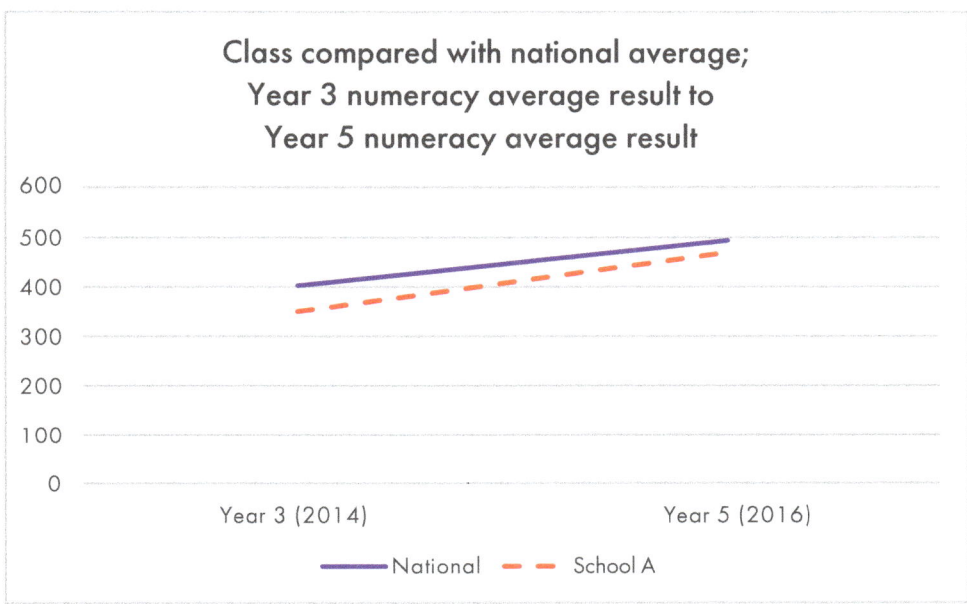

Figure 6.2: NAPLAN numeracy results for a particular student cohort over time
SOURCE: Association of Independent Schools Western Australia (2018)

What is noticeable here is that the students in Year 5 at School A have improved since their previous numeracy test in 2014. While it would be expected that they would improve since they have had a further two years of teaching and schooling, they have improved slightly more than the average improvement for all students in Year 5 across the nation. This can be seen in the fact that the slope of their improvement line is steeper than the slope of the national improvement line.

The improvement of the Year 5 students at School A can be attributed primarily to their teachers and one would hope this has been the result of a whole-school approach designed and committed to through school improvement planning processes led by school leaders. While these students are still behind the national average, the goal of the teachers and school would be to ultimately ensure the students' achievement is the same or better than the national average. They would continue using the same strategies but might also supplement others as part of their ongoing whole-school planning and monitoring processes.

Teachers can use filters to consider the progress (or lack thereof) of individual students in their class. For example, figure 6.3 reveals the progress made by a specific Year 5 student in numeracy since their NAPLAN numeracy test in Year 3, compared with the average for the whole class.

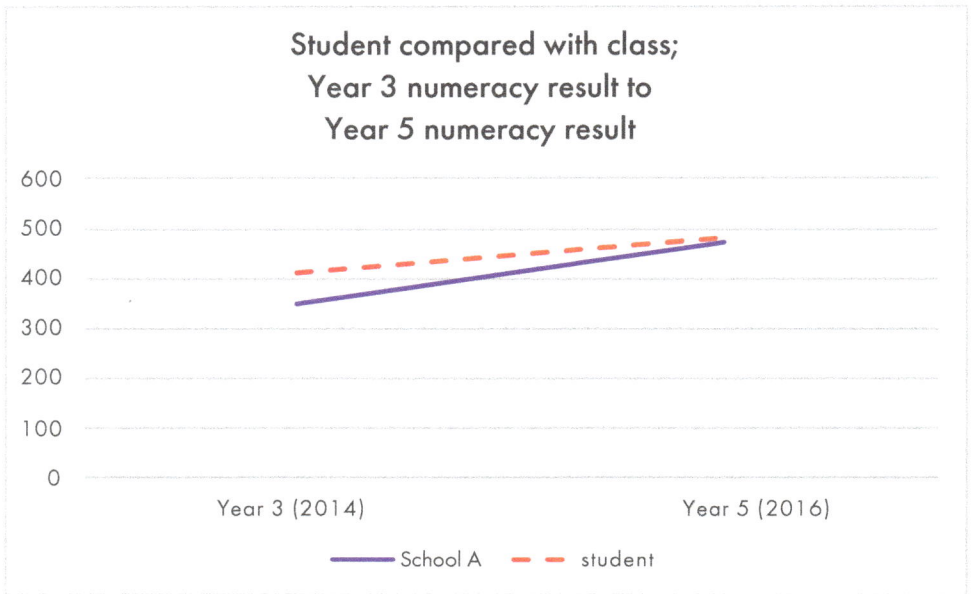

Figure 6.3: NAPLAN numeracy results for a specific student over time
SOURCE: Association of Independent Schools Western Australia (2018)

The Year 5 teacher might, on observing the results of this student, consider that the progress made by the student is not good enough. Questions such as 'Why isn't this student improving at the same rate (at least) as other students in the class?' may need to be considered. Being aware that the student is being compared with the class average (shown in figure 6.3), the teacher would know – due to their understanding of how averages work – that other students in the class must also be improving at a greater rate than that shown for the class average.

The teacher would further investigate the student's result. They may ask questions such as 'Is this what I expected for this student? Are there events occurring in the child's life that might be impeding progress? Is this reliable? What might have affected this result during the test itself? How does this compare with the student's in-class maths results so far this year and over the past two years?' The class teacher might talk to the student's previous teachers to see what they think, investigating the result by examining other circumstances that may have affected this result. The teacher might then examine their own teaching. Do other students' results reveal patterns like this? What does the student's raw data show? Are

Evidence-based whole-school approaches to numeracy improvement

there certain topics that this student didn't do well in? How many questions about fractions, measurement, data and so on did this student get wrong?

By examining the raw data the teacher can better consider the reasons for the student's lack of progress and action intervention strategies to address this.

Collaborative data assessment

To drill down into the data collaboratively, leaders facilitate discussions about test questions and students' responses, working with teachers to consider hypotheses for reasons behind the results. Note that these sessions need to be blame-free and take place in an environment of trust. Remember that incorrect understanding of a concept by a student can be the result of six years of teaching if the student is in Year 5; it is not the Year 5 teacher's fault! The focus is on improvement for all – teachers and students – not blame. School leaders should work hard to build this collaborative culture.

Consider the following extract of raw data for a small group of students on part of a NAPLAN numeracy test. Note: all names have been changed.

Table 6.1: NAPLAN numeracy test achievement data extract

	Number and algebra			Statistics and probability			Geometry and measurement		
Question	2	10	12	7	15	25	1	6	11
Correct answer	d	c	a	b	c	a	d	b	a
Australian % correct	54	79	47	63	59	61	76	77	81
Students % correct	63	68	51	61	64	73	67	78	69
Name									
Di Smith	b	c	a	b	a	a	d	b	a
Jason Jones	b	d	d	b	c	a	b	b	a
Jeremy Brown	d	c	a	c	d	d	d	b	a
Fiona Frobe	a	a	a	b	c	d	d	c	c
Ross Edwards	b	c	b	d	c	a	d	b	c
Amber Long	d	a	a	b	d	d	d	b	a
Toby Potter	a	a	c	b	a	d	d	d	a
Melanie Masters	b	d	a	c	c	d	a	b	a
David Hurst	d	a	a	b	c	a	b	d	c

SOURCE: Association of Independent Schools Western Australia (2017)

Individual questions and what choices students made

Looking at individual questions on the test and the responses selected by individual students can raise questions about possible reasons behind the choices. The discussions generated provide insight into the teaching and learning process.

For example, leaders and teachers might consider that only a small proportion of students chose answer *c* for question 10 – why might this be? Have they been taught the concept deeply? Are there any patterns in their errors or are they random?

With question 2 the answer is *d*, but many children chose *b* – let's look at the test question and consider why children might be choosing that response.

Look at question 25 – why are students choosing answer *d*? Are our teaching practices contributing to this result?

Individual students and patterns in their responses

Some students have greater understanding in some strands than they do in others. Knowing this can give teachers insight into the support needed in certain strands by individual students.

For example, let's look at Jason Jones. I note that he got all of the number and algebra questions wrong, but this is not the case with the other strands. Let's have a look at questions 2, 10 and 12 – they are all questions about fractions. We will write this down as his focus area for targeted improvement. Let's talk about how we each teach the concept of fraction so that students in Year 5 can get these questions correct.

Strand questions and the overall responses they elicited

If large proportions of students in a class respond incorrectly on certain strands then this can lead the teacher to question their own understanding of the strand and ability to teach it well – it may even indicate that the material has not been taught.

For example, more students got geometry and measurement questions wrong than anything else. What might the reasons for this be? Are we all including measurement in our planning? Do we all feel confident about teaching it? Do we leave it out if we run out of time? Fran, tell me how you teach shapes. Dion, which of the strands are you more confident to teach? Georgie, you teach measurement well – can you perhaps mentor Dion with this? What about if you team-teach? Every time you are teaching measurement you could join classes and Georgie could take the lead – perhaps swap over when you're learning about place value since that's your strength, Dion. Does anyone need professional learning in any of these areas or concepts? Let's go through the test paper and look at how all the students went on questions about time. Questions 5, 17 and 29 are all time questions. Highlight student responses to these and see if there are any patterns that we should consider.

Whole-school improvement

Schools and teachers use their student achievement data to answer the question: What can we do to improve the results of underachieving students? Deliberate intervention to improve student results across the entire school requires a whole-school approach. Specifically, it means not only designing and implementing strategies but also engaging with achievement data generated by assessment tasks to see if strategies are working and, if not, investigating, designing and implementing other strategies that lead to significant improvement. Monitoring of data must be ongoing to ensure learning gains are sustained and, if not, further strategies must be developed and employed.

Fullan et al., (2006) assert that a whole-school approach to improving learning must work from the following requirements:

- ✦ Schools need to work from the classroom out.
- ✦ Professional learning by staff must be in context.
- ✦ Teachers must interact in relation to teaching and learning.

At the classroom level, there must be:

- ✦ personalisation (every teacher has skills in putting each individual student at the centre of the learning)
- ✦ precision (taking the analysed data and using it to inform instruction)
- ✦ professional learning embedded into the daily learning experiences of students and teachers. (Fullan et al., 2006)

Capacity building

In implementing any change across a whole school it is essential the desired change is embedded rather than 'bolted on'. In other words, there needs to be a personal commitment to undertaking the changes required by staff involved. Staff, over time, need to see the benefits and commit to the change so that any additional work required by them comes from an internalised paradigm shift, rather than because they have been 'told to do it' (compliance).

Fullan (2005) defines *capacity building* as:

> *actions that lead to an increase in the collective power of a group to improve student achievement, especially by raising the bar and closing the gap for all students. Capacity building synergizes three things: new skills and dispositions; enhanced and focused resources; new and focused motivation or commitment.* (para. 4)

Sometimes teachers commence new activities because they've been asked to, and the shift in their commitment occurs gradually as they personally see the advantages to the learning of their students and as they feel empowered through the learning of new skills.

Building school capacity is often the work of a skilled school leader. School leaders who manage changes to bring about improvements to student learning through increased and refocused staff collaboration understand the benefits to building capacity in their school communities. Schools have 'come alive' as a result of a renewed focus where they can see the benefits of their new learning and their hard work.

Intervention

In Chapter 4 we looked at what individual teachers can do in their classrooms to intervene and improve learning. Strategies such as aligning and differentiating the curriculum, having high expectations and encouraging student growth mindsets, and focusing on learning quality to extend all students to achieve to high levels were discussed. Similarly, a whole-school approach to intervention can improve learning for all students and have far-reaching benefits for the school community. DuFour (2004) asserts:

> *When a school begins to function as a professional learning community . . . teachers become aware of the incongruity between their commitment to ensure learning for all students and their lack of a coordinated strategy to respond when some students do not learn. The staff addresses this discrepancy by designing strategies to ensure that struggling students receive additional time and support, no matter who their teacher is.* (p. 8)

Intervention in a school has historically been perceived to be the role of specialists. For example, leaders might recognise that there is a problem with poor literacy results and a literacy expert is contracted to work with staff to build their capacity in that area or to work with struggling students outside the classroom or after school. However, a PLT works together to focus the strategies in classrooms with trained teachers as the experts. This makes the withdrawal of students unnecessary; experts in teaching students with additional needs work instead with students in their classrooms.

Similarly, the focus of intervention has often, historically, been located *within* the child or group of students. This sometimes results in low expectations of students by schools and teachers, which can translate into low-level curriculum. This in turn may result in even lower achievement. Research indicates, however, that when students from marginalised backgrounds are presented with intellectually demanding work, their outcomes are likely to improve (Hayes et al., 2006). When all staff work together to ensure that *all* students learn – not merely those in their own class – they realise what Fullan (2015) calls the *moral imperative*: to provide every child with a fair and equitable opportunity to learn.

What typically happens when teachers are faced with students who are not learning (the third of the four core PLC questions) is that they often feel compelled to move forward in teaching the course rather than taking time out to provide additional instruction for these students. This results in the underachieving students falling further behind. DuFour (2004) states:

> *Almost invariably, the school leaves the solution to the discretion of individual teachers, who vary widely in the ways they respond. Some teachers conclude that the struggling students should transfer to a less rigorous course or should be considered for special education. Some lower their expectations by adopting less challenging standards for subgroups of students within their classrooms. Some look for ways to assist the students before and after school. Some allow struggling students to fail.* (p. 8)

As discussed in Chapter 4, it is integral that intervention occurs to support these students. It is neither fair nor sufficient to leave this work up to individual teachers, especially if they feel inadequate or unsupported to respond. Sharing student needs and discussing the challenges with colleagues can be difficult for teachers.

Decision-making and shared problem-solving

The most powerful part of a whole-school approach is that it calls on total transparency in teaching and decision-making, and de-privatisation of practice. DuFour (2004) explains:

> *Collaborative conversations call on team members to make public what has traditionally been private – goals, strategies, materials, pacing, questions, concerns and results. These discussions give every teacher someone to turn to and talk to, and they are explicitly structured to improve the classroom practice of teachers – individually and collectively.* (p. 10)

Or as Lunenburg (2010) explains, the team 'will analyze those results and work together to come up with new ideas for improving those results' (p. 2). There is nothing like teamwork to solve a problem. Professional dialogue can transform a school into a PLC (DuFour, 2004). The collective research cited in this chapter shows that whole-school approaches where communities of educators focus on collective problem-solving using agreed evidence result in sustainable improvements in student achievement.

Motivation

Finnegan (2013) states, 'Teachers behave in ways that will enhance their views of themselves as competent teachers' (p. 18). If their students fail in spite of teacher effort, the teacher's subsequent effort, persistence and resilience, and the amount of stress that can result are all impacted. To maintain their self-belief and limit stress, many disengage and are less likely to persevere in preparation and delivery of instruction (Tollefson, 2000). McNaughton and Lai (2009) assert:

> *Bandura (1995) describes a depressing cycle in which a sense of unsolvable problems lowers beliefs in personal effectiveness, which in turn results in a decreased commitment to teaching and innovating. The resulting impact on students further reduces teachers' sense of being effective.* (p. 11–12)

In analysing this and similar research, Finnegan (2013) and Bandura (1995) conclude that two of the major influences in developing teachers' personal sense of efficacy include immersion in an effective community where school administrators provide them with resources, such as time for planning, and the powerful experience of having been effective in the past.

A powerful spin-off of a whole-school approach to shared problem-solving is that collective and personal sense of self-efficacy is developed. As Mulford (2003) states, 'collective teacher efficacy is the important intervening variable between leadership and teacher work and then improved student outcomes' (p. 4). Research shows that when teachers focus on seemingly insurmountable difficulties in areas outside their immediate control (such as low socioeconomic status, poverty, literacy of families, lack of parental interest) there is a low collective sense of efficacy that undermines teachers' own personal sense of efficacy, or their ability to make a difference. Self-efficacy is a theory from psychology about self-worth. It is generated mainly through the improvements in output as a result of doing things differently and through the performances of others around them, inspiring, motivating and persuading. Bandura (1995) found that a sense of achievement or positive self-efficacy is created when teachers can see and experience the effects of their efforts.

Sharing student achievement

We need to celebrate successes! Improvements result from much hard work and strategic planning. School improvement successes should be shared with the school community, including the students themselves. Teachers and students are motivated to continue to work even harder so that improvement may continue. This is enhanced if the school publicly values and celebrates student improvements. It is important that 'Members of the [professional learning] community thoughtfully study multiple sources of student data to discover where students are performing well, and thus where staff members can celebrate' (Hord, 2009, p. 40).

Many schools have found a range of ways of doing this through publications such as school newsletters, social media, principal reports and even local newspapers. They also celebrate improvements internally as a school community through morning teas and other rewards.

Benefits of whole-school improvement for all

A number of benefits to students, teachers and school communities result from whole-school improvement.

When teachers gain more specific knowledge about the targeted support their students need, they are better able to foster discussion with their students. Not only does this result in students receiving more explicit feedback about how to improve, but they also gain a greater sense of agency and control over their own learning. This increased level of teacher–student conversation enhances this relationship, leaving students with a stronger belief that their teacher really cares about them and their learning.

Teachers, too, benefit from these collaborative ways of working, feeling they are not alone and finding comfort in knowing other teachers may be having the same challenges. Their learning supports them to grow, develop and engage more closely with the elements of the curriculum, as depicted in figure 4.1 (page 65). They gain a greater knowledge of the links and alignment between teaching and pedagogy and between pedagogy and assessment. Their changed focus on student learning removes some of the drive to 'get through the course' as they become centred on the question 'Are my students learning what I'm teaching, and if not, why not?' Another benefit for teachers working in school teams is that they develop a shared professional language and discourse through discussing student work samples, assessment criteria and standards, and evidence-based literacy and numeracy practices.

With teachers and staff growing and developing also comes benefit to the school and its community. There are stronger partnerships forged with parents and carers through a shared commitment to improved student results. This raises the perception of the school in the community, particularly in terms of its focus on maximising learning for individual students (which can in turn result in increased parent and carer engagement in the school).

The problem-solving processes by staff result in earlier identification of students at risk rather than a 'wait to fail' process and hence there are fewer students referred for special education or other support – for example, from the school psychologist, special needs teacher, speech therapist and so on. Also reduced is the over-identification of students from culturally and linguistically diverse backgrounds for intervention purposes.

Roles in a whole-school approach

Using a whole-school approach usually demands that school staff change their roles significantly. The educational research has focused specifically on the changed nature of the role of the school principal in the last few decades.

The role of the principal in a whole-school approach

There is no doubt that it is the teacher in the classroom that makes the biggest single difference to improving learning (Hattie, 1992, 2003; Rowe, 2003). At the same time, it is the principal and other school leaders who are in the best position to influence the practice of the teacher. Indeed, research indicates that individual teachers alone cannot bring about sustained and enduring improvements to student learning (Elmore, 2004; Fullan, 2002; Fullan et al., 2006; Hopkins, 2013; Sharratt & Fullan, 2009). Increasing evidence over the last two decades, however, points to the role and decision-making of the principal – in particular, the allocation of resources – in focusing on teaching and learning as the core business of the school (Blankstein, 2010; Lunenburg, 2010).

> *Principals have a key responsibility for developing a culture of effective teaching, for leading, designing and managing the quality of teaching and learning and for students' achievement in all aspects of their development. They set high expectations for the whole school through careful collaborative planning, monitoring and reviewing the effectiveness of learning.* (AITSL, 2015, p. 14)

Principals are in the best and most authoritative position to ask critical questions – such as 'Are all our students learning?' – that can shift and keep the focus of teachers on learning rather than on teaching. They set direction, manage teaching and learning, and lead professional learning teams, creating the conditions in schools that bring about improvements in student achievement (AITSL, 2014; Bandura, 1995; Blasé & Blasé, 1998; Boudett & Steele, 2007; Chenoweth, 2009; Dinham, 2016; DuFour et al., 2004; Elmore, 2000; Fullan, 2002; Gupton, 2003; Hopkins, 2013; Leader, 2008; Lunenberg, 2010; Marzano et al., 2005; Reeves, 2004; Robinson, 2007; Sharratt & Fullan, 2009; Timperley et al., 2007).

Instructional leadership requires that principals – sometimes sharing or distributing this responsibility with other school leaders such as deputies and curriculum leaders, depending on the size of the school – focus on learning and instruction. They use student data collaboratively to determine the needs of students, supporting teachers to align their curriculum, pedagogy and assessment, and develop the skills needed (Lunenberg, 2010). They are also responsible for providing clear leadership about the learning expected at each learning phase or year level and creating and enabling processes for addressing gaps in learning at whole-school, learning phase, class and individual student levels. As discussed by Mulford (2003), 'Good leadership helps foster the kind of school climate in which learning flourishes, rather than directly inspiring students to achieve' (p. 25).

The research cited here, and a plethora of other similar research, clearly demonstrates that principals, leading either directly or indirectly, are intrinsic in supporting school staff to effectively improve student learning, particularly in complex environments (Mulford, 2003). Schools with clear principal leadership share similar characteristics, including:

- ✦ Clarity of purpose. The principal articulates an expectation that all staff begin from the belief and premise that schools exist to help all students learn essential knowledge and skills without expecting additional resources.

- ✦ Collaborative culture. The principal and school leaders ensure that time is built in for staff to meet, together or in teams, and that their collaborative work focuses on student learning. Teachers are given opportunities to talk about planning, teaching strategies, assessment strategies and achievement data.

- ✦ Collective inquiry and problem-solving. Principals, school leaders and teachers examine student achievement data, hypothesise about the reasons for not all students learning or not learning to their potential, gather data to test their hypotheses – including teachers reflecting on their practice – develop and implement strategies to improve learning, monitor effectiveness and discard strategies that do not show improvement.

- ✦ Action orientation. Principals, school leaders and teachers engage with an unrelenting focus and sustained effort on teaching and learning. They know that plans and vision statements don't make a difference unless they act differently in collaborative ways.

- ✦ Commitment to continuous improvement. There is a well-defined process of continuous improvement and ongoing renewal as well as recognition that there is always room for improvement, no matter how well students are doing. This recognition is captured in the principal's articulated vision for the school.

- ✦ Focus on results. Under the principal's guidance and direction, schools assess the impact of their efforts and decisions based on student achievement data.

- ✦ Commitment to face adversity, conflict and anxiety. Sometimes staff are passively or aggressively resistant to the whole-school approach and their resulting behaviours can undermine teamwork. Principals meet privately with each of these staff, outlining their unacceptable behaviour and explaining the consequences if the behaviour continues. They will identify specific steps each teacher needs to take to remedy the situation and ask how they might support them to make the identified changes.

- Strong principals and school leaders. As previously stated, effective PLTs are critical to student achievement gains. Principals and school leaders who lead these teams are committed to empowering their teachers to improve teaching and learning. Successful principals delegate and distribute leadership and work with their staff, leading inquiry approaches around student achievement data.

The role of other school leaders in a whole-school approach

School leaders other than the principal, such as assistant principals and curriculum leaders, play an important role in any whole-school approach. They often have additional time to collate and present data needed by PLTs to support discussion and decision-making. At all levels, careful and fine analysis of achievement data combined with analysis of other important information, such as teacher professional development needs and student agency, leads to planning and practices that meet the needs of all parties involved.

These leaders are well placed to support decision-making about additional resources needed for intervention and how these might be used in the most efficient ways. School leaders can lead PLTs and drive improvement and learning in team members. While the principal makes decisions about resource allocation to improve teaching and learning, it is the other school leaders who are involved in setting group goals and targets, celebrating gains and monitoring improvements. Significantly they can table professional reading and set expectations about what is read and by when, and then facilitate discussions about what can be learned from the experiences of others. School leaders can ensure that the precious time of teachers is focused on the learning through engaging with student achievement data and discussing about what can be done about it. This leadership is critical and a realisation that learning is the work (Fullan, 2014).

> *Learning is not an add-on to the role of the professional. It is a habitual activity where the group learns how to learn together continuously.*
> (Hord, 2009, p. 40)

School leaders other than the principal also play a significant role in sourcing student data and formatting it in ways that can be read and understood by teachers. They can also provide an essential function in teaching staff to read and interpret the data so that it makes sense to them and informs decision-making.

> *Reviewing, studying, and interpreting data is the foundation of professional learning communities. Someone must be responsible for organizing the various sources of data in formats that are user-friendly . . . Eventually, all teachers should learn how to do this task so that they have ready access to current data.* (Hord, 2009, pp. 42–43)

The role of teachers in a whole-school approach

As has been shown, teachers are integral to student intervention and improvement. Coaching by trained support teachers or classroom teachers also constitutes a useful form of professional development because it includes collaborative analysis of classroom practice, values and builds on teacher expertise, and encourages the growth of a PLC.

The role of family and community in a whole-school approach

Clearly, schools cannot do it all. Research cited earlier by Hattie (2003), Rowe (2003) and Marzano et al. (2005), while indicating that teachers make the biggest single difference to student learning, acknowledges the role that parents, carers and families play. They do this, for example, by encouraging their children to learn at home, providing children with a suitable learning space free from distractions wherever possible, and by holding and verbalising high expectations of their children for their learning outcomes.

Schools should build strong relationships with parents, carers and communities to ensure that these stakeholders understand their important role in bringing their children to the learning environment before the teaching and learning work at school can begin. Children and young people also need to take responsibility for their learning. This is more likely to happen when teachers provide quality feedback to students that generates thinking and reasoning about what they can do to improve. Teachers also need to be explicit in ensuring that students know exactly what they are required to learn (Leahy et al., 2005; Wiliam, 2013).

Whole-school numeracy focus

When focusing on the improvement of numeracy outcomes in a school, the spotlight must be onthe numeracy achievement of its students.

All decision-making starts with a clear understanding of who the students are and what they bring with them into the learning environment. This involves scrutinising both demographic data and achievement data, as discussed earlier.

Evidence-based whole-school approaches to numeracy improvement

To answer the first two core PLC questions in the context of numeracy learning and development, there needs to be:

+ a common and shared understanding of what numeracy outcomes students should learn – intended curriculum and the expected learning of their same-age cohort

+ design and implementation of valid and reliable assessments of numeracy and maths that produce evidence of student learning – national and classroom achievement data

+ processes in place for school staff to collaboratively examine the evidence produced from shared assessment tasks in aggregated student reporting.

The third question requires that members of the PLT believe as a group that their students can produce better numeracy results than they are currently producing, and the fourth question requires that teachers move on and challenge children to transform what they currently know, as explained in Chapter 4.

The whole-school numeracy improvement process

The processes concerned with intervention and extension as outlined in Chapter 4 are at the centre of a successful whole-school approach. Student achievement from individual teacher intervention feeds directly into the data scrutinised by teachers in the PLT. As discussed, PLTs use a specific process to work collaboratively on school improvement and address the four critical PLC questions. This process can be shown diagrammatically in figure 6.4.

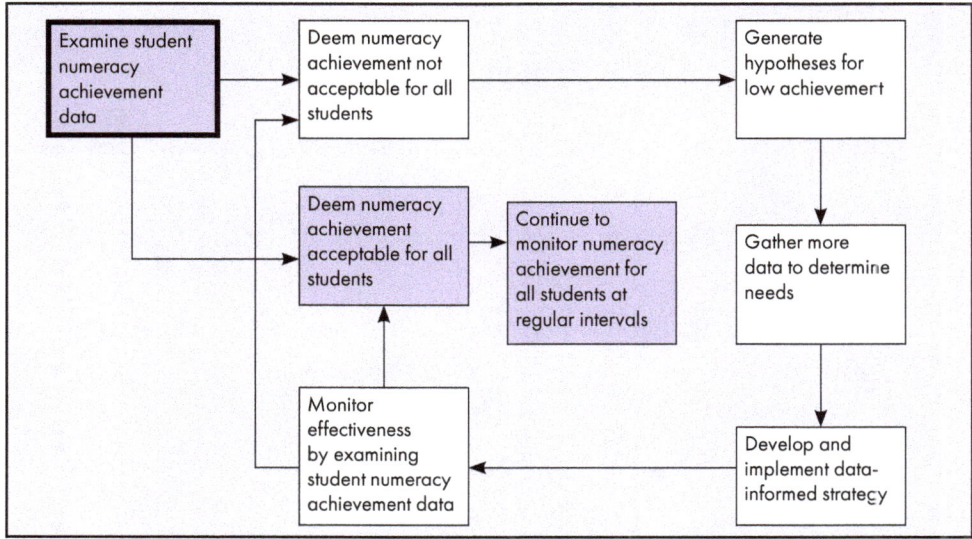

Figure 6.4: PLC and PLT approach for improving numeracy learning

Schools and teachers use their student achievement data to answer the question: What can we do to improve the results of underachieving students in mathematics and numeracy?

Teachers often find generating hypotheses the most difficult part of the process to enact. A hypothesis is a possible suggestion for why something is happening. In discussion teachers might suggest, for example, that low achievement is a result of:

- teachers' uncertainties around the intended maths learning for their students
- teachers not teaching maths for deep understanding
- teachers focusing on moving through the content rather than ensuring students are understanding what is taught
- teachers not explicitly teaching problem-solving skills
- teachers not teaching the skills of comprehension needed to understand contexts.

These are just some examples. In short, the earlier chapters outline a myriad of reasons for students not achieving the numeracy required for learning.

By examining any one of these hypotheses, teachers might intuitively know which reasons are likely and be able to cite their evidence. Teachers might have a clear enough idea that they may not need to gather additional data as suggested as the next step of the model. They might decide that they will all focus to a greater degree on designing and teaching a whole-school approach to problem-solving, using the framework suggested in Chapter 1. Alternatively, they might agree that they need more professional development in understanding the mathematical concepts that they are teaching or how to better assess them.

The approach shown in figure 6.4 (page 131) is underpinned by the following principles:

- All students have the potential for achieving equal and challenging maths and numeracy outcomes.
- Whole-school numeracy improvement is effective when achievement data indicates student progress in classroom-based results and national testing results.
- Whole-school improvement in numeracy is efficient when it results in considered and strategic use of the total resources available to a school for maximum gain for the most students at any given point in time

+ Intervention strategies and choices are defensible when using evidence-based decision-making processes concerning individual students in maths and numeracy.

Teacher reflection on practice is pivotal. This reflection may result in teachers reteaching a concept using a different strategy – not necessarily to the whole class, but to students who have yet to grasp the concept. When this practice is scaled up to the whole-school level and teachers share the effectiveness of their practices and try approaches that have proved effective for others, large gains can be achieved. Hord (2009), in her work with PLTs, relates the following anecdote:

> *As we studied and interpreted item analysis data, the young science teacher leaped to his feet and loudly proclaimed, 'They didn't get it.' After a long pause, he added, 'Next time, I will have to learn how to teach that differently.' This young teacher got it! And he got it through examining data in concert with his peers.* (p. 40)

All schools should operate in a paradigm of continuous improvement. The aim of schooling is to add value to the learning of students to maximise the education potential of each and every one. An effective and efficient approach to improvement is to focus on whole-school intervention processes within data-based inquiry approaches – that are evidence based – taken by teachers and endorsed, led and enabled by the principal (figure 6.4, page 131). This means that the design process presented as curriculum alignment in figure 4.1 (page 65) is operationalised by all classroom teachers, who together enact the process shown in figure 6.4.

A model for whole-school intervention

Just as figure 6.4 (page 131) depicts the scaling up of alignment from classroom to sub- or whole-school, the whole-school approach to intervention shown in figure 6.5 depicts the scaled-up version of classroom intervention discussed in Chapter 4.

An evidence-based response for whole-school intervention is built around three levels of intervention (Wanzek & Vaughn, 2011).

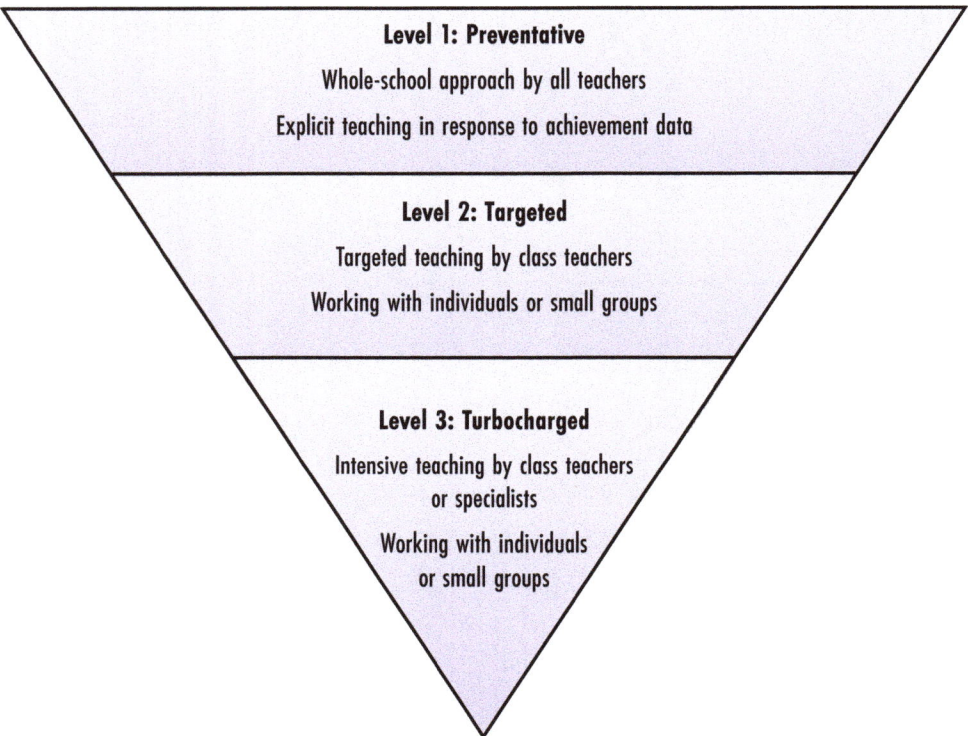

Figure 6.5: Whole-school approach to intervention

SOURCE: Adapted from Wanzek & Vaughn (2011)

The three levels of the approach can be summarised as follows:

Table 6.2: The three levels of the whole-school approach to intervention

Intervention level	Description
Level 1: Preventative	◆ Schools plan for numeracy learning based on the expectations of the national mathematics and numeracy expectations for students for their same-age cohort as indicated in the Australian Curriculum. ◆ They put strategies and policies in place to ensure that all teachers are delivering high-quality, explicit teaching of mathematics (aimed at developing conceptual understanding). ◆ Teachers collaborate to use high-quality assessment tasks and procedures to ensure valid data is generated. They collectively analyse data for patterns indicating any subgroups requiring more support (for example, more than half the class achieving D grade in last mathematics test; girls requiring greater support with spatial mathematics concepts than boys). ◆ Schools develop curriculum responses including hypotheses and strategies for intervention, then implement, monitor and review these based on further student achievement data generated. ◆ For patterns revealed in demographic data (for example, students from culturally or linguistically diverse backgrounds) curriculum responses are designed in consultation with the community, including professional development for staff, as needed.
Level 2: Targeted	◆ Teachers and support staff (if available) collaborate to examine classroom student achievement data and determine responses that can be implemented through targeted pedagogy in the classroom (for example, 'My students have done poorly on the measurement sections of the national numeracy tests; what pedagogies for teaching these concepts can I learn from other teachers? Am I addressing all the intended curriculum expected for this age cohort in measurement? Do I need professional development to teach measurement better?' or 'Most of my students are not demonstrating standards greater than C; are my assessment tasks giving them access to an A or B? Maybe I'm marking them too low – is my judgement-making valid?' or 'Are my gifted students being sufficiently stretched and intellectually challenged? How do I know, and do I know how to do this in both my pedagogy and my assessment?' or 'Are students with learning difficulties accessing the curriculum on the same basis as their peers? Do I need PD in how to help them? Should they be receiving intensive (Level 3) intervention?' ◆ If teachers implement strategies that are not effective, it is likely that professional development programs are needed for them and schools need to make funds available for this, either for all teachers or for a school leader who then uses their knowledge to develop teachers and support them in implementing new intervention strategies.
Level 3: Turbocharged	◆ Teachers, in collaboration with specialists, examine individual student achievement data in order to develop responses that include intensive and highly scaffolded pedagogies. Individual education plans are developed in consultation with parents and carers. If the curriculum's goals are lower than the same-age cohort curriculum goals, parents must agree. (Note that these students are generally a very small proportion of the year cohort and should be included in mainstream classrooms rather than withdrawn except for short periods of time.) ◆ This level is sometimes referred to as the 'intensive intervention/teaching' level. In this approach a third level of intervention involves the use of intensive pedagogy for short periods of time or instruction in the use of compensatory tools such as assistive technology. It should be implemented by trained teachers having the in-depth knowledge of the progression of skills that the learning area requires. Too often this group of students is supported by parents, volunteers, paraprofessionals who do not have these skills (DuFour & Marzano, 2011). Students who do not respond to this third level of teaching should be referred for a comprehensive evaluation by special education service provider. They may have learning difficulties and require specific strategies to enable them to access the curriculum.

Different intervention at each level

The levels respond in flexible ways to students and the intervention they receive. Ideally, no student should be removed from the mainstream class, even when receiving intensive support. The ultimate goal for each student, given an agentic teacher response — that is, having an attitude of believing all students will achieve what they are expected to achieve or beyond — is to be part of the mainstream class and learning what is their expected learning and curriculum entitlement.

At all levels, teachers continue to closely monitor student responsiveness to pedagogy using the feedback loop. Student learning is monitored at increasing levels of intensity at each layer with increasing involvement of other staff in providing support.

This approach has been successfully used by a number of schools and has produced benefits for all learners including:

- earlier identification of students who require support and intervention
- a reduction in the number of students referred for special education services
- a reduction in the over-identification of students from culturally and linguistically diverse backgrounds for intervention support
- more instructionally relevant data by monitoring progress through the use of curriculum-based, classroom-based assessment, student portfolios, teacher observations and criterion-referenced standard achievement measures (COAG, 2008; Meiers et al., 2013).

While the response to intervention model is a powerful whole-school approach to improving student achievement, it is only as good as the data used to inform the evidence base for discussions and the data literacy skills of the teachers using it (see figure 6.4, page 131). If the data is not generated through quality assessment and the teachers reviewing and analysing it do not have the skills to interpret it, they will be unable know what the data is saying and rely on it to inform the choices of intervention that might be needed.

Whole-school numeracy planning

In their PLTs teachers, led by the school principal or other school leaders, should examine their data sources (NAPLAN, classroom and data from other sources), including drilling down into individual student and class results. They might agree that more work is needed. If achievement results are not improving, they will need to consider further hypotheses for what the problems and challenges might be and what the possible solutions might be, as shown in figure 6.4 (page 131). It may not be possible to determine one specific reason why results are not improving; often reasons are complex and a range of responses are needed, at both individual and whole-school levels. Schools should do whatever it takes to maximise the learning of their students. They might try a single strategy or a group of strategies and monitor and review them over time to gauge their effectiveness.

By considering all the aspects of numeracy presented in this book and the reasons why results are lower than expected, hypotheses such as the following might result:

- All teachers having a better understanding of the difference between maths and numeracy will improve student results.
- Considering the intended learning outcomes together and discussing them ensures we share the understandings and will result in us better and more consistently teaching the intended learning.
- A whole-school approach to teaching problem-solving by all teachers will improve students' numeracy achievement.
- Teaching students higher-order skills will improve student results.
- A whole-school approach to teaching mental computation and estimation will improve student results.
- Undertaking professional learning to better understand maths concepts will improve teaching and hence student results.
- Undertaking professional learning in problem-solving or numeracy across the curriculum will improve student results.

These hypotheses will then lead to proposed strategies being documented with timelines for monitoring and review, as included in the following example school numeracy plan (table 6.3, page 138). Note the inclusion of literacy focus areas as part of improving numeracy. (Note also that this plan is one section of a school improvement plan rather than a separate plan.)

Table 6.3: Example of a school numeracy plan

Priority area	Goal	Targets	Strategies	Tasks	Responsibility
Numeracy	Improve numeracy achievement in the school	◆ 20% more students reaching national benchmarks ◆ In Years 5 and 7 move from pink to at least white — if not light green — for next year, on My School	In Years 3–6: ◆ use NAPLAN questions (one a day) to increase problem-solving skills and strategies ◆ include more estimation in all classes (including in sport) to improve concept understanding	◆ Run PLT on data literacy for all teachers ◆ All teachers engage in one NAPLAN question a day ◆ Get NAPLAN questions from hard copy onto ppt for teachers to use in one question a day ◆ Teachers use daily maths chants for memorisation	Deputy or school leader All teachers Deputy or school leader All teachers
Student agency	Students become equal learning partners with teachers	◆ Learning goals are mutually negotiated through a culture of high expectations	◆ Students work in groups to develop real-life and engaging problem-solving tasks ◆ Students develop and use rubrics which they use to check other groups' work	◆ Students develop and use rubrics	All teachers

(continued)

Evidence-based whole-school approaches to numeracy improvement

Priority area	Goal	Targets	Strategies	Tasks	Responsibility
Assessment quality	Improve assessment quality to ensure valid data is generated	◆ All assessment tasks align to intended learning ◆ Intended learning understanding is shared ◆ All teachers use rubrics to describe learning quality	◆ Teachers write learning goals on the board each lesson ◆ Teachers work with students to develop rubrics ◆ Posters of Bloom's taxonomy should be placed on walls in every classroom ◆ Teachers explicitly teach students higher-order skills ◆ Parents understand the new approach to assessment and learning quality	◆ PLTs examine Australian Curriculum content descriptors together and moderate understanding ◆ All assessment tasks should be reviewed to include higher-order skills ◆ Posters of Bloom's taxonomy made and laminated for each room ◆ PLTs focus on developing teacher skills in writing rubrics ◆ Meetings held for parents to explain assessment approach and goals	PLT leaders and deputy or school leader Deputy or school leader initially Deputy, school leader or administrative staff PLT leaders, deputy or school leader Principal
Literacy	Improve comprehension skills	◆ Whole-school approach to comprehension and use of higher-order skills in all classes using written texts	◆ Teachers use one NAPLAN question a day approach with past questions ◆ Teachers focus on reading comprehension in all learning areas		All teachers All teachers

All plans to improve numeracy in a school need to be set within a greater context: a holistic school perspective. For example, if students are not achieving the results they should be achieving in numeracy, PLTs might hypothesise that students are not reading and comprehending questions well enough to know which maths to apply to the context. They might then triangulate this data with their NAPLAN reading data to see if this confirms that fact. One of their improving numeracy strategies might be to raise student levels of comprehension, which might include professional learning for all teachers in teaching comprehension as well as using the one NAPLAN numeracy question a day strategy across the school. This might be part of a literacy improvement plan which connects to numeracy improvement. The principal and school leaders might also decide, in consultation with staff, to address critical thinking, improving higher-order thinking skills through changing the way assessment is done, using rubrics to support teachers to understand learning quality, and so on.

In this way, the principal strategically orchestrates and manages changes with other school leaders by making connections across areas to avoid a siloed-approach to improvement in the school.

School leaders know that the planning is more important than the resulting plan; the plan needs to be a living document – revisited frequently to monitor and evaluate the strategies included to gauge effectiveness. They are prepared to make changes and manage these as needed to minimise potential negative feedback from staff and parents and carers. They share their evidence and ensure that teachers are themselves able to interpret data that justify school decisions, thereby sharing the ownership of these.

School leaders know that addressing student numeracy achievement needs to occur on a number of fronts, including the amount of change needed, staff capacity for change, number of school priorities and so on. They consider all the evidence, propose a vision for improvement and describe steps that are achievable to attain it. They then put this proposal to staff and discuss the support staff might need to implement it.

Case study: Mundaring Christian College

Mundaring Christian College is a small school in the hills about 28 kilometres east of Perth in Western Australia. At the time of writing, I was working at the school directing teaching and learning and was employed to support the principal during a time of expansion. This involved the principal spending much of his time working with contractors and architects on a new building program. The transition to having a primary school and early learning centre on one campus and Years 7–12 on another campus 10 kilometres away would occur over a three-year period. The physical relocation of the secondary school to a new campus – Years 7–10 in the first year – and the addition of senior schooling – Years 11 and 12 – in subsequent years, required much strategic planning, especially since the new campus for the first year was only at stage one of a three-stage build and hence did not have sufficient capacity to hold all the classes. This meant that other spaces such as the canteen and hallways would have to be used for classes while the other building phases occurred in the following years. In addition, adding Years 11 and 12 required an additional layer of policy from the state curriculum authority, hiring and training Years 7–10 staff to teach these years, and an increased level of accountability. This meant a large amount of additional work and planning involving a focus on raising standards at the school to ensure growth and to make the college a viable 'school of choice'.

As well as supporting the principal with school operations, training staff in the teaching and requirements of senior schooling and other operational matters, my brief was to raise learning standards across the school. On arriving at the school, I engaged with achievement data, demographic data and informal data gathered through conversations with staff. PLTs already existed in the school: one for each of early childhood to Year 2, Years 3–6, Years 7–10 (English and HASS), Year 7–10 (maths and science) and 7–10 (options and electives), but they had not yet engaged with any data to inform planning, and teachers and school leaders had limited data literacy skills.

I ascertained that the most efficient and effective way to raise standards and lift achievement in the school was to address the assessment process. I briefed staff on the quality dimension of learning and outlined a vision for quality assessment tasks. All teachers would be challenged and supported to write rubrics describing the learning quality of assessment tasks that they would use. Our shared goal would be for the current A-grade standard in the school to be the C standard. This would naturally involve educating students, teachers, and parents and carers about the quality dimension of learning. It would also require teachers to explicitly teach higher-order and reasoning skills and to ensure these were included in all lessons.

This strategic approach would see staff working together to:

- address the general capabilities of the Australian Curriculum, in particular, literacy, numeracy, and critical and creative thinking
- improve the quality of assessment tasks to ensure they were valid, explicit and gave all students the opportunity to access and demonstrate their learning
- give all students agency in their learning and feedback on how they might improve
- shift students' perceptions of their grades from 'This is what my teacher *gave me* for this work' to 'This is what *I earned* on this task'
- enable teacher capability of data literacy, as required by the APST, and an understanding of the primacy of assessment in driving excellence in teaching and learning

- enable deep learning about curriculum alignment as well as the development of assessment tasks before the teaching program commences to maximise validity and ensure a focus on instructional goals in teaching
- connect the school A–E grades with a consistent and shared scale describing learning quality, which should tightly articulate the qualities demonstrated in student work and be written into a rubric, understood by both parents and students
- minimise the effect of an implementation bump between Years 10 and 11 and ensure seamlessness in the way assessment was approached and undertaken across the entire school
- help build an understanding across the school of school improvement and strategic planning processes and, in particular, the use of data in providing an evidence base to inform the plan and for monitoring and reviewing progress.

Note that the strategy was aimed at raising student learning standards by raising teacher professional standards.

The focus was not aimed at numeracy improvement. I knew from experience and research that addressing all other areas would raise student numeracy and literacy achievement. The strategy therefore included a number of fronts that were strategically connected and combined.

The plan required me to critique the validity and rigour of all assessment tasks in every learning area, developed by teachers from across the school — a time-consuming process. The focus was that all tasks assessed the content descriptors they were designed to assess, that all students were able to access some of each task and that tasks designed to address Bloom's (1956) taxonomy actually did. I frequently met with teachers to discuss and provide feedback, coaching them in what was required for improvement. In working with PLT leaders, I modelled this process, developing their skills regarding learning quality and developing rubrics so that they could eventually coach others themselves.

Processes for improved assessment included having teachers work together to consider learning qualities in content descriptors, critiquing each other's tasks and rubrics, justifying evaluations and discussing criteria for learning tasks which could be stretched across the levels of Bloom's taxonomy. After tasks had been administered, PLT members then supported each other to judge grades and feedback using the rubrics; moderation became a normal part of the assessment process.

In addition, table 6.3 (page 138) indicates other strategies that were implemented and monitored during the fifteen-month period prior to the release of the 2016 NAPLAN data results and then continued following review through 2017. Teachers worked hard at using strategies such as 'one question a day'; analysing student NAPLAN data from 2015 and 2016; reading, discussing and using professional development materials in their teaching; as well as learning about numeracy and how it depends on teachers teaching maths content and concepts, problem-solving and application across all learning areas and school contexts.

I would like to note that it should be reiterated that improving school numeracy was not the sole focus of my work. Workshops concerning the development of maths teaching and learning during that time were minimal. Instead, teachers trialled and used resources independently or were facilitated by a teacher with particular interest in this learning area.

Standards did indeed improve over time at Mundaring Christian College. Student standards increased in all aspects of literacy and numeracy and in all learning areas. Teacher capabilities greatly increased so that many teachers subsequently became proficient in the APST and were able to demonstrate their learning in all areas of their teaching practice. PLT leaders had over time gained expertise in all areas and are now able to continue to provide mentoring in these areas, without my input.

Following the release of the 2016 NAPLAN data, I celebrated the improvement in the college newsletter.

NAPLAN celebration: School improvement on NAPLAN

I am so proud of our students and teachers!

Although we don't go into league tables and school comparisons, we do give a lot of credence to our annual NAPLAN results. The main reason for this is that the data that is made available to schools about what students did or did not do in the tests is invaluable to us to inform our planning:

- Which students need more help and in what areas?
- Which students need to be extended and further challenged and in what areas?
- What areas aren't our students doing well in and how can we improve the way we do things?

Figure 6.6: College newsletter NAPLAN celebration *(continued)*
SOURCE: Mundaring Christian College leadership (personal communication)

So we use the NAPLAN data to inform and improve our practice. While we acknowledge that the tests are done on one day of the year and have reliability issues (due to sicknesses or lack of attendance for some students) we read the data they generate with appropriate skepticism; *Is this what we were expecting?* If results for a particular student are too different from what we were expecting, we disregard them. In other words, we control what is useful for our improvement – we don't disregard the data due to minor reliability issues.

The following table reveals how successful the use of student data has been for us this year. Our teachers have been diligently learning how to interpret it, discuss what it means and make necessary changes to their teaching if students aren't improving in the ways we expect them to. The table reveals school improvements since 2015 (note there were some decreases, but these were very insignificant – national averages remain fairly constant from year to year).

	National average	MCC 2015 average	MCC 2016 average	Result
Numeracy				
Year 3	402	400	401	About the same
Year 5	493	470	483	Increase
Year 7	550	522	552	Significant increase
Year 9	589	600	597	About the same
Reading				
Year 3	426	449	440	About the same
Year 5	502	501	493	About the same
Year 7	541	543	558	Significant increase
Year 9	581	588	599	Increase
Writing				
Year 3	421	422	433	Increase
Year 5				Decrease
Year 7				
Year 9	548	561	574	Significant increase

(continued)

	National average	MCC 2015 average	MCC 2016 average	Result
Spelling				
Year 3	420	388	444	Significant increase
Year 5				Increase
Year 7	543	534	553	Significant increase
Year 9				Decrease
Grammar and punctuation				
Year 3	436	433	467	Significant increase
Year 5				Decrease
Year 7	540	520	551	Significant increase
Year 9		570	578	Increase

Out of a total of twenty measures (four tests in each of five areas) our results as a school have increased in twelve, and seven of these increases were significant! These results are outstanding, and we have much to celebrate!

Please join me in congratulating our wonderful teachers who work so hard! Remember, for example, an improved result in Year 7 is the result of the hard work of teachers and students in Years 5, 6 and 7. Similarly, outstanding results in Year 3 are the results of teachers and educators in pre-kindy, kindy, pre-primary, Year 1, Year 2 and Year 3! Every teacher is responsible and deserves our thanks.

Thank you for all your support as we make these improvements and continue to strive for excellence in our teaching and learning programs.

Thelma Perso
Director, teaching and learning

Making improvements to student achievement through learning with teachers takes time and a large investment. To make the gains discussed in fifteen months was very challenging and also very rewarding for all those involved. Teachers saw the benefits of their hard work and also the power of working collaboratively with student achievement data. They became aware that the most difficult work was in making the initial gains, but improvements continued as they pushed forward.

NAPLAN results from 2017 continued to show improvements. However, as with most schools, priorities, staff movements and cohort changes had considerable impact on three of the phases of schooling. Two of the teachers in the F–2 phase of schooling were new during the 2015–2017 period and had not participated in the F–2 PLT in previous years. The move to the new campus had attracted a new stream of students (half the cohort) in Year 7 and, with all secondary teachers having to teach Year 11 and 12 courses for the first time, their efforts in Years 7–9 intervention were not as rigorous as in subsequent years. These changes in teacher learning and focus are an expected and normal part of the life of most schools. The goal is to stabilise over time and continue to build teacher capability that maximises learning for every student.

Despite these changes, the Year 3–6 phase of schooling PLT was stable between 2015 and 2017. This group of teachers had worked collaboratively for three years and increased their capabilities and expertise enormously. Student results from this group on the 2017 NAPLAN numeracy test (and all other areas) showed remarkable improvements, as indicated in figure 6.7. The school community greatly celebrated these achievements.

There may be some readers who believe this progress in the numeracy area was made possible only because of my expertise in numeracy and mathematics. It is for this reason I have included student progress graphs for all NAPLAN areas to indicate that the *process* was effective regardless of the domain. Less progress occurred in numeracy than in the other three domains, probably due to the fact that there was more staff expertise in literacy – as is the case in most schools. It was the PLTs and the school improvement processes that made the difference.

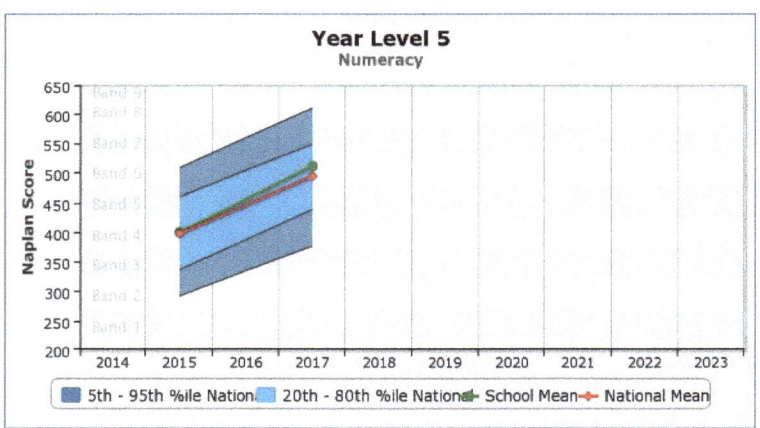

Figure 6.7: Mundaring Christian College NAPLAN cohort growth, Years 3–5, 2015–2017
SOURCE: Association of Independent Schools Western Australia (2017)

Evidence-based whole-school approaches to numeracy improvement

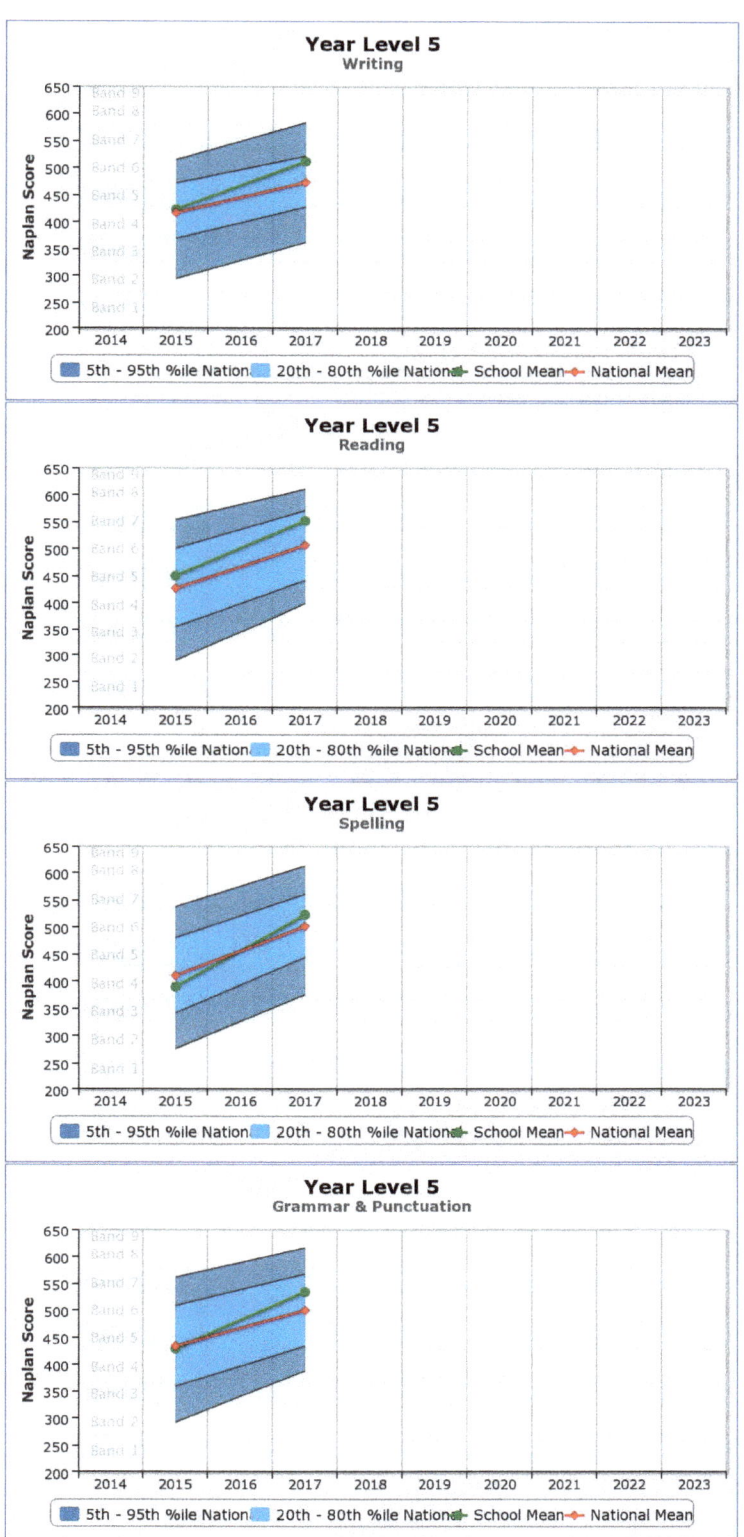

Conclusion

This chapter has presented a discussion about numeracy improvement through whole-school approaches. It reveals the complexities of improving student numeracy achievement and development. It outlines the processes and considerations that schools need to undertake to design, plan and implement strategies aimed at making these improvements.

The Mundaring Christian College case study shows how one school improved using the approaches outlined. This improvement was led by school leaders who understand school improvement and have evidence-based processes in place to manage and lead a whole-school approach. They also understand the many facets of numeracy and that improving teacher understanding of maths is but one of these. A concerted effort to improve both literacy and numeracy, with evidence-informed strategies that were monitored and tweaked as needed, resulted in improved numeracy results in all school phases in fifteen months, with greatly increased results in thirty months in one of these. Note that these strategies were enabled by the pre-existence of PLTs in which teachers continued to learn and work together using the model shown in figure 6.4 (page 131).

The amount of development teachers need can vary from school to school and site to site. It is also a function of the numeracy attainment by teachers through their own schooling experiences and as they enter the profession. Strong instructional leadership has been shown to build whole-school capability through fostering and enabling the conditions for regular collaborative teacher work, which also plays a major role in teacher professional development.

Personal numeracy of prospective and in-service teachers, and the online numeracy test developed by ACER for this purpose, will be discussed in the following chapter.

Professional and personal numeracy

The community holds teachers in high regard, not least because of the responsibility they have in educating their children. Educators are held accountable for the literacy and numeracy of the current and future generations of Australian children and young people and of the adults of tomorrow. Teachers must be numerate if their students are to be so.

As we have seen in the pages of this book, effective teachers of numeracy are those who help pupils acquire maths knowledge, learn how to apply the knowledge and learn them in sufficient depth to enable the confidence required to apply them in a range of contexts and situations where it is helpful to do so. Askew et al. (1997) agree and add, 'students learn how to apply these skills and knowledges … through both explicit teaching and through immersing them in the modelling behaviours of teachers' (p. 10).

Ultimately, teachers will not be able to teach their students the knowledge, skills and dispositions unless they themselves first have them. This chapter explores some of the personal and professional numeracy behaviours that teachers in Australian schooling settings need.

Initial teacher education student testing

There are current standards in place for the literacy and numeracy capabilities of teachers (AITSL, 2018). The development of these standards was subsequently followed by calls to bring into play a benchmark or standard that might be used to determine whether students enrolling in teacher education courses in Australian universities were sufficiently literate and numerate to commence, and indeed complete, their teacher preparation.

In 2011 all education ministers from Australian states and territories agreed to a national approach to the accreditation of initial teacher education programs. Two standards were subsequently developed to describe the levels of literacy and numeracy required by new teachers:

> *3.1 All entrants to initial teacher education will successfully demonstrate their capacity to engage effectively with a rigorous higher education program and to carry out the intellectual demands of teaching itself. To achieve this, it is expected that applicants' levels of personal literacy and numeracy should be broadly equivalent to those of the top 30 per cent of the population; and*
>
> *3.2 Providers who select students who do not meet the requirements in 3.1 above must establish satisfactory additional arrangements to ensure that all students are supported to achieve the required standard before graduation. (AITSL, 2011, as cited in ACER, 2015, p. 25)*

AITSL (2018), which developed the existing APST, contracted ACER in 2013 to develop the literacy and numeracy test for initial teacher education students (LANTITE). Following the decision of education ministers to introduce the test as a requirement from 1 July 2016, the then Australian Government contracted ACER to deliver the test nationally on behalf of all jurisdictions. As part of test delivery, ACER is also responsible for ongoing test item development, refreshment and validation.

The test aims to assess whether the levels of personal literacy and numeracy of applicants are broadly equivalent to those of the top 30 per cent of the adult population. Both the ACSF and the Programme for the International Assessment of Adult Competencies (PIAAC) are relevant to the tests and were drawn on in developing the assessment framework for the tests. The ACSF describes adult literacy and numeracy in Australia (Commonwealth of Australia, 2012). The framework is used to support adult teaching and learning, but also provides a benchmark for adult learners against prescribed levels. PIAAC similarly provides frameworks for adult literacy and numeracy, and hence provided useful content informing the development of the test framework.

The numeracy test framework draws on the definitions of numeracy from the ACSF and PIAAC. Developed by members of the ACER project team, in consultation with AITSL and expert advisory groups (of which I was part), it reflects an education context where:

> *Personal numeracy, for the purpose of the Test, is defined as: interpreting and communicating important non-technical mathematical information, and using such information to solve relevant real-world problems to participate in an education community, to achieve one's goals, and to develop one's knowledge and potential as a teacher.* (ACER, 2015, p. 21)

The numeracy test questions are categorised using the same content headings as the Australian Curriculum: Mathematics, namely number and algebra, measurement and geometry, and statistics and probability. The use of 'non-technical' in the definition means that the maths demanded by the questions is aligned closely to the maths used in ordinary everyday life in society and the workplace. This would not include, for example, formal algebra, measurement theorems or trigonometry.

The numeracy test questions and framework are also categorised by process: identifying mathematical information and meaning in activities and texts, using and applying mathematical knowledge and problem-solving processes, and interpreting, evaluating, communicating and representing maths (ACER, 2015). They align well with both the ACARA numeracy definition and the problem-solving processes presented and discussed in Chapter 1.

The numeracy test situates maths in contexts that are relevant to education provision in schools, some examples of which are provided in figure 7.1 (page 152). These include 'situations that teachers are likely to come across as part of their everyday life that require the application of important mathematical skills to solve relevant real-world problems' (ACER, 2015, p. 28). The three contexts are: personal and community, schools and teaching, and further education and professional learning.

Numeracy sample question 1
EDUCATION EXPENDITURE

Government operating expenditure on education refers mainly to money spent on schools and tertiary education.

Of the total operating expenditure on education in 2011–2012, 51% was spent on primary and secondary education and 36% on tertiary education (universities and TAFEs).

What percent of the total operating expenditure on education in 2011–2012 was spent on the remaining aspets of the education budget?

_____ %

Numeracy sample question 10
GEOGRAPHICAL DISTRIBUTION OF AUSTRALIANS

The Australian Bureau of Statistic conducts a census every five years.

In 2011, the population of Australia was 22 million.

About 2% of these people lived in remote or very remote areas.

About how many people lived in remote or very remote areas in Australia in 2011?

A	11 000
B	44 000
C	110 000
D	440 000

Figure 7.1: Examples of numeracy questions from the LANTITE
SOURCE: ACER (2015). Used with permission.
NOTE: ACER regularly releases retired test questions and practice materials on the ACER test website. This set of questions is an early set of sample questions.

Professional and personal numeracy

Numeracy sample question 8
BAND ACHIEVEMENT

This graph shows the percentage of Year 3 students in six achievement bands for reading, for a selected school.

It also shows comparable percentages for statistically similar schools and for all Australian schools.

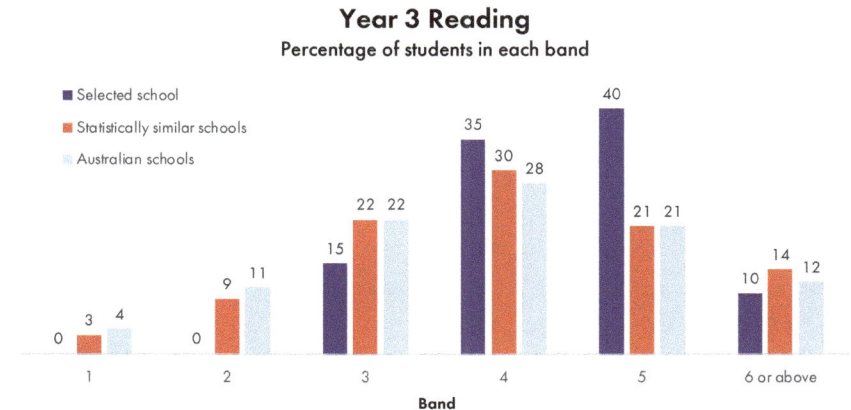

The table below contains some statements about the graph.

Click on 'True' of 'False' for each statement.

Statement	True	False
A higher percentage of Year 3 students at the selected school achieved at Band 4 compared to students at statistically similar schools.	○	○
At the selected school, more Year 3 students achieved at Band 4 than at any other band.	○	○
A greater percentage of the Year 3 students at the selected school achieved above Band 3 compared to Year 3 students at statistically similar schools.	○	○

Test standards

The minimum requirement to pass, as the public would expect for a test of this nature, is reasonably high. The non-technical maths demanded by the test aligns approximately to the Year 6–7 Australian Curriculum: Mathematics. This in turn, aligns with Level 4 of the ACSF; however, some of the questions connect with Levels 2 or 3 of the ACSF (Commonwealth of Australia, 2012). There are some who might say that this level of maths is insufficient for people teaching Australia's children. However, it is a numeracy test, not a maths test. We would therefore expect that the problem-solving and context dimensions are also considered. Hence, the level of difficulty of the test is well beyond the standard of maths learning required of a Year 6–7 student. The standard is primarily set by the complexity of the contexts, which in turn require student teachers to use their problem-solving skills in determining what maths is needed and then applying this knowledge.

Since most questions are situated in educational settings or schooling contexts, with which many prospective teachers may be unfamiliar, the candidates are required to transfer their numeracy capability to these unfamiliar contexts. The language describing the contexts is often quite complex with a high literacy demand. This requires students not only read complex texts (including tables and graphs), but also demonstrate a high level of comprehension to determine which maths to apply in the context to obtain a successful response. The questions themselves demand a reasonably high level of numeracy, despite many not necessarily demanding a high level of maths.

Australian state ministers for education expect students to successfully complete the tests prior to graduating as teachers. All initial teacher education students must possess personal literacy and numeracy skills in the top 30 per cent of the adult population. The test has been used to demonstrate students have achieved this standard since 2016. The Australian Government requires that:

> *Any initial teacher education student undertaking a qualification that enables them to register to teach in a school setting is expected to meet the standard of the test prior to graduation. There are no exemptions or alternative assessments to the test requirement.*
>
> *Some states and territories also require prospective teachers to meet the test standard before registration or employment as a teacher.* (Department of Education, Skills and Employment, 2021, para. 8–9)

Australian Professional Standards for Teachers

In 2011, AITSL released the APST. The standards recognise the significant role of the teacher in student learning. They also recognise that teachers develop their teaching ability over time. The standards subsequently are described over four developmental levels, articulating what teachers are expected to know and be able to do, at the graduate, proficient, highly accomplished and lead stages of their careers (AITSL, 2018). They describe the qualities and capabilities that the nation expects of teachers in Australian schools with a concomitant expectation that teachers will continue to develop professionally over the duration of their careers.

There are seven standards for teachers in three domains: professional knowledge, professional practice and professional engagement (AITSL, 2015). The standards and focus areas are not written as a checklist. That is, although literacy and numeracy strategies are mentioned specifically in Standard 2, Focus area 2.5, teachers are not expected to address this focus in isolation from each of the other standards. Literacy and numeracy are capabilities and tools for learning; they cannot be turned on and off but must be embedded in every aspect of a teachers' work. Each of the standards and their focus areas listed demand literate and numerate behaviours.

However, it is important to note the phrasing of the focus area – *literacy and numeracy strategies* – and the placement of literacy and numeracy strategies in Standard 2: Know the content and how to teach it (AITSL, 2018). In considering the term *literacy and numeracy strategies* with the understanding of literacy and numeracy as general capabilities, this placement makes sense. All the other five focus areas of Standard 2 refer to the work of teaching what students need to learn. These can be paraphrased as:

2.1 the work of choosing the content using pedagogical content knowledge

2.2 the work of choosing the content, paying attention to the sequence and Vygotsky's Zone of Proximal Development (ZPD) and constructivist approaches to organise and choose the content appropriate for the readiness of their students

2.3 the work of aligning content to appropriate assessment and reporting on what has or hasn't been learned

2.4 the work of understanding and respecting, and subsequently embedding First Australians perspectives in the content to minimise cultural bias in delivery and maximise cultural safety for students

2.5 the work of choosing literacy and numeracy strategies to enhance understanding of and access to the desired learning

2.6 the work of using ICT to enhance understanding and support presentation of the content and access to it (AITSL, 2015).

Focus area 2.5 can be further broken down, based on our deeper understanding of literacy and numeracy, as:

- the work of recognising and attending to literacy and numeracy demands and opportunities in the learning areas
- the choosing and using of literacy and numeracy skills – as tools for learning – by the teacher in accessing the content, to enable students to do the same.

Numeracy strategies

What are numeracy strategies? We have learned in earlier chapters that numeracy is not a subject or body of knowledge, but rather a capability that encompasses confidence resulting from deep learning of maths, a recognition of when it is needed and an understanding of how to apply it in context. Numeracy strategies then, in the context of Standard 2, include approaches and methods to:

- teach maths content in ways that promote confidence and deep understanding
- teach problem-solving
- teach ways to understand and make sense of contexts to determine whether maths will help and what maths will help (see Chapter 1).

Teaching numeracy strategies must extend beyond teaching maths well, as you will understand by now. It must include being able to recognise both the numeracy demands and the numeracy opportunities in all learning areas and cross-curriculum contexts.

The quality of Focus area 2.5 is described at the 'graduate', 'proficient', 'highly accomplished' and 'lead' stages. While graduate teachers are expected to demonstrate knowledge and understanding in the focus areas, proficient teachers are able to develop and design strategies and activities in each of the focus areas as well as implement them. Highly accomplished teachers work collaboratively with colleagues, providing advice, innovation and support based on their experience, including by modelling high-level practice. Lead teachers lead school-based initiatives both directly and by virtue of their exemplary practice and understanding of school and system policy, and they demonstrate excellence in all aspects of their teaching practices.

In the context of Focus area 2.5, graduate teachers, while they may have the knowledge and capability to know and understand strategies and application, first need to implement the teaching strategies derived from their knowledge and subsequently reflect on their success, modifying the strategies as necessary, in order to improve student learning (see Focus area 5.4, AITSL, 2018, p. 19).

Pre-service and graduate teachers should learn through professional development, including through learning from proficient, highly accomplished and lead teachers, to help them develop and become increasingly proficient in numeracy strategies.

More experienced teachers are expected to demonstrate competence beyond the proficient level. Responses beyond proficient will depend largely on the depth of knowledge learned from self-reflection on successful or unsuccessful practice through personal engagement and application in classrooms, and implemented interventions and modification.

Experienced teachers will use their knowledge and experience to design, model and lead effective programs targeted at the needs of all students. This progression is not possible without self-reflection and evaluation of the effectiveness of their responses, particularly with respect to increased achievement of their students, as revealed through achievement data.

Financial literacy

Should teachers be financially literate? Do they learn financial literacy at school? Is financial literacy part of being numerate?

The practice of attaching the word *literacy* to a context to describe a facility and a confidence with something is common in the Western world. *Financial literacy* is having facility and confidence to work with and critique finances. Maths knowledge and understanding is essential – though not sufficient – to having facility with money.

Financial literacy is not the same as numeracy in the context of money. Financial literacy requires capabilities and elements of curriculum areas and disciplines other than maths. These include:

- knowledge of what money is for and how it is used, including making the distinction between needs and wants (HASS)
- knowledge of how to calculate with money (maths)
- knowledge of risk and how to manage it (maths, business administration and accountability)

- understanding the fine print (critical literacy and English)
- managing self and wellbeing (health and physical education)
- a sense of right and wrong (ethics and values)
- *nous* (common sense).

Moreover, financial literacy includes the confidence and capacity to choose to apply knowledge of money to a situation – knowing financial maths is insufficient to make one financially literate. As with mathematical literacy, the question of tolerated error is critical and the understanding of risk is consequently a very important part of financial literacy.

PISA defines financial literacy as the:

> *knowledge and understanding of financial concepts and risks, and the skills, motivation and confidence to apply such knowledge and understanding in order to make effective decisions across a range of financial contexts, to improve the financial well-being of individuals and society, and to enable participation in economic life.* (OECD, 2017, p. 87)

Note that the knowledge and understanding of financial concepts is insufficient on its own – financial literacy is a capability. Adding it to the general capabilities table (table 1.1, page 7) it would show as:

Table 7.1: Financial literacy as a general capability

General capability	Knowledge and skills	Attitudes and behaviours
Financial literacy	Financial concepts and risks	Confidence in choosing, using and applying financial concepts and risks in different contexts

The content descriptors in the Australian Curriculum for F–6 generally do not provide the opportunity for teaching and learning of maths with sufficient depth to enable financial literacy in the everyday life of an adult. Contexts are relevant to the age of the students studying the given topics. Those from Years 7–10 (including from the numeracy continuum) are included in table 7.2 in support of this argument.

Professional and personal numeracy

Table 7.2: Australian Curriculum: Mathematics content descriptors and numeracy continuum learning descriptions for money, Years 7–10

	Australian Curriculum: Mathematics content descriptors			
	Year 7	Year 8	Year 9	Year 10
Money and financial mathematics	Investigate and calculate 'best buys', with and without digital technologies. (ACMNA174)	Solve problems involving profit and loss, with and without digital technologies. (ACMNA189)	Solve problems involving simple interest. (ACMNA211)	Connect the compound interest formula to repeated applications of simple interest using appropriate digital technologies. (ACMNA229).
	Australian Curriculum numeracy continuum			
	Level 5		Level 6	
Use money	Identify and justify 'best value for money' decisions.		Evaluate financial plans to support specific financial goals.	

SOURCE: Adapted from ACARA (n.d.-b) and ACARA (n.d.-d)

Generally, people will not be sufficiently financially literate to cope with the financial issues of everyday life if they don't have the mathematical knowledge and facility with money (to at least Year 10 level) to draw on with confidence in contexts where it is needed. However, a word of caution about applying this statement too literally – recall that a component of financial literacy is common sense learned through an understanding and familiarity of contexts. There are many cases of people who are extremely competent in money matters who have had very little formal learning of maths.

Personal diagnosis of mathematics for numeracy

As indicated earlier, the LANTITE has an unwritten requirement that prospective teachers know, at least, the Australian Curriculum: Mathematics Year 6–7 content deeply enough for them to recognise that some maths will help and which maths to use in the professional and personal contexts presented.

Table 7.3 (page 160) outlines the maths and numeracy standards required at Year 6–7 level, aligned to the Australian Curriculum. Examples indicate the applications of the maths in contexts to represent the numeracy required. Teachers, both pre-service and in-service, might use this table for personal diagnosis to determine whether they need support or further study to better or more deeply understand the maths they will need to teach, or that they currently teach.

Table 7.3: Year 6–7 maths standards with numeracy examples

By the end of Year 6, students must be able to:

Topic	Requirement	Example
Number	Read, say, write (in words and digits), interpret, compare and order all whole numbers.	Compare and order the populations of Australian capital cities from largest to smallest and explain which city has the largest population, correctly reading the numbers.
	Locate and mark all positive and negative integers on a number line and compare them in real contexts.	Know that if they owe $16 this can be represented on a number line as −16, and that if the temperature in Canberra is −2° at night and rises to 16° during the day then it has risen by 18°.
Fraction	Read and say numbers with up to three decimal places correctly.	Say 'thirty-five point zero eight two' and also as 'thirty-five and eighty two thousandths', being aware that saying 'thirty-five point zero eight two' is not correct and explaining why when asked.
	Compare and order decimal numbers in practical contexts.	Determine first, second and third places in a running race given five finishing times (to hundredths of a second) or locate books on a library shelf.
	Understand that the decimal point separates whole numbers from fractional parts of a number and that when operating with fractional parts whole numbers can result.	Explain why (using diagrams or objects) 0.3 + 0.9 = 1.1 and not 0.11.
	Add and subtract decimal numbers using digital technologies or written methods by estimating first and reasoning whether the solution is what is expected.	
	Read a situation and decide whether multiplication or division is needed. Estimate expected result before calculating for greater accuracy (with calculator or written method). Interpret the remainder of a decimal division by the context.	When faced with the problem 'How many buses holding fifteen people will be needed to transport eighty people?' can estimate about five buses are needed, enter 80 ÷ 15 = 5.33 and determine that 6 buses are needed
	Find the percentage of an amount using efficient mental methods where possible.	Calculate what they'd pay if there's a '20% off' sale by determining 10% of the marked price and doubling this to take the result from the total.
	Use proportional reasoning to think about and solve ratio or rate problems that occur across the curriculum.	Calculate the quantity of salt required in a science experiment when using 1 litre of water, based on requirement of 5 g salt to 200 mL water.

SOURCE: Informed by ACARA (2020) and ACARA (n.d.-d)

(continued)

Professional and personal numeracy

Topic	Requirement	Example
Money	Calculate 50%, 25% and 75% by mentally using fractional equivalents.	Find 25% by halving and halving again
	Interpret calculator display when operating in money context.	Know a display showing 6.5 is $6.50 and display of 2.034 may need to be rounded or truncated depending on context.
Patterns and algebra	Write, describe in words and continue patterns with whole numbers, decimals and fractions that result from adding and subtracting, and describe the rule that was used to create the pattern.	
	Know that the order in which operations are done in number sentences can result in different answers.	Know that 6 + 3 × 4 is 36 if done one way and 18 if done another way.
Measurement	Visualise common volumes, such as a cubic metre, and use these to estimate spaces, such as volume of a room, capacity of a trailer or cupboard or amounts such as a pile of sand.	
	Determine whether perimeter, area or volume is needed for a task and whether estimation or exact measurement is needed, explaining why.	Recognise that estimating the distance around the school oval as about 400m is fine when practising but know accurate measurement is needed for sports day to determine the school record.
	Estimate capacity of a variety of cups by first visualising a cubic centimetre and a litre.	
	Estimate volume of liquid in the same cup or jug filled to different levels.	
	Choose and use units, measuring instruments and graduated scales for particular purposes and justify their choice based on the degree of precision required by the context.	Choose to use a graduated cup and grams to measure the flour for a cake but knows that a pinch will do to measure the salt.
	Measure volume accurately to the nearest graduation in L and mL by first choosing an appropriate measuring instrument that allows for the level of precision needed for the purpose.	Choose a graduated jug to measure 200 mL for recipe or teaspoon for cough mixture.
	Read meters and scales in the environment for interest and action.	Read an odometer to see if they should slow down or thermometer to check the temperature.
	Know the connection between decimal numbers and the metric system.	Know that 3.45 km is not the same as 3 km and 45 metres.

(continued)

Topic	Requirement	Example
Time	Read, interpret and use timetables, timelines and calendars in everyday situations.	Read a calendar to determine how many Fridays until the end of term or read a timeline and discuss that First Australians were here long before the First Fleet.
	Solve elapsed-time problems for 24-hour time.	Calculate how long a flight will take if it leaves at 0930 and arrives in Adelaide at 1315 on the same day.
Location	Read a standard map with scales, legends and compass points for a practical purpose.	Determine which provincial town is closer to the capital city.
	Find 'you are here' on a public map and follow or explain a route using directions.	Follow or explain a route using directions such as 'turn 90° clockwise and walk about 100 metres in a south-west direction'.
	Create a simple bird's-eye view map of a familiar environment to show someone how to get to a location.	Show or explain how to get to the shop or post office.
Data	Interpret pie charts and other graphs in the media.	
	Create pie charts using technology to show collected data and relate the amount of the whole pie to the proportion of the number of students.	
	Understand why and how sampling is done and how this might potentially bias results.	
	Create and interpret a graph of data of the same variable collected over time and describe why it might vary by considering the things that influence it (including inaccurate measurements).	Measure the height of a plant over a term, graph measurements and question a data point that indicates a 'dip' in the data.
	Know that average is a measure of centeredness or one number roughly in the centre that can represent a group of numbers and estimate it by visualising the group of numbers on a number line.	
Chance	Compare risk based on published data.	Having researched data on lung cancer, determine the risks for smokers and non-smokers.

> **Time to reflect**
>
> Do you know and understand the maths outcomes listed in table 7.3 (page 160)?
>
> Do you know and understand them deeply? Do you know and understand the concepts, or the methods to find the answers? Could you explain or teach the concepts to someone else and, most importantly, to students?
>
> Would you be able to do all the things described in the examples in table 7.3?

Numeracy disposition diagnosis

In Chapter 1 we analysed the components of numeracy, including the confidence and disposition to use maths to meet the demands of life. Table 7.3 (page 160) provides an opportunity for us to individually diagnose how well we know the maths. The reflection questions that follow the table provided prompt us to think deeply about the word *know*. While we may think we know, the level of cognitive knowing may not be deep enough to result in the confidence needed to choose to use the maths in contexts or, even further, to teach the concept to someone else.

Scales for self-diagnosis

The following scales provide an opportunity for self-diagnosis regarding confidence with choosing and using maths. Standards or answers have not been provided. The intention of these questions is to prompt self-reflection only.

1. When confronted with a situation in which I recognise that some maths will help, I confidently proceed and think, 'Which maths?'
    - Never
    - Rarely
    - Sometimes
    - Always

2. I recognise when some maths will help in everyday contexts.
    - Never
    - Rarely
    - Sometimes
    - Always

3. I know which maths to apply in contexts.
    - ○ Never
    - ○ Rarely
    - ○ Sometimes
    - ○ Always

4. I avoid using maths whenever I can.
    - ○ Never
    - ○ Rarely
    - ○ Sometimes
    - ○ Always

5. I am confident using maths when I need to.
    - ○ Never
    - ○ Rarely
    - ○ Sometimes
    - ○ Always

6. I attempt to apply maths, being sure I've chosen the appropriate maths for the context.
    - ○ Never
    - ○ Rarely
    - ○ Sometimes
    - ○ Always

7. If someone questions my maths, I give up and think I must be wrong.
    - ○ Never
    - ○ Rarely
    - ○ Sometimes
    - ○ Always

Professional and personal numeracy

8. I get anxious when I'm confronted with a maths problem to solve.
- ○ Never
- ○ Rarely
- ○ Sometimes
- ○ Always

9. I am reluctant to choose and use maths in front of other people.
- ○ Never
- ○ Rarely
- ○ Sometimes
- ○ Always

10. I confidently apply maths to contexts but give up if it gets too hard.
- ○ Never
- ○ Rarely
- ○ Sometimes
- ○ Always

11. When problem-solving and using maths with a group I sit back and allow others with more confidence to do most of the work.
- ○ Never
- ○ Rarely
- ○ Sometimes
- ○ Always

Time to reflect

Do you have the disposition and confidence to apply maths in contexts where it is helpful to do so?

Are you modelling this to your students?

Conclusion

This chapter has focused on some of the personal and professional numeracy behaviours that prospective and practising teachers need. Prospective teachers need to confront the fact that they need a certain level of proficiency with maths and the confidence to apply it, in both teaching maths to their students and in undertaking other professional roles such as planning, budgeting and analysing achievement data.

All teachers are teachers of numeracy and hence the need for all teachers to deeply consider their own numeracy capability is imperative. If this capability is not sufficiently rigorous for them to successfully undertake teaching duties, or to teach the maths and other skills that students need to become numerate themselves, then teachers must do something about it. This might include participating in further study or seeking professional help from school leaders. This is critical for the future of numeracy learning in Australia's schools.

Numeracy into the future

Educators affecting numeracy outcomes

There are four critical questions that drive the work of educators, including classroom teachers, school leaders, principals and PLCs:

1. Are our students learning and achieving what's expected of their age cohort?

2. How do we know if they are learning what's expected?

3. What are we doing if they aren't learning what's expected?

4. What are we doing if they already know what's expected? (DuFour et al., 2010)

The first question is the intended curriculum question, and this depends on whether we know what our students are expected to know. Are we clear about the standards expected and do we view them as standards? The answer to this in the context of numeracy has been discussed in Chapters 1, 2 and 3.

The second question is the assessment question, and the value of the answer depends on the quality of the assessment tasks. Are our assessments valid? Are they rigorous? The answer to this in the context of numeracy has been discussed in Chapter 5 and parts of Chapter 6.

The third and fourth questions are the intervention questions. What evidence-informed strategies can we draw on to improve the learning of all our students? These strategies have been described for individual teachers in Chapter 4 and for school leaders and whole schools in parts of Chapter 6. A case study in Chapter 6 indicates that these strategies work to drive improvements when considered and implemented by instructional leaders in schools, supported by teachers willing to work collaboratively to improve the learning outcomes of all their students.

As a profession, we must first attempt to understand the four questions. Improving numeracy outcomes of students is the work that we are accountable for to the Australian public. It is only in understanding the questions and their answers, and acknowledging that students' numeracy standards nationally are not as good as they should be, that we have the motivation and moral imperative to address the current challenges.

The chapters in this book reveal the complexities of numeracy and what is required if we want our students to be competitive internationally and to live fulfilling and capable lives.

Society, policymakers and numeracy outcomes

The rate of change in our society is rapidly increasing. What do we know about the levels of numeracy that students in today's schools will need for learning, employment and life in general?

Declining results

Reports published by the Foundations for Young Australians, *The new work order* (2015) and *The new work mindset* (2016), indicate that employers increasingly want young employees to have enterprising skills such as digital skills and digital literacy, critical thinking skills, problem-solving and financial literacy. The 2015 report reveals that about 35 per cent of Australian fifteen-year-olds demonstrated low proficiency in problem-solving, 27 per cent demonstrated low proficiency in digital literacy and 29 per cent showed low proficiency in financial literacy.

Further, the results of the 2019 TIMSS reveal that Australia's students have plateaued or flatlined in Year 4 (not improving since 2007), while Year 8 results showed small improvement in 2019 (Thomson et al., 2020). Twenty-two of the participating countries performed significantly higher than Australia's Year 4 students on the maths test. Reasons cited for these poor results include the lower standard of maths set in the national curriculum than other countries, students' ability to read and problem-solve, and levels of teacher anxiety about maths (Buckley et al., 2016)

In addition, results from the 2019 PISA indicate similar results for mathematical literacy as defined in Chapter 1 (Carey & Hunter, 2019). The PISA mathematical literacy test is, in fact, a test of numeracy administered to fifteen-year-olds. Results from the 2019 test indicate that Australian students recorded their worst ever results internationally and it has been estimated that they are about a full school year behind where Australian students were at the turn of the millennium (Carey & Hunter, 2019).

Since both PISA and TIMSS are primarily comprised of problem-solving tasks, it is reasonable to hypothesise that our students simply are not being taught the problem-solving and higher-order reasoning skills they need to meet the numeracy demands that will be placed on them into the future.

Unless we, as a society, and our policymakers, address this issue and change school practices, our students will continue to be taught low-level maths thinking and reasoning skills, resulting in a perpetuation of current practices and achievements. These practices will, in turn, not deliver the twenty-first century competencies or enterprising skills that our students need and deserve. Nor will they be able to take increased agency over their learning which allow them to adapt to their changing world (Treadwell, 2017). We risk that our children and young people will not be able to live fulfilling lives but also that our society and economy will lack the benefits of their potential skills. This has major implications for our nation (Fullan et al., 2017; Gonski et al., 2018; Griffin et al., 2012; Ontario Ministry of Education, 2016).

While we continue to prioritise facts over concepts in our intended curriculum and delivery of it, we fail to recognise that the workplace is changing. While being able to access knowledge is one thing, 'what is more important is being able to take that knowledge and develop it into a deeper understanding and then apply those understandings to be innovative and ingenious, allowing the creation of new products, systems, environments and media' (Treadwell, 2017, p. 142).

The path to improvement

We all have a responsibility to improve these outcomes. As indicated in this book, improving numeracy is complex and multifaceted. It begins with:

- national recognition of the importance of problem-solving and critical thinking in both literacy and numeracy as necessary skills for learning and life in a changing world
- strategic approaches for addressing the need for higher-order thinking and conceptual reasoning and a greater focus on capabilities
- policy, training and incentives that demand, enable and reward new standards of achievement.

Discussions in this book indicate that we need to raise standards across our schools. This must begin with recognising the relatively low level of cognitive demand occurring in a large proportion of the nation's classrooms. There is little incentive for teachers to change their practices to teach deep learning and rigour. Current achievement standards of the Australian Curriculum are too often an amalgamation of low-level skills and knowledges. More demanding, higher-order cognition in the curriculum for all where an A level of achievement gained by those students who can evaluate, create and transform their learning, rather than an A for students who can merely apply their learning, is essential. The emphasis must be on higher-order thinking and reasoning skills to provide teachers with the incentives to aim their programs higher and demand more from their students (with the support needed for training). The goal is not that students achieve better grades but that they are more engaged and interested in what is worthwhile, enduring and relevant, and that they gain greater understanding of reflection, reasoning, analysis and critique.

We can drive national improvement through raising standards of achievement in schools, teaching teachers how to do this both in pre-service teacher education and in the workplace. This can only be achieved if policy writers and school leaders share this vision and are prepared to do whatever it takes for the national good as a national learning community.

In addition, use of the problem-solving model is a framework for not only supporting literacy and numeracy development, but also addressing the twenty-first century competencies. These competencies are currently being heralded as necessary for all children and young people 'to meet the demands of democracy, competitiveness and life' (Harvard Advanced Leadership Initiative, 2014, p. 2). Moreover, the Alice Springs (Mparntwe) Education Declaration publicly proclaims a national commitment to all young Australians becoming successful lifelong learners who, among other things:

- 'have the essential skills in literacy and numeracy as the foundation for learning …
- 'are able to think deeply and logically, and obtain and evaluate evidence as the result of studying fundamental disciplines
- 'are creative, innovative and resourceful, and are able to solve problems in ways that draw on a range of learning areas and disciplines and deep content knowledge …
- 'are confident and motivated to reach their full potential' (Education Council, 2019, p. 7).

In the context of the Australian Curriculum, we might, as a nation, consider the possibility of a revised set of general capabilities becoming the framework for school curriculum planning and delivery with the learning areas as contexts. While this may have been considered and disregarded a decade ago (McGaw,

2013), a current and increasing international focus on twenty-first century competencies may require a rethink of this in the future. This would position literacy, numeracy, critical thinking and creativity where they belong: as the most significant skills students must attain throughout their schooling in preparation for further study, employment, and maximum community and society participation.

Finally

There has been a plethora of recommendations concerning teaching and learning maths for numeracy in the past two decades, including those in the *National numeracy review report* (COAG, 2008) and the *Numeracy across the curriculum* report (DEST, 2004). The majority of these have not been widely implemented or included beyond isolated small-scale programs and single education sites.

Suggestions following recent international results that the Australian 'laid-back attitude' is partially to blame indicate the possible depth of the problem. Deep-seated beliefs and misconceptions about our ability as a nation to 'be good at maths' must be challenged and laid to rest. A focus on teaching students a growth mindset – that they can become smarter with effort and hard work – has been shown to help students overcome low self-belief.

An accountability requirement at state and national level to teach maths for both understanding of concepts and acquisition of skills, accompanied by national support for teachers to do so, would help to address some of the concerns raised throughout this book, including the ever-widening gap between what many students should know and what they do know at the commencement of each year of schooling.

On a personal note

Some of the workshops I have delivered to schools include material and messages I was delivering over twenty years ago, albeit using different curriculum documentation. While teachers and school leaders have the will to make changes and improvements in their work, they do not always have the skill and support they need to make these changes. It breaks my heart to know that in many schools maths is still being taught as it was in the sixties and seventies, in spite of advances in technologies and research into how children learn maths.

The ongoing depletion of expertise in support needed for schools continues across the nation, under the banner of cost cutting, at the nation's peril.

Governments must realise that teaching is becoming more challenging as a result of increased societal complexities, not easier.

Further reviews of the problems in numeracy attainment by our students are not what is needed. National policymakers and state education authorities need to address recommendations already made if they still have currency. They must work together with a sense of moral purpose to find ways to articulate achievement standards more clearly and support schools to implement the changes needed to attain them, holding them accountable.

Appendix: Numeracy across the curriculum

The arts

Year	Strand or focus	Content descriptor	Numeracy demand
F–2	Communicating ideas through their artworks	Recognise that visual and spatial ideas are developed and understood in different ways.	Students need to be able to sort and name simple 2D and 3D shapes and objects. (ACMMG009, 022; ACMNA005, 018) Students need to demonstrate understanding of words of position (*behind* and *above* etc.) and words of movement (e.g. *forward, backward, left, right*) in all art forms.
	Dance	Explore, improvise and organise ideas to make dance sequences using the elements of dance. (ACADAM002)	Students need to know movements of the body, repeating patterns and sequences, and timing (understand 'how long it takes'). (ACMMG007, 023; ACMNA005)
	Music	Develop aural skills by exploring and imitating sounds, pitch and rhythm patterns using voice, movement and body percussion. (ACAMUM080)	Students need to know combinations of long and short sounds, duration of time and patterns in movements and sounds. (ACMMG007; ACMNA005)

(continued)

Year	Strand or focus	Content descriptor	Numeracy demand
3–4	Imagining and improvising	Explore how to express ways of seeing and imagining their world, working with images, forms, objects and spaces.	Students need to know the language of shapes and their names. (ACMMG042, 043) Students need to be able to close their eyes and visualise shapes and make and draw them, and use familiar words to describe things in their environment (e.g. *symmetry, angles*). Students can make shapes, letters, and turns using their bodies and limbs in dance. Students can replicate patterns (repeating and growing) in their environment in drawings, dance and music. (ACMNA005) Students need to know what 2D and 3D are in shapes and objects in visual arts, music and dance. (ACMMG063, 065)
	Practising skills and techniques	Experiment with techniques, tools and forms to develop skills and refine their art-making.	Students need to visualise, sort, identify and describe symmetry, shapes and angles in their environment, experimenting with these in their artwork in all art forms. (ACMMG64, 066, 089, 091)
	Communicating ideas through their artworks	Share and display visual artworks focusing on the details, intentions and techniques used.	Students need to know words of position, and shapes and objects to describe ideas and creations in their own artworks and those of others. (ACMMG063, 065, 088)
	Dance	Improvise and structure movement ideas for dance sequences. (ACADAM005)	Students need to know movements of the body, repeating patterns and sequences, and timing (understand duration and 'how long it takes'). (ACMMG007, 023; ACMNA005)
	Music	Develop aural skills by exploring, imitating and recognising elements of music including dynamics, pitch and rhythm. (ACAMUM084) Practise singing, playing instruments and improvising music, using elements of music including rhythm, pitch, dynamics and form. (ACAMUM085)	Students need to understand combinations of long and short sounds like duration of time and patterns in movements and sounds. (ACMMG007; ACMNA005) Students need to understand that subdivision of sound within a beat equal parts of a whole (fraction). (ACMNA016, 033, 058, 077)

(continued)

Appendix: Numeracy across the curriculum

Year	Strand or focus	Content descriptor	Numeracy demand
5–6	Imagining and improvising	Experiment with and create 2D and 3D images and objects based on imagination and a deepening understanding of their world.	Students need to know what 2D and 3D are in shapes and objects in visual arts, music and dance. (ACMMG114)
	Communicating ideas through their artworks	Share visual artworks and investigate and respond to ways their own and others' artworks communicate to an audience.	Students need to know words of position, and shapes and objects to describe ideas and creations in their own artworks and those of others. (ACMMG114)
	Linking their artworks to other arts subjects and learning areas	Combine arts subjects and other learning areas to communicate meaning in and through visual arts.	Students need to know and understand how mathematical shapes and objects, and words of position and direction are used in the arts (e.g. patterns, angles and lines in dance; fractions in music) and use these to make meaning.
	Dance	Explore movement and choreographic devices using elements of dance. (ACADAM009) Develop technical and expressive skills in movements. (ACADAM010) Perform dance using expressive skills to communicate a choreographer's ideas. (ACADAM011)	Students need to know recognise and use repetition or sequence, shapes in the environment and understand position and movement. (ACMMG010, 114, 142) Students need to be able to describe position and movement. (ACMMG010, 114, 142)
	Media arts	Develop skills with media technologies to shape space, time, movement and lighting within images, sounds and text. (ACAMAM063)	Students need to develop a short digital sequence that uses camera angles such as close-ups. (ACMNA005; ACMMG115)

Technologies

Design and technologies

Year	Strand or focus	Content descriptor	Numeracy demand
F–2	Generating	Visualise, generate, develop and communicate design ideas through describing, drawing and modelling. (ACTDEP006)	Students need to have a sense of relative size and scale (e.g. understanding whether something is bigger or smaller). (ACMMG006) Students can record data such as types of features in a table to make comparisons.

(continued)

Year	Strand or focus	Content descriptor	Numeracy demand
F–2	Collaborating and managing	Sequence steps for making designed solutions and working collaboratively. (ACTDEP009)	Students need to understand duration of time to sequence steps in a plan, including orders such as first, second and third. Students can describe duration using months, weeks and days. (ACMMG006, ACMNA289)
3–64	Engineering principles and systems	Investigate how forces and the properties of materials affect the behaviour of a product or system. (ACTDEK011)	Students need to be able to use a table to record and organise data such as input and output data (e.g. to compare behaviours of foods or toys when they drop different distances).
	Food and fibre productions and food specialisations	Investigate food and fibre production and food technologies used in modern and traditional societies. (ACTDEK012)	Students need to organise data generated in investigations, in a table (e.g. recording information about climate and soil types for plant production). (ACMSP050)
	Materials and technologies specialisations	Investigate the suitability of materials, systems, components, tools and equipment for a range of purposes. (ACTDEK013)	Students need to be able to organise and record data generated when conducting tests (e.g. to understand properties of materials). (ACMSP050)
5–6	Engineering principles and systems	Investigate how forces or electrical energy can control movement, sound or light in a designed product or system. (ACTDEK020)	Students need to be able to organise and record data generated when conducting tests (e.g. to measure the amount of movement produced). (ACMSP069)
	Generating	Generate, develop, communicate and document design ideas and processes for audiences using appropriate technical terms and graphical representation techniques. (ACTDEP026)	Students need to be able to draw representations such as front, top and side views or 2D drawings of 3D objects to represent their designs.

Digital technologies

Year	Strand or focus	Content descriptor	Numeracy demand
F–2	Knowledge and understanding	Recognise and explore patterns in data and represent data as pictures, symbols and diagrams. (ACTDIK002) Sort objects and events using digital systems to represent patterns in data (e.g. birthdates using seasonal symbols).	Students need to be able to sort and classify objects based on features and copy and continue and create patterns. (ACMNA005) Students need to be able to generalise about patterns (e.g. say, 'Most kids who live a long way from school get driven.'). Students can recognise patterns (e.g. that email addresses have '@bigpond.com' etc.).

(continued)

Appendix: Numeracy across the curriculum

Year	Strand or focus	Content descriptor	Numeracy demand
F–2	Processes and production skills	Collect, explore and sort data and use digital systems to present the data creatively. (ACTDIP003) Collect and sort data through play (e.g. toys they like or dislike). Locate using visual or text data (e.g. search digital photo library for photo).	Students need to be able to answer 'yes' or 'no' to simple questions, choose simple questions and gather responses and data relevant to a question. (ACMSP011, 048, 262) Students need to collect and organise data by first classifying it into categories. (ACMSP049)
		Follow, describe and represent a sequence of steps and decisions (algorithms) needed to solve simple problems. (ACTDIP004)	Students need to describe position and movement using words such as *left*, *right*, *forwards*, *backwards* (e.g. by following a path of a robotic device or writing a set of instructions). (ACMMG010, 023, 044)
3–4	Knowledge and understanding	Explore and use a range of digital systems and peripheral devices for different purposes and transmit different types of data. (ACTDIK007)	Students need to be able to interpret data displays such as column graphs, and picture graphs (1:1 and many:1; e.g. from a mobile device or interactive whiteboard).
		Recognise different types of data and explore how the same data can be represented in different ways. (ACTDIK008)	Students need to know that data can be numbers, images, codes and symbols and that these can be differently represented.
	Processes and production skills	Collect, access and present different types of data using simple software to create information and solve problems. (ACTDIP009)	Students need to be able to choose different formats to present and manage data depending on audience and purposes (e.g. use spreadsheets to produce column graphs, or sum large amounts of data).
		Define simple problems and describe and follow a sequence of steps and decisions (algorithms) needed to solve them. (ACTDIP010)	Students need to be able to clarify problems and write the steps needed to solve them.
		Implement simple digital solutions as visual programs with algorithms involving branching and user input. (ACTDIP011)	Students create storyboards or flowcharts using software to show relationships and steps in a process or program. Students understand the order steps need to be conducted in.
5–6	Knowledge and understanding	Investigate how digital systems use whole numbers as a basis for representing all types of data. (ACTDIK015)	Students need to understand what whole numbers are and their properties and how binary numbers work. (ACMNA051, 071)

(continued)

WOULD YOU LIKE MATHS WITH THAT?

Year	Strand or focus	Content descriptor	Numeracy demand
5–6	Processes and production skills	Acquire, store and validate different types of data and use a range of commonly available software to interpret and visualise data in context to create information. (ACTDIP016)	Students need to understand how numbers are input differently in different contexts (e.g. data inputs in spreadsheets or formula to make calculations in spreadsheets).
		Define problems in terms of data and functional requirements, and identify features similar to previously solved problems. (ACTDIP017)	Students need to check data to troubleshoot (e.g. recognise outliers or digits input incorrectly or omissions in data entry or mistakes in formulae).
		Design, modify and follow simple algorithms represented diagrammatically and in English involving sequences of steps, branching, and iteration (repetition). (ACTDIP019)	Students need to understand that the order of steps needed to solve problems is critical. Students need to know some simple logic such as 'if' and 'then', and identify the steps used in sequence.
		Implement digital solutions as simple visual programs involving branching, iteration and user input. (ACTDIP020)	Students need to understand the cognitive function of checking their own mathematical working out, using repetition to meet an expected solution.

Health and physical education

Year	Strand or focus	Content descriptor	Numeracy demand
F	Movement and physical activity	Practise fundamental movement skills and movement sequences using different body parts and in response to stimuli. (ACPMP008)	Students need to know that repeating patterns can occur in numbers, movements, shapes (e.g. stamp, hop, shake, stamp, hop, shake etc.). (ACMNA005)
		Identify and describe how their body moves in relation to effort, space, time, objects and people. (ACPMP011)	Students need to be able to determine which movements take a long time and which take less time. (ACMMG008) Students need to know words of position to describe how their body moves (e.g. *up, down, along, next to*). (ACMMG009)

(continued)

Appendix: Numeracy across the curriculum

Year	Strand or focus	Content descriptor	Numeracy demand
1–2	Movement and physical activity	Construct and perform imaginative and original movement sequences in response to stimuli. (ACPMP025)	Students need to know what sequences are, know that repeating patterns can occur in numbers, movements, shapes etc. (e.g. stamp, hop, shake, stamp, hop, shake etc.), and determine which movements take a long time and which take less time. (ACMMG008; ACMNA001, 005)
		Create and participate in games. (ACPMP027)	Students need to understand steps (first, second, third), and use position and patterns to both create and participate. (ACMMG009, 019; ACMNA001, 005)
		Incorporate elements of effort, space, time, objects and people in performing simple movement sequences. (ACPMP029)	Students need to be able to determine which movements take a long time and which take less time. (ACMMG008) Students need to know words of position to describe how their body moves (e.g. *up, down, along, next to*). (ACMMG009) Students need to know ordinal numbers (first, second, third). (ACMNA001)
3–4	Movement and physical activity	Perform movement sequences which link fundamental movement skills. (ACPMP043)	Students need to be able to use numbers in sequences and as connected to patterns, and describe movements in 2D and 3D. (ACMMG009; ACMNA001)
		Combine the elements of effort, space, time, objects and people when performing movement sequences. (ACPMP047)	Students need to be able to determine which movements take a long time and which take less time. (ACMMG008) Students need to know words of position to describe how their body moves (e.g. *up, down, along, next to*). (ACMMG009) Students need to know ordinal numbers (first, second, third). (ACMNA001)
5–6	Movement and physical activity	Design and perform a variety of movement sequences. (ACPMP061, 063)	Students need to be able to determine which movements take a long time and which take less time. (ACMMG008) Students need to know words of position to describe how their body moves (e.g. *up, down, along, next to*). (ACMMG009) Students need to know ordinal numbers (first, second, third). (ACMNA001)

Humanities and social sciences (HASS)

Geography

(Note: Italics indicate a numeracy opportunity.)

Year	Strand or focus	Content descriptor	Numeracy demand or opportunity
F	Knowledge and understanding	Represent the location of places and their features on maps and globe. (ACHASSK014, 015)	Students need to have a sense of what a map is and that the globe is a 3D object that is a model of the world. *Students can create story maps and describe how the world globe represents the world and locate Australia on it.*
	Inquiry skills	Draw simple conclusions based on discussions, observations and information displayed in pictures, in texts and on maps. (ACHASSI008)	Students need to be able to visualise 2D shapes and 3D objects by first knowing what they are and interpret simple maps. (ACMMG009, 044)
1	Knowledge and understanding	Understand the natural, managed and constructed features of places, their location, how they change and how they can be cared for. (ACHASSK015, 017)	Students know how to give and follow directions to familiar locations such as a park, river or bank. (ACMMG023) *Students can locate natural and constructed features on a map.*
		Understand the weather and seasons of places and the ways in which different cultural groups, including First Australians, describe them. (ACHASSK032)	Students need to know what seasons are and their order. (ACMMG040)
		Know the ways that space within places, such as the classroom or backyard, can be rearranged to suit different activities or purposes. (ACHASSK033)	Students can describe position and movement. (ACMMG010) *Students can rearrange the room space for different activities.*
	Inquiry skills	Collect and record geographical data and information (e.g. by observing, or interviewing, or from sources such as photographs, plans, satellite images, storybooks and films).	Students understand simple plans or maps (e.g. of the classroom). (ACMMG044)
		Sort and record information and data, including location, in tables and on plans and labelled maps. (ACHASSI020)	Students need to know how to represent data (1:1) in a table. (ACMSP050) Students understand simple plans or maps (e.g. of the classroom). (ACMMG044)
		Draw simple conclusions based on discussions, observations and information displayed in pictures, in texts and on maps. (ACHASSI025)	Students can apply sorting skills after considering features. *Students can sort and categorise drawings or images.*

(continued)

Appendix: Numeracy across the curriculum

Year	Strand or focus	Content descriptor	Numeracy demand or opportunity
1	Inquiry skills	Present narratives information and findings in oral, graphic and written forms using simple terms to denote the passing of time and to describe direction and location. (ACHASSI027)	Students need to be familiar with words such as *near* and *far*, used to give and follow directions. (ACMMG023) *Students can use words such as north and south. (ACMMG065)*
2	Knowledge and understanding	Locate the major geographical divisions of the world in relation to Australia. (ACHASSK047)	Students need to interpret simple maps and identify relative positions of key features. (ACMMG044) Students need to be familiar with words such as *near* and *far*, used to give and follow directions. (ACMMG023), *Students can use words such as north and south. (ACMMG065)* *Students can use a globe, map or Google Earth to locate continents and oceans and describe locations using north, south, opposite, near, far etc.*
		Define places as parts of the Earth's surface that have been given meaning by people, and understand how places can be defined using a variety of scales. (ACHASSK048)	Students can talk about scale using measurement words of comparison (e.g. *bigger* and *smaller*) and words of distance (e.g. *further* and *closer*).
		Understand the influence of purpose, distance and accessibility on the frequency with which people visit places. (ACHASSK051)	Students have an understanding of actual distance compared with relative distance or position in discussing how close things are to each other. (ACMMG044)
	Inquiry skills	Represent data and location of places and their features by constructing tables, plans and labelled maps. (ACHASSI036)	Students need to interpret simple maps. (ACMMG044) *Students can develop a treasure map with map symbols showing features and routes.*
		Draw simple conclusions based on discussions, observations and information displayed in pictures, in texts and on maps. (ACHASSI041)	Students can sort and categorise, using a table to organise data. *Students can produce a timeline of the development of ICT (on foot, horse and cart, telephone etc.) and interpret the information gathered.*
		Present narratives, information and findings in oral, graphic and written forms using simple terms to denote the passing of time and to describe direction and location. (ACHASSI043)	Students need to be familiar with words such as *near* and *far*, used to give and follow directions. (ACMMG023) *Students can use words such as north and south. (ACMMG065)*

(continued)

Year	Strand or focus	Content descriptor	Numeracy demand or opportunity
3	Knowledge and understanding	Understand the representation of Australia as states and territories and as countries and places of First Australians peoples. (ACHASSK066)	Students need to be able to interpret grid maps to read language maps and determine survey and natural boundaries. (ACMMG065)
		Recognise the location of Australia's neighbouring countries and their diverse characteristics. (ACHASSK067)	Students need to be able to interpret grid maps and show position to locate New Zealand, Timor-Leste etc. on maps and determine their direction from Australia. (ACMMG065)
		Know the main climate types of the world and the similarities and differences between the climates of different places. (ACHASSK068)	Students need to be able to interpret grid maps to locate, identify and compare places with similar or different climates. (ACMMG065)
	Inquiry skills	Record, sort and represent data and the location of places and their characteristics in different forms, including simple graphs, tables and maps. (ACHASSI054)	Students need to be able to create data displays using lists, tables and picture or column graphs by first measuring using metric units. (ACMSP050)
		Represent the location of places and their features by constructing large-scale maps that include scale, legend, title and north point, and describe location using simple grid references, compass direction and distance. (ACHASSI054)	Students need to be able to create simple grid maps. (ACMMG065)
		Interpret geographical data and information displayed in different formats, to identify and describe distributions and patterns and draw conclusions. (ACHASSI057, 058)	Students must be able to interpret displays of data in tables and graphs. (ACMSP070)
		Present ideas, findings and conclusions in texts and modes that incorporate digital and non-digital representations and use geographical terminology. (ACHASSI061)	Students choose and use displays when presenting information such as maps showing populations living near the ocean or numbers. (ACMSP096)

(continued)

Appendix: Numeracy across the curriculum

Year	Strand or focus	Content descriptor	Numeracy demand or opportunity
4	Knowledge and understanding	Recognise the location of the major countries of Africa and South America in relation to Australia and their main characteristics, including the types of natural vegetation and native animals in at least two countries from each continents. (ACHASSK087, 088)	Students need to be able to read grid maps (latitude and longitude) to locate and recognise countries outside Australia. (ACHGK065)
		Understand the types of natural vegetation and the significance of vegetation to the environment and to people. (ACHASSK088, 089)	Students need to be able to interpret and map of different vegetation types. (ACMMG090)
		Consider the custodial responsibility First Australians have for Country and how this influences their past and present views about the use of resources. (ACHASSK089, 090)	Students need to be able to use legends on maps to read the location of different people groups prior to colonisation. (ACMMG090) *Students determine from maps where First Australians lived prior to colonisation.*
	Inquiry skills	Collect and record relevant geographical data and information (e.g. by observing, interviewing, conducting surveys, measuring, or from a range of other sources). (ACHASSI074)	Students need to be able to use scales and legends on maps to read the location and extent of vegetation types. (ACMMG090) *Students can map the extent of vegetation in an area.*
		Represent data by constructing tables and graphs. (ACHASSI075)	Students need to know how to construct tables and graphs. (ACMSP096)
		Represent the location of places and their features by constructing large-scale maps that include scale, legend, title and north point, and describe location using simple grid references, compass direction and distance. (ACHASSI075)	Students need to be able to create simple grid maps. (ACMMG065)
		Interpret geographical data to identify distributions and patterns and draw conclusions. (ACHASSI078)	Students must be able to interpret displays of data in tables and graphs. (ACMSP070)
		Present ideas, findings and conclusions in texts and modes that incorporate digital and non-digital representations and use geographical terminology. (ACHASSI082)	Students choose and use displays when presenting information such as a map showing populations living near the ocean or numbers of people travelling to Bali from Perth. (ACMSP096)

(continued)

Year	Strand or focus	Content descriptor	Numeracy demand or opportunity
5	Knowledge and understanding	Recognise the location of the major countries of Europe and North America in relation to Australia and the influence of people on the environmental characteristics of places in at least two countries from each continents. (ACHASSK111, 112)	Students need to be able to identify relative locations of other continents in relations to Australia. (ACMMG090)
	Inquiry skills	Collect and record relevant geographical data and information, using ethical protocols, from primary and secondary sources (e.g. people, maps, plans, photos and reports). (ACHASSI094)	Students need to be able to read a map to collect information, estimate and calculate, read settlement patterns, measure distances and interpret data displays. (ACMMG184; ACMNA099; ACMSP120)
		Evaluate sources for their usefulness and represent data in different forms such as maps, plans, graphs and tables. (ACHASSI094, 096)	Students must be able to choose to represent data with a range of displays. (ACMSP096)
		Interpret geographical data and other information, using digital and spatial technologies as appropriate, and identify spatial distributions, patterns and trends, and infer relationships to draw conclusions. (ACHASSI100)	Students must know how maps work, interpret them and infer relationships (e.g. between bushfire events in a bar graph and population movement).
		Present ideas, findings, viewpoints and conclusions in a range of texts and modes (e.g. graphs, tables, maps) using digital and non-digital representations and using geography terms. (ACHASSI105)	Students must understand relative location, scale and legends in a map, and the relationships between these elements (e.g. skills to present a report on a local issue such as location of a new bridge or road).
6	Knowledge and understanding	Recognise the location of the major countries of the Asia region in relation to Australia and the geographical diversity within the region. (ACHASSK138)	Students need to be able to interpret maps. (ACMMG113)
		Understand the differences in the economic, demographic and social characteristics between countries across the world. (ACHASSK139)	Students need to be able to estimate and calculate with whole numbers to compare populations and economic wealth. (ACMNA072)

(continued)

Appendix: Numeracy across the curriculum

Year	Strand or focus	Content descriptor	Numeracy demand or opportunity
6	Inquiry skills	Collect and record relevant geographical data and information from sources. (ACHASSI123)	Students need to be able to estimate and calculate with whole numbers to compare populations and economic wealth. (ACMNA072) Students need to be able to interpret graphs and tables. (ACMSP147, 148) *Students should compare language group sizes.*
		Evaluate sources for their usefulness and represent data in different forms (e.g. maps, plans, graphs and tables). (ACHASSI123, 124, 126, 127)	Students must be able to choose to represent data with a range of displays. (ACMSP096)
		Represent the location and features of places and different types of geographical information by constructing large-scale and small-scale maps that conform to cartographic conventions including border, source, scale, legend, title and north point, using spatial technologies as appropriate. (ACHASSI124)	Students need to be able to create grid maps using scales, legends and north point. (ACMMG090)
		Interpret geographical data and other information using digital and spatial technologies as appropriate, and identify spatial distributions, patterns and trends, and infer relationships to draw conclusions. (ACHASSI128)	Students must know how maps work, interpret them and infer relationships (e.g. between population distribution in Australia compared with China).
		Present ideas, findings, viewpoints and conclusions in a range of texts and modes (e.g. graphs, tables, maps) using digital and non-digital representations and using geography terms. (ACHASSI133)	Students must understand relative location, scale and legends in a map, and the relationships between these elements (e.g. to be able to present a report using geographical terminology on a global event such as migration from Africa to Italy).

Economics and business

Year	Strand or focus	Content descriptor	Numeracy demand
5	Knowledge and understanding	Recognise influences on consumer choices and methods that can be used to help make informed personal consumer and financial choices. (ACHASSK121)	Students need to know that cost is a significant factor influencing purchases and be able to determine costs differences by rounding when appropriate. (ACMNA099)
		Develop questions to guide an investigation of an economic or business issue or event, and gather data and information from observation, and print and online sources. (ACHASSK119, 120, 121)	Students need to be able to interpret displays of data such as advertising material and draw tables to organise gathered data (e.g. comparing costs for items from various supermarkets). (ACMSP069)
6	Knowledge and understanding	Recognise the effect that consumer and financial decisions can have on the individual, the broader community and the environment. (ACHASSK150)	Students need to understand money: how it is represented and compared, and how to solve problems involving purchases. (ACMNA080)
		Develop questions to guide an investigation of an economic or business issue or event, and gather data and information from observation, and print and online sources. (ACHASSK149, 150, 151)	Students need to be able to interpret displays of data such as advertising material and draw tables to organise gathered data (e.g. comparing costs for items from various supermarkets). (ACMSP069)

History

Year	Strand or focus	Content descriptor	Numeracy demand
F	Historical skills	Sequence familiar objects and events. (ACHASSI004)	Students need to know that time passes in sequences or cycles and that days, months and years can be marked off one by one on calendar or timeline. (ACMMG008, 021)
		Distinguish between the past, present and future. (ACHASSI004)	Students need to be able to show they know the difference between past, present and future by comparing and ordering events using everyday language such as *yesterday*, *last night*, *today* and *tomorrow*. (ACMMG006)

(continued)

Appendix: Numeracy across the curriculum

Year	Strand or focus	Content descriptor	Numeracy demand
1	Knowledge and understanding	Recognise differences and similarities between students' daily lives and life during their parents' and grandparents' childhoods, including family traditions, leisure time and communications. (ACHASSK028, 029, 030) Distinguish between the past, present and future. (ACHASSK029)	Students need to be able to distinguish between events and when they occur (or occurred) using words of time such as before, after, today and next week. (ACMMG008, 021)
	Historical skills	Sequence familiar objects and events. (ACHASSI021)	Students need to know that time passes in sequences or cycles and that days, months and years can be marked off one by one on calendar or timeline. (ACMMG008, 021)
2	Historical skills	Sequence familiar objects and events. (ACHASSI037)	Students need to be able to connect objects and events to points in time (e.g. photos of parents and grandparents). (ACMMG008, 021)
4	Knowledge and understanding	Explain the journey(s) of at least one world navigator, explorer or trader up to the late eighteenth century, including their contacts with other societies and any impacts. (ACHASSK084)	Students need to be able to plot or read a journey made by someone on a map. (ACMMG065)
	Historical skills	Sequence historical people and events. (ACHASSI076)	Students need to be able to place events and people groups on timelines (i.e. know how to order times chronologically and show these visually on a number line). (ACMNA013, 027, 052)
		Pose a range of questions about the past. (ACHASSI073)	Students need to understand the passing of time in order to pose questions about 'when', distinguishing between events and when they occurred. (ACMMG008, 021)
6	Historical skills	Sequence information about people's lives, events, developments and phenomena. (ACHASSI125)	Students need to be able to place events and people groups on timelines (i.e. know how to order times chronologically and show these visually on a number line). (ACMNA013, 027, 052)

WOULD YOU LIKE MATHS WITH THAT?

Science

Year	Strand or focus	Content descriptor	Numeracy demand
F	Science understanding	Understand the way objects move depends on a variety of factors, including their size and shape. (ACSSU005)	Students need to be able to describe the movement of objects using words such as *forwards*, *backwards* and *sideways* and visualise 2D and 3D objects moving. (ACMMG009, 010)
1	Inquiry skills	Use informal measurement in the collection and recording of observations, with the assistance of digital technologies as appropriate. (ACSIS026)	Students need to be able to measure using informal units such as handspans. (ACMMG019)
		Use a range of methods to sort information, including drawings and provided tables. (ACSIS027)	Students need to be able to organise their information into categories shown in tables. (ACMSP263)
2	Inquiry skills	Respond to and pose questions, and make predictions about familiar objects and events. (ACSIS037)	Students need to distinguish between real and fantasy by saying words like *will happen* or *won't happen*. (ACMSP024)
		Use a range of methods to sort information, including drawings and provided tables. (ACSIS040)	Students need to be able to organise their information into categories shown in tables and draw picture graphs to show information. (ACMSP050, 263)
3	Science understanding	Understand the Earth's rotation on its axis causes regular changes, including night and day. (ACSSU048)	Students need to understand repeating patterns in time such as the cycles of day and night. (ACMNA005)
	Science as human endeavour	Recognise that science involves making predictions and describing patterns and relationships. (ACSHE050)	Students need to distinguish between real and fantasy by saying words like *will happen* and *certain* or *won't happen*, *unlikely*, *impossible*, *uncertain*. (ACMSP024, 047)

(continued)

Appendix: Numeracy across the curriculum

Year	Strand or focus	Content descriptor	Numeracy demand
3	Inquiry skills	Safely use appropriate materials, tools or equipment to make and record observations, using formal measurements and digital technologies as appropriate. (ACSIS055)	Students need to be able to measure and read measurement scales for metric units of length, mass and capacity. (ACMMG061)
		Use a range of methods including tables and simple column graphs to represent data and to identify patterns and trends. (ACSIS057)	Students need to know how to construct simple column graphs and identify patterns and trends in data. (ACMSP069, 070)
		Compare results with predictions, suggesting possible reasons for findings. (ACSIS215)	Students need to distinguish between degrees of likelihood of something occurring (e.g. more likely and less likely). (ACMSP092)
		Represent and communicate ideas and findings in a variety of ways such as diagrams, physical representation and simple reports. (ACSIS060)	Students need to be able to represent findings in flowcharts, schematics diagrams or map as well as graphs. (ACMSP069; ACMMG044)
4	Knowledge and understanding	Know that forces can be exerted by one object on another through direct contact or from a distance. (ACSSU076)	Students need to be able to estimate measurements in metric units. (ACMMG061)
	Science as human endeavour	Recognise that science involves making predictions and describing patterns and relationships. (ACSHE061)	Students need to distinguish between degrees of likelihood of something occurring (e.g. more likely and less likely) and to identify patterns in data. (ACMSP070, 092)

(continued)

Year	Strand or focus	Content descriptor	Numeracy demand
4	Inquiry skills	Safely use appropriate materials, tools or equipment to make and record observations, using formal measurements and digital technologies as appropriate. (ACSIS066)	Students need to be able to estimate and measure in metric units. (ACMMG061)
		Use a range of methods including tables and simple column graphs to represent data and to identify patterns and trends. (ACSIS068)	Students need to know how to construct simple column graphs and identify patterns and trends in data. (ACMSP069, 070)
		Compare results with predictions, suggesting possible reasons for findings. (ACSIS216)	Students need to distinguish between degrees of likelihood of something occurring (e.g. more likely and less likely). (ACMSP092)
		Reflect on an investigation including whether a test was fair or not. (ACSIS069)	Students need to know that fair means as having equal chances of occurring. (ACMSP092)
		Represent and communicate ideas and findings in a variety of ways such as diagrams, physical representations and simple reports. (ACSIS071)	Students need to be able to represent findings in flowcharts, schematics diagrams or map as well as graphs. (ACMMG044; ACMSP069)
5	Science as human endeavour	Recognise science involves testing predictions by gathering data and using evidence to develop explanations of events and phenomena. (ACSHE081)	Students need to be able to interpret predictions, distinguish between degrees of likelihood of something occurring (e.g. more likely and less likely) and organise data displays. (ACMSP092, 096)
	Inquiry skills	Decide which variable should be changed and measured in fair tests and accurately observe, measure and record data, using digital technologies as appropriate. (ACSIS087)	Students need to be able to estimate and measure in metric units and organise measurement data. (ACMMG061; ACMSP096)
		Construct and use a range of representations, including tables and graphs, to represent and describe observations, patterns or relationships in data, using digital technologies as appropriate. (ACSIS090)	Students need to be able to choose and construct column graphs, dot plots and tables and observe or notice variability in data displays. (ACMSP097)
		Compare data with predictions and use as evidence in developing explanations. (ACSIS218)	Students need to be able to interpret data displays. (ACMSP097, 120)

(continued)

Appendix: Numeracy across the curriculum

Year	Strand or focus	Content descriptor	Numeracy demand
6	Science as human endeavour	Recognise science involves testing predictions by gathering data and using evidence to develop explanations of events and phenomena. (ACSHE098)	Students need to be able to interpret predictions, distinguish between degrees of likelihood of something occurring (e.g. more likely and less likely) and organise data displays to help understand. (ACMSP092, 096)
	Inquiry skills	Decide which variable should be changed and measured in fair tests and accurately observe, measure and record data, using digital technologies as appropriate. (ACSIS104)	Students need to be able to estimate and measure in metric units and organise measurement data. (ACMMG061; ACMSP096)
		Construct and use a range of representations, including tables and graphs, to represent and describe observations, patterns or relationships in data, using digital technologies as appropriate. (ACSIS107)	Students need to be able to choose and construct column graphs, dot plots and tables, and observe or notice variability in data displays. (ACMSP097)
		Compare data with predictions and use as evidence in developing explanations. (ACSIS221)	Students need to be able to interpret data displays. (ACMSP097, 120)

English

Year	Strand or focus	Content descriptor	Numeracy demand
1	Language	Understand concepts about print and screen, including how different types of texts are organised using page numbering, tables of content, headings and titles, navigation buttons, bars and links. (ACELA1450)	Students need to understand that page numbers and chapter numbers in a text are used in an ordinal sense (showing the order or sequence of the pages). (ACMNA001, 013) Students need to understand the use of words of time to show a sequence in a text or create cohesion (e.g. *once upon a time*, *finally* and *for ever and ever*). (ACMMG007)
2	Literature	Identify, reproduce and experiment with rhythmic, sound and word patterns in poems, chants, rhymes and songs. (ACELT1592)	Students need to understand repeating patterns to recognise them in songs, poems and other forms. (ACMNA005)
3	Language	Identify the effect on audience of techniques (e.g. shot size, vertical camera angle and layout) in picture books, advertisements and film segments. (ACELA1483)	Students need to understand relative angle and comparative size and be able to visualise these differences in 2D and 3D to know that this can be used as a literary device to show power. (ACMMG022, 037)
	Literature	Create texts that adapt language features and patterns encountered in literary texts (e.g. characterisation, rhyme rhythm, mood, music, sound effects and dialogue). (ACELT1791)	Students need to understand that repeating patterns can be created in different forms (e.g. 1, 1, 2, 1, 1, 2) as a repeating pattern can be written in sounds and words (e.g. clap, clap, stamp, clap, clap, stamp). (ACMNA035)
5	Language	Explain sequences of images in print texts and compare these to the ways hyperlinked digital texts are organised, explaining their effect on viewers' interpretations. (ACELA1512)	Students need to understand what a sequence is and that the order is important. (ACMNA001, 012, 026)
6	Language	Identify and explain how analytical images like figures, tables, diagrams, maps and graphs contribute to our understanding of verbal information in factual, fictional and persuasive texts. (ACELA1524)	Students can make sense of a map, table or graph inserted in a text (e.g. a map of Hobbiton in *The lord of the rings*, the use of a graph in an advertisement). (ACMSP097)

References

Ahn, R., & Class, M. (2011). Student-centered pedagogy: Co-construction of knowledge through student-generated midterm exams. *International Journal of Teaching and Learning in Higher Education, 23*(2), 269–281. https://www.isetl.org/ijtlhe/pdf/IJTLHE1023.pdf

Alberta Education. (2011). *Framework for student learning: Competencies for engaged thinkers and ethical citizens with an entrepreneurial spirit*. Alberta Education. https://open.alberta.ca/dataset/4c47d713-d1fc-4c94-bc97-08998d93d3ad/resource/58e18175-5681-4543-b617-c8efe5b7b0e9/download/5365951-2011-Framework-Student-Learning.pdf

Anderson, J. (2009, October 2–4). *Mathematics curriculum development and the role of problem solving* [Paper presentation]. Australian Curriculum Studies Association National Biennial Conference, Canberra, ACT, Australia. https://www.acsa.edu.au/pages/images/judy%20anderson%20-%20mathematics%20curriculum%20development.pdf

Anderson, L. W., & Krathwohl, D. R. (Eds.). (2001). *A taxonomy for learning, teaching, and assessing: A revision of Bloom's taxonomy of educational objectives*. Addison Wesley Longman.

Askew, M., Rhodes, V., Brown, M., Wiliam, D., & Johnson, D. (1997). *Effective teachers of numeracy: Report of a study carried out for the Teachers Training Agency*. King's College, University of London. https://www.ru.ac.za/media/rhodesuniversity/content/sanc/documents/Askew_et_al._-_1997_-_Effective_teachers_of_numeracy.pdf

Association of Independent Schools of Western Australia (AISWA). (2017). NAPLAN cohort growth, Year 3 to Year 5, 2015–2017. Mundaring Christian College.

Association of Independent Schools of Western Australia (AISWA). (2018). NAPLAN results, Mundaring Christian College.

Australian Association of Mathematics Teachers (AAMT). (1997). *Numeracy = everyone's business: The report of the numeracy education strategy development conference May 1997*.

Australian Association of Mathematics Teachers (AAMT). (1998). *The Australian Association of Mathematics Teachers policy on numeracy education in schools*. https://makeitcount.aamt.edu.au/content/download/724/19518/version/5/file/numpol.pdf

Australian Council of Education Research (ACER). (2015). *Literacy and numeracy test for initial teacher education students: Assessment framework*. Retrieved May 6, 2021, from https://teacheredtest.acer.edu.au/files/Literacy-and-Numeracy-Test-for-Initial-Teacher-Education-Students-Assessment-Framework.pdf

Australian Curriculum, Assessment and Reporting Authority (ACARA). (n.d.-a). *Numeracy*. Retrieved August 2, 2016, from https://www.australiancurriculum.edu.au/f-10-curriculum/general-capabilities/numeracy/

Australian Curriculum, Assessment and Reporting Authority (ACARA). (n.d.-b). *Numeracy learning continuum*. https://docs.acara.edu.au/resources/General_capabilities_-_NUM_-_learning_continuum.pdf

Australian Curriculum, Assessment and Reporting Authority (ACARA). (n.d.-c). *Mathematics proficiencies*. Retrieved August 7, 2016, from https://www.australiancurriculum.edu.au/resources/mathematics-proficiencies/

Australian Curriculum, Assessment and Reporting Authority (ACARA). (n.d.-d). *F–10 Curriculum: Mathematics*. Retrieved August 7, 2016, from https://www.australiancurriculum.edu.au/f-10-curriculum/mathematics/

Australian Curriculum, Assessment and Reporting Authority (ACARA). (n.d.-e). *General capabilities*. Retrieved June 3, 2021, from https://www.australiancurriculum.edu.au/f-10-curriculum/general-capabilities/

Australian Curriculum, Assessment and Reporting Authority (ACARA). (n.d.-f). *Learning areas*. Retrieved June 3, 2021, from https://www.australiancurriculum.edu.au/f-10-curriculum/learning-areas/

Australian Curriculum, Assessment and Reporting Authority (ACARA). (2008). Year 7 numeracy non-calculator test. https://docs.acara.edu.au/resources/200808_NAPLAN_2008_Final_Test_Numeracy_year_7_non_calculator.pdf

Australian Curriculum, Assessment and Reporting Authority (ACARA). (2010). Year 3 numeracy test. https://docs.acara.edu.au/resources/201005_NAPLAN_2010_Final_Test_Numeracy_Year_3.pdf

Australian Curriculum, Assessment and Reporting Authority (ACARA). (2013). General capabilities information sheet. https://docs.acara.edu.au/resources/General_Capabilities_2011.pdf

Australian Curriculum, Assessment and Reporting Authority (ACARA). (2018). *Introduction to the national literacy and numeracy learning progressions*. https://www.australiancurriculum.edu.au/media/3637/introduction.pdf

Australian Curriculum, Assessment and Reporting Authority (ACARA). (2020). *National numeracy learning progression: Version 3.0*. https://www.lpofai.edu.au/media/pphia1eq/national-numeracy-learning-progression-v3-for-publication.pdf

Australian Institute for Teaching and School Leadership (AITSL). (2014). *Australian professional standard for principals and the leadership profiles*. https://www.aitsl.edu.au/docs/default-source/national-policy-framework/australian-professional-standard-for-principals-and-the-leadership-profiles-(web).pdf?sfvrsn=c07eff3c_10

Australian Institute for Teaching and School Leadership (AITSL). (2015). *Accreditation of initial teacher education programs in Australia: Standards and procedures*. https://www.aitsl.edu.au/docs/default-source/national-policy-framework/accreditation-of-initial-teacher-education-programs-in-australia.pdf?sfvrsn=e87cff3c_28

Australian Institute for Teaching and School Leadership (AITSL). (2018). *Australian professional standards for teachers*. https://www.aitsl.edu.au/docs/default-source/national-policy-framework/australian-professional-standards-for-teachers.pdf

Bandura, A. (1995). Exercise of personal and collective efficacy in changing societies. In A. Bandura (Ed.), *Self-efficacy in changing societies* (pp. 1–45). Cambridge University Press. https://doi.org/10.1017/CBO9780511527692.003

Biggs, J. B., & Collis, K. F. (1982). *Evaluating the quality of learning: The SOLO taxonomy (structure of the observed learning outcome)*. Academic Press.

Bishop, R., Berryman, M., Cavanagh, T., & Teddy, L. (2007). *Te Kotahitanga Phase 3 whanaungatanga: Establishing a culturally responsive pedagogy of relations in mainstream secondary school classrooms*. Ministry of Education, New Zealand. https://www.educationcounts.govt.nz/__data/assets/pdf_file/0004/9922/Te_Kotahitanga_Phase3.pdf

Black, P., & Wiliam, D. (1998). Inside the black box: Raising standards through classroom assessment. *Phi Delta Kappan, 80*(2), 139–144, 146–148. https://doi.org/10.1177/003172171009200119

Black, P., Harrison, C., Lee, C., Marshall, B., & Wiliam, D. (2004). Working inside the black box: Assessment for learning in the classroom. *Phi Delta Kappan, 86*(1), 8–21. https://doi.org/10.1177/003172170408600105

References

Blackwell, L. S., Trzesniewski, K. H., & Dweck, C. S. (2007). Implicit theories of intelligence predict achievement across an adolescent transition: A longitudinal study and an intervention. *Child Development, 78*(1), 246–263. https://doi.org/10.1111/j.1467-8624.2007.00995.x

Blankstein, A. M. (2010). *Failure is not an option: 6 principles for making student success the only option* (2nd ed.). Corwin Press.

Blasé, J., & Blasé, J. (1998). *Handbook of instructional leadership: How really good principals promote teaching and learning.* Corwin Press.

Bloom, B. S. (1956). *Taxonomy of educational objectives.* Allyn & Bacon.

Boudett, K. P., & Steele, J. L (2007). *Data wise in action: Stories of schools using data to improve teaching and learning.* Harvard Education Press.

Bransford, J. D., Brown, A. L., Cocking, R. R. (Eds.). (2000). *How people learn: Brain, mind, experience, and school.* National Academy Press.

Brophy, J. E. (1983). Research on the self-fulfilling prophecy and teacher expectations. *Journal of Educational Psychology, 75*(5), 631–661. https://doi.org/10.1037/0022-0663.75.5.631

Brophy, J. E. (2008). Developing students' appreciation for what is taught in school. *Educational Psychologist, 43*(3), 132–141. https://doi.org/10.1080/00461520701756511

Buckley, S., Reid, K., Goos, M., Lipp, O. V., & Thomson, S. (2016). Understanding and addressing mathematics anxiety using perspectives from education, psychology and neuroscience. *Australian Journal of Education, 60*(2), 157–170. https://doi.org/10.1177/0004944116653000

Byrne, C. (2016). Familiarising oneself with Understanding by Design. *e-Leading: Management strategies for school leaders, 18*. http://www.acel.org.au/acel/ACEL_docs/Publications/e-Leading/2016/e-Leading_2016_18.pdf

Cai, J., & Nie, B. (2007). Problem-solving in Chinese mathematics education: Research and practice. *ZDM – Mathematics Education, 39*, 459–473. https://doi.org/10.1007/s11858-007-0042-3

Carey, A., & Hunter, F. (2019, December 3). 'Alarm bells': Australian students falling behind in maths, science and reading. *Sydney Morning Herald.* https://www.smh.com.au/politics/federal/alarm-bells-australian-students-falling-behind-in-maths-science-and-reading-20191203-p53gho.html

Chenoweth, K. (2009). *How it's being done: Urgent lessons from unexpected schools.* Harvard Education Press.

Cimpian, A., Arce, H.-M. C., Markman, E. M., & Dweck, C. S. (2007). Subtle linguistic cues affect children's motivation. *Psychological Science, 18*(4), 314–316. https://doi.org/10.1111/j.1467-9280.2007.01896.x

Clarke, D. J., & Sullivan, P. (1990). Is a question the best answer? *The Australian Mathematics Teacher, 46*(3), 30–33.

Clarke, D. J., & Sullivan, P. (1991, November 20–24). *The assessment implications of open-ended tasks* [Paper presentation]. Assessment and the Mathematical Sciences Conference, Geelong, Victoria, Australia.

Cockroft, W. H. (1982). *Mathematics counts: Report of the Committee of Inquiry into the Teaching of Mathematics in Schools.* Her Majesty's Stationery Office.

Commonwealth of Australia. (2012). *Australian core skills framework.* Department of Industry and Science. https://www.dese.gov.au/skills-information-training-providers/australian-core-skills-framework/download-acsf

Council of Australian Governments (COAG). (2008). *National numeracy review report.* Commonwealth of Australia. https://apo.org.au/sites/default/files/resource-files/2008-07/apo-nid4016.pdf

Department of Education, Employment and Workplace Relations (DEEWR). (2009). *Belonging, being & becoming: The early years learning framework for Australia.* https://www.dese.gov.au/national-quality-framework-early-childhood-education-and-care/resources/belonging-being-becoming-early-years-learning-framework-australia

Department of Education, Science and Training (DEST). (2004). *Numeracy across the curriculum.*

Department of Education, Skills and Employment. (2021). *Literacy and numeracy test for initial teacher education students.* Retrieved July 12, 2021, from https://www.dese.gov.au/teaching-and-school-leadership/literacy-and-numeracy-test-initial-teacher-education-students

Dinham, S. (2016). *Leading learning and teaching.* ACER Press.

DuFour, R. (2004). What is a 'professional learning community'? *Educational Leadership, 61,* 6–11.

DuFour, R., DuFour, R., Eaker, R., & Karhanek, G. (2004). *Whatever it takes: How professional learning communities respond when kids don't learn.* Solution Tree.

DuFour, R., DuFour, R., Eaker, R., & Many, T. (2010). *Learning by doing: A handbook for professional learning communities at work* (2nd ed.). Solution Tree.

DuFour, R., & Marzano, R. J. (2011). *Leaders of learning: How district, school, and classroom leaders improve student achievement.* Hawker Brownlow Education.

Dweck, C. S. (2008). *Mindsets and math/science achievement.* Carnegie-IAS Commission on Mathematics and Science Education. http://www.nationalnumeracy.org.uk/sites/default/files/dweck_2008_mindsets_and_math-science_achievement.pdf

Dweck, C. S. (2012). *Mindset: How you can fulfil your potential.* Constable & Robinson.

Dweck, C. S., Walton, G. M., & Cohen, G. L. (2014). *Academic tenacity: Mindsets that promote long-term learning.* Bill and Melinda Gates Foundation. https://files.eric.ed.gov/fulltext/ED576649.pdf

Education Council. (2015). *National STEM school education strategy: A comprehensive plan for science, technology, engineering and mathematics education in Australia.* https://files.eric.ed.gov/fulltext/ED581690.pdf

Education Council. (2019). *Alice Springs (Mparntwe) Education Declaration.* https://www.dese.gov.au/alice-springs-mparntwe-education-declaration/resources/alice-springs-mparntwe-education-declaration

Elmore, R. F. (2000). *Building a new structure for school leadership.* Albert Shanker Institute.

Elmore, R. F. (2004). *School reform from the inside out: Policy, practice, and performance.* Harvard Education Press.

Erickson, H. L. (2012). *Concept-based teaching and learning.* International Baccalaureate Organization. http://www.ibmidatlantic.org/Concept_Based_Teaching_Learning.pdf

Erickson, H. L. (2017). What are the essential elements of concept-based curriculum design?. In J. Stern, K. Ferraro, & J. Mohnkern (Eds.), *Tools for teaching conceptual understanding, secondary: Designing lessons and assessments for deep learning* (pp. 9–27). Corwin.

Ferguson, R. F. (2002). *What doesn't meet the eye: Addressing racial disparities in high-achieving suburban schools.* North Central Regional Educational Laboratory.

Finnegan, R. S. (2013). Linking teacher self-efficacy to teacher evaluation. *Journal of Cross-Disciplinary Perspectives in Education, 6*(1), 18–25. https://jcpe.wmwikis.net/file/view/Finnegan_Linking_Efficacy_to_Evaluations.pdf

Forgasz, H., Leder, G., & Tan, H. (2014). Public views on the gendering of mathematics and related careers: International comparisons. *Educational Studies in Mathematics, 87*(3), 369–388. https://doi.org/10.1007/s10649-014-9550-6

The Foundation for Young Australians. (2015). *The new work order: Ensuring young Australians have skills and experience for the jobs of the future, not the past.* https://www.fya.org.au/app/uploads/2021/09/new-work-order-2015.pdf

The Foundation for Young Australians. (2016). *The new work mindset: 7 new job clusters to help young people navigate the new work order.* https://www.fya.org.au/app/uploads/2021/09/The-New-Work-Mindset_2016.pdf

Fullan, M. (2002). *Principals as leaders in a culture of change.* https://michaelfullan.ca/wp-content/uploads/2016/06/13396053050.pdf

References

Fullan, M. (2005). *The tri-level solution: School/district/state synergy*. Society for the Advancement of Excellence in Education. https://www.saee.ca/analyst/C_023.1_BII_LON.php

Fullan, M. (2014, July 29). *Topic series 19 – Learning is the work* [Video]. YouTube. https://www.youtube.com/watch?v=-GRd4ifz-Yk

Fullan, M. (2015, March 17). *Topic series 10 – The moral imperative* [Video]. YouTube. https://www.youtube.com/watch?v=tQYvruRPeLU

Fullan, M., Hill, P., & Crévola, C. (2006). *Breakthrough*. Corwin Press.

Fullan, M., Hill, P., & Rincón-Gallardo, S. (2017). *New pedagogies for deep learning whitepaper: Deep learning: Shaking the foundations* (Deep Learning Series, Issue 3). New Pedagogies for Deep Learning: A Global Partnership. https://deep-learning.global/wp-content/uploads/2017/04/npdl_shaking_the_foundations.pdf

Fullan, M., & Scott, G. (2014). *New pedagogies for deep learning whitepaper: Education PLUS: The world will be led by people you can count on, including you!*. Collaborative Impact. https://www.michaelfullan.ca/wp-content/uploads/2014/09/Education-Plus-A-Whitepaper-July-2014-1.pdf

Good, C., Aronson, J., & Inzlicht, M. (2003). Improving adolescents' standardized test performance: An intervention to reduce the effects of stereotype threat. *Journal of Applied Developmental Psychology, 24*(6), 645–662. https://doi.org/10.1017/CBO9780511527692.003

Goos, M., Geiger, V., & Dole, S. (2012a, July 8–15). *Changing classroom practice through a rich model of numeracy across the curriculum* [Paper presentation]. Twelfth International Congress on Mathematics Education, Seoul, South Korea. https://espace.library.uq.edu.au/view/UQ:278741/UQ278741_fulltext.pdf

Goos, M., Geiger, V., & Dole, S. (2012b). Auditing the numeracy demands of the Australian Curriculum. In J. Dindyal, L. P. Cheng, & S. F. Ng (Eds.), Mathematics education: Expanding horizons (Proceedings of the 35th Annual Conference of the Mathematics Education Research Group of Australasia, Volume 2, pp. 314–321). MERGA. https://files.eric.ed.gov/fulltext/ED573240.pdf

Goos, M., Geiger, V., Bennison, A., & Roberts, J. (2015). *Numeracy teaching across the curriculum in Queensland: Resources for teachers: Final report*. The University of Queensland. https://cdn.qct.edu.au/pdf/Numeracy_Teaching_Across_Curriculum_QLD.pdf

Griffin, P., McGaw, B., & Care, E. (Eds.). (2012). *Assessment and teaching of 21st century skills*. Springer.

Gross, M. U. M. (2004). *Gifted and talented education: Professional development package for teachers* (Module 3). Gifted Education Research, Resource and Information Centre. https://www.unsw.edu.au/content/dam/images/photos/campus/kensington/2021-06-gerric-documents/2021-06-gerric-module3-primary.pdf

Gross, M. U. M. (2015). Characteristics of able gifted highly gifted exceptionally gifted and profoundly gifted learners. In H. E. Vidergor & C. R. Harris (Eds.), *Applied practice for educators of gifted and able learners* (pp. 3–23). SensePublishers. https://doi.org/10.1007/978-94-6300-004-8_1

Gupton, S. L. (2003). *The instructional leadership toolbox: A handbook for improving practice*. Corwin Press.

Hammond, J., & Gibbons, P. (2005). Putting scaffolding to work: The contribution of scaffolding in articulating ESL education. *Prospect, 20*(1), 6–30. http://www.ameprc.mq.edu.au/__data/assets/pdf_file/0008/229760/20_1_1_Hammond.pdf

Harvard Advanced Leadership Initiative. (2014). *Education for the 21st century: A synthesis of ideas from the Harvard University advanced leadership initiative think tank*. https://globaled.gse.harvard.edu/files/geii/files/2014_education_report_web.pdf

Hattie, J. (1992). Measuring the effects of schooling. *Australian Journal of Education, 36*(1), 5–13. https://doi.org/10.1177/000494419203600102

Hattie, J. (2003, October 19–21). *Teachers make a difference: What is the research evidence?* [Paper presentation]. ACER Research Conference, Melbourne, Australia. https://research.acer.edu.au/cgi/viewcontent.cgi?article=1003&context=research_conference_2003

Hattie, J. (2009). *Visible learning: A synthesis of over 800 meta-analyses relating to achievement*. Routledge.

Hattie, J. (2012). *Visible learning for teachers: Maximising impact on learning*. Routledge.

Hayes, D., Mills, M., Christie, P., & Lingard, B. (2006). *Teachers & schooling making a difference: Productive pedagogies, assessment and performance*. Routledge. https://doi.org/10.4324/9781003117643

Hopkins, D. (2013). *Exploding the myths of school reform*. ACER Press.

Hord, S. M. (1997). Professional learning communities: What are they and why are they important? *Issues About Change*, *6*(1), 1–8. https://sedl.org/change/issues/issues61/Issues_Vol6_No1_1997.pdf

Hord, S. M. (2009). Professional learning communities: Educators work together toward a shared purpose – improved student learning. *Journal of Staff Development*, *30*(1), 40–43. http://www.ecap-videos.ca/ecap/resources/Hord2009.pdf

Kamins, M. L., & Dweck, C. S. (1999). Person versus process praise and criticism: Implications for contingent self-worth and coping. *Developmental Psychology*, *35*(3), 835–847. https://doi.org/10.1037/0012-1649.35.3.835

Krakovsky, M. (2017, September 20). Why Mindset Matters. *Stanford Magazine*. https://stanfordmag.org/contents/why-mindset-matters

Kruse, S. D., & Louis, K. S. (1993, April 12–16). *An emerging framework for analyzing school-based professional community* [Paper presentation]. Annual Meeting of the American Educational Research Association, Atlanta, Georgia, United States.

Kusimo, P., Ritter, M. G., Busick, K., Ferguson, C., Trumbull, E., & Solano-Flores, G. (2000). *Making assessment work for everyone: How to build on student strengths*. WestEd. https://eric.ed.gov/?id=ED447237

Leader, G. C. (with Stern, A. F.). (2008). *Real leaders, real schools: Stories of success against enormous odds*. Harvard Education Press.

Leaf, C. (2015). *Switch on your brain: The key to peak happiness, thinking, and health*. Baker Publishing Group.

Leahy, S., Lyon, C., Thompson, M., & Wiliam, D. (2005). Classroom assessment: Minute by minute, day by day. *Educational Leadership*, *63*(3), 19–24.

Limeri, L. B., Carter, N. T., Choe, J., Harper, H. G., Martin, H. R., Benton, A., & Dolan, E. L. (2020). Growing a growth mindset: Characterizing how and why undergraduate students' mindsets change. *International Journal of STEM Education*, *7*(35). https://doi.org/10.1186/s40594-020-00227-2

Lunenburg, F. C. (2010). The principal as instructional leader. *National Forum of Educational and Supervision Journal*, *27*(4), 1–6. http://www.nationalforum.com/Electronic%20Journal%20Volumes/Lunenburg,%20Fred%20C.%20The%20Principal%20as%20Instructional%20Leader%20NFEASJ%20V27%20N4%202010.pdf

Maker, C. J., & Shciever, S. W. (2005). *Teaching models in the education of the gifted, third edition*. Pro-Ed.

Marr, B., & Hagston, J. (2007). *Thinking beyond numbers: Learning numeracy for the future workplace*. National Centre for Vocational Education Research. https://www.ncver.edu.au/__data/assets/file/0017/5426/nl05002.pdf

Marzano, R. J., Waters, T., & McNulty, B. A. (2005). *School leadership that works: From research to results*. Association for Supervision and Curriculum Development.

References

McGaw, B. (2013, September 22–24). *Developing 21st century competencies through disciplines of knowledge* [paper presentation]. International Symposium on Education and 21st Century Competencies, Muscat, Sultanate of Oman. http://docs.acara.edu.au/resources/Developing_21st_century_competencies_Prof_Barry_McGaw.pdf

McNaughton S, & Lai, M. K. (2009). A model of school change for culturally and linguistically diverse students in New Zealand: A summary and evidence from systematic replication. *Teaching Education, 20*(1), 55–75. https://doi.org/10.1080/10476210802681733

McTighe, J., & Wiggins, G. (2012). *Understanding by Design® framework.* ASCD. http://www.ascd.org/ASCD/pdf/siteASCD/publications/UbD_WhitePaper0312.pdf

Mehta, J., & Fine, S. (2015). *The why, what, where and how of deeper learning in American secondary schools.* Jobs of the Future.

Meiers, M., Reid, K., McKenzie, P., & Mellor, S. (2013). *Literacy and numeracy interventions in the early years of schooling: A literature review.* Australian Council for Educational Research. http://research.acer.edu.au/policy_analysis_misc/20

Mueller, C. M., & Dweck, C. S. (1998). Praise for intelligence can undermine children's motivation and performance. *Journal of Personality and Social Psychology, 75*(1), 33–52. https://doi.org/10.1037/0022-3514.75.1.33

Mulford, B. (2003). *School leaders: Changing roles and impact on teacher and school effectiveness.* Organization for Economic Co-operation and Development. https://www.oecd.org/education/school/2635399.pdf

Munro, J. (2010, July 29–August 1). *Using the Victorian Essential Learning Standards to differentiate pedagogy for gifted and talented learners* [Paper presentation]. The 11th Asia Pacific Conference on Giftedness, Sydney, NSW, Australia.

Munro, J. (2012, August 27–28). *Effective strategies for implementing differentiated instruction* [Paper presentation]. ACER Research Conference, Sydney, NSW, Australia. http://research.acer.edu.au/cgi/viewcontent.cgi?article=1144&context=research_conference

Munro, J. (2013a). *Gifted students as experts + knowers: A teaching friendly model of gifted knowing and understanding* (CSE Seminar Series, Paper 225). Centre for Strategic Education.

Munro, J. (2013b). *Teaching gifted students: A knowing and thinking-based framework for differentiation.* (CSE Seminar Series, Paper 227). Centre for Strategic Education.

National Curriculum Board. (2009). *Shape of the Australian Curriculum: Mathematics.* Commonwealth of Australia. https://docs.acara.edu.au/resources/Australian_Curriculum_-_Maths.pdf

National Research Council. (2012). *Education for life and work: Developing transferable knowledge and skills in the 21st century.* The National Academies Press. https://doi.org/10.17226/13398

Northcote, M., & McIntosh, A. (1999). What mathematics do adults really do in everyday life? *Australian Primary Mathematics Classroom, 4*(1), 19–21.

Nottingham, J. (2017). *The learning challenge: How to guide your students through the learning pit to achieve deeper understanding.* Corwin.

Ontario Ministry of Education. (2016). *21st century competencies: Foundational document for discussion.* http://edugains.ca/resources21CL/About21stCentury/21CL_21stCenturyCompetencies.pdf

Organization for Economic Co-operation and Development (OECD). (2009). *PISA 2009 assessment framework: Key competencies in reading, mathematics and science.* http://www.oecd.org/pisa/pisaproducts/44455820.pdf

Organization for Economic Co-operation and Development (OECD). (2017). *PISA 2015 assessment and analytical framework: Science, reading, mathematic, financial literacy and collaborative problem solving.* https://doi.org/10.1787/9789264281820-en

Perso, T. (2013). *Numeracy: What classroom teachers should know.* Australian Association of Mathematics Teachers.

Perso, T., & Hayward, C. (2015). *Teaching Indigenous students: Cultural awareness and classroom strategies for improving learning outcomes*. Allen & Unwin.

Reeves, D. B. (2004). *Accountability for learning: How teachers and school leaders can take charge*. ASCD.

Robinson, V. (2007, August 12–14). *The impact of leadership on student outcomes: Making sense of the evidence* [Paper presentation]. The leadership challenge: Improving leadership in schools, ACER Research Conference, Melbourne, Vic, Australia. https://research.acer.edu.au/cgi/viewcontent.cgi?article=1006&context=research_conference_2007

Rowe, K. (2003, October 19–21). *The importance of teacher quality as a key determinant of students' experiences and outcomes of schooling* [Paper presentation]. Building leadership quality: What does the research tell us?, ACER Research Conference, Melbourne, Vic, Australia. https://research.acer.edu.au/cgi/viewcontent.cgi?article=1001&context=research_conference_2003

Sadler, D. R. (1989). Formative assessment and the design of instructional systems. *Instructional Science, 18*, 119–144. http://dx.doi.org/10.1007/BF00117714

Sarra, C. (2005). Strong and smart: Reinforcing Aboriginal perceptions of being Aboriginal at Cherbourg State School (Doctoral thesis, Murdoch University]. https://researchrepository.murdoch.edu.au/id/eprint/1687/

Schill, B., & Howell, L. (2011). Concept-based learning. *Science & Children, 48*(6), 40–45.

Scoular, C., Ramalingam, D., Duckworth, D., & Heard, J. (2020). *Assessment of general capabilities: Skills for the 21st-century learner, final report*. Australian Council for Educational Research. https://research.acer.edu.au/ar_misc/47

Sergiovanni, T. J. (1992). Why we should seek substitutes for leadership. *Educational Leadership, 49*(5), 41–45. http://www.ascd.org/ASCD/pdf/journals/ed_lead/el_199202_sergiovanni.pdf

Sharratt, L., & Fullan, M. (2009). *Realization: The change imperative for deepening district-wide reform*. Corwin Press.

Smale-Jacobse, A. E, Meijer, A., Helms-Lorenz, M., & Ridwan, M. (2019). Differentiated instruction in secondary education: A systematic review of research evidence. *Frontiers in Psychology*. https://doi.org/10.3389/fpsyg.2019.02366

Smith, P., Ladewig, M., & Prinsley, R. (2018). *Improving the mathematics performance of Australia's students* (Occasional paper series). Office of the Chief Scientist. https://www.chiefscientist.gov.au/sites/default/files/Improving-the-mathematics-performance-of-Australias-students.pdf

State of Queensland Department of Education, Training and The Arts. (2018). *P–12 Curriculum Framework: Policy and guidelines for Queensland State Schools*.

Soland, J., Hamilton, L. S., & Stecher, B. M. (2013). *Measuring 21st century competencies: Guidance for educators*. Asia Society. http://asiasociety.org/files/gcen-measuring21cskills.pdf

Southern Regional Education Board (SREB). (2004). *Ten strategies for creating a classroom culture of high expectations: Site development guide #13*. https://www.sreb.org/sites/main/files/file-attachments/04v03_ten_strategies_0.pdf

Stacey, K. (2005). The place of problem solving in contemporary mathematics curriculum documents. *Journal of Mathematical Behaviour, 24*(3–4), 341–350. https://doi.org/10.1016/j.jmathb.2005.09.004

Steen, L. A. (2001). *Mathematics and democracy: The case for quantitative literacy*. National Council on Education and the Disciplines.

Sullivan, P. (2003, July 6–10). *The potential of open-ended tasks for overcoming barriers to learning* [Paper presentation]. Annual conference of the Mathematics Education Research Group of Australia, Geelong, Vic, Australia. javascript://[Uploaded%20files/Annual%20Conference%20Proceedings/2003%20Annual%20Conference%20Proceedings/_Symposium_2Sullivan.pdf]

Thomson, S., Wernert, N., Rodrigues, S., & O'Grady, E. (2020). *TIMSS 2019 Australia highlights*. Australian Council for Education Research. https://doi.org/10.37517/978-1-74286-616-1

References

Timperley, H., Wilson, A., Barrar, H., & Fung, I. (2007). *Teacher professional learning and development: Best evidence synthesis iteration [BES]*. Ministry of Education, New Zealand. http://www.oecd.org/education/school/48727127.pdf

Tollefson, N. (2000). Classroom applications of cognitive theories of motivation. *Educational Psychology Review, 12*, 63–83. https://doi.org/10.1023/A:1009085017100

Tomlinson, C. A., & McTighe, J. (2006). *Integrating differentiated instruction and Understanding by Design*. Hawker Brownlow Education.

Treadwell, M. (2017). *The future of learning: The global curriculum project*. Retrieved on March 3, 2021, from https://www.academia.edu/36103044/The_Future_of_Learning

Unger, C. (1994). What teaching for understanding looks like. *Educational Leadership, 51*(5), 8–10. http://www.ascd.org/publications/educational-leadership/feb94/vol51/num05/What-Teaching-for-Understanding-Looks-Like.aspx

Vygotsky, L. S. (1978). *Mind in society: The development of higher psychological processes* (M. Cole, V. John-Steiner, S. Scribner, & E. Souberman, Eds.). Harvard University Press.

Wanzek, J., & Vaughn, S. (2011). Is a three-tier reading intervention model associated with reduced placement in special education?. *Remedial and Special Education, 32*(2), 167–175. https://doi.org/10.1177/0741932510361267

Weiner, B. (1972). Attribution theory, achievement motivation, and the educational process. *Review of Educational Research, 42*(2), 203–215. https://doi.org/10.3102/00346543042002203

Wiliam, D. (2013). Assessment: The bridge between teaching and learning. *Voices from the Middle, 21*(2), 15–20. https://library.ncte.org/journals/VM/issues/v21-2/24461

Willis, S. (1992, October 9–11). *Being numerate: Whose right? Who's left?* [Keynote address]. The right to literacy: The rhetoric, the romance, the reality: Australian Council for Adult Literacy National conference, Sydney, NSW, Australia.

Willis, S. (1998). Which numeracy? *UNICORN, 24*(2), 32–41.

Index

Note: Page numbers in italics indicate information appearing in tables or illustrations.

A

AAMT (Australian Association of Mathematics Teachers), 5, 97, 98–99
ACARA (Australian Curriculum, Assessment and Reporting Authority), 5, 32. *see also* Australian Curriculum
acceleration, 79–80, 82
achievement data. *see* data
ACSF (Australian core skills framework), 150, 153
AEDC (Australian Early Development Census), 60
AITSL (Australian Institute for Teaching and School Leadership), 115, 150–154, 155–157
Alice Springs (Mparntwe) Education Declaration, 27, 89, 170
APST (Australian Professional Standards for Teachers), 115, 143, 155–157
    numeracy testing, 150–154
assessment. *see also* data; NAPLAN (National Assessment Program – Literacy and Numeracy)
    definition, 89–90
    grading, 79, 80, 84, 99, *99–100*
    higher-order skills, 94–95
    improving, 141–142
    lesson planning, 66
    maths concepts, 93–96
    NAPLAN tests, 101–110
    numeracy, 97–102
    open-ended questions, 95–96
    quality, 90–93
    test formats, 104–105
    types, 90, 92
attitude, 6, 25, 163. *see also* confidence
    can do attitude, 50
    cultural mindset, 171
    growth mindset, 76, 78–79, 171
    motivation, 124–125
    praise, 78–79, 125
    role of expectations, 77–78
    self-efficacy, 125
    students, 75–79, 141
Australian Association of Mathematics Teachers. *see* AAMT (Australian Association of Mathematics Teachers)
Australian core skills framework. *see* ACSF (Australian core skills framework)
Australian Curriculum. *see also* general capabilities
    across school years, 61–62, *69, 72*, 173–192 (*see also under specific* Years)
    assessment, 97
    differentiation, 64, 66, 67–68, 80, 86
    gaps in student knowledge, 63–66
    learning areas, 38–45
    lesson planning, 64–66
    maths, 29–31, 57, *69*, 159–162
    numeracy, 5, 27–34, *29, 39–41, 43–45*, 159–162
Australian Curriculum, Assessment and Reporting Authority. *see* ACARA (Australian Curriculum, Assessment and Reporting Authority)
Australian Early Development Census. *see* AEDC (Australian Early Development Census)
Australian Institute for Teaching and School Leadership. *see* AITSL (Australian Institute for Teaching and School Leadership)
Australian Professional Standards for Teachers. *see* APST (Australian Professional Standards for Teachers)

B

Bloom's taxonomy, 54, 55–57, *81*, 142

C

capabilities, 170
    assessment of, 101
    context, 10–12, 13
    definition, 5, 6–7
    financial literacy, *158*
    importance of, 27
    literacy, 9–10
    numeracy, 6–7, 27–28
    in teaching, 155
capacity building in schools, 121–122
case study: Mundaring Christian College, 140–147
cognitive conflict, 110
cognitive struggle, 25, 58
collaboration, 8
    benefits, 124, 126

culture, 128
data analysis, 119–121, 131–132, 136–137
PLCs (professional learning communities), 113–114, 167–168
PLTs (professional learning teams), 114–115, 131
communication skills, 8, 23–24
concept-focused teaching, 51–52, 82, 104
    assessment, 96
    versus content-focused teaching, 51–55, 57–59, 169
    rooted in content-focused teaching, 53
confidence, 11, 17, 32, 42. *see also* attitude
    financial literacy, 157–158
    increasing, 23, 34, 38, 48
    praise, 78–79
    in teachers, 149, 163
content-focused teaching, 51–55, 57–59, 82, 169
context-specific numeracy, 13, 15
continuous improvement, 128, 133. *see also* lifelong learning
core skills framework. *see* ACSF (Australian core skills framework)
critical and creative thinking, 7, 8, 17, 18, 170
critical numeracy, 12–13, 17, 22–23
curriculum. *see* Australian Curriculum
curriculum differentiation, 64, 66, 67–68, 80, 86

D

data
    analysis, 114, 120–121, 131–133, 141
    from assessments, 90, 93–95, 136
    collaborative analysis, 119–121, 131–132, 136–137
    data literacy, 33, 115, 136, 141
    hypotheses, 132, 136
    importance of, 89
    intervention planning, 86
    from NAPLAN tests, 105–106, 116–118, 143–145
    numeracy improvement, 115–121, 130, 131–132, 136
    on students, 118–120
data over time, 116–119, 147
data sources, 86
    AEDC (Australian Early Development Census), 60
    assessment, 90, 93–95, 136
    NAPLAN tests, 105–106, 116–118
    school records, 60
deep learning, 17, 32, 62, 82
    assessment of, 104
    big idea concepts, 51, 53, 59
    teaching, 50–58
digital literacy, 168

E

employment, 8, 168–169
equity in learning, 82–85, 93, 123
extension, 63, 79–82, *85*
EYLF (Early Years Learning Framework), 30, 61

F

families, *16,* 60, 130
financial literacy, 157–159, 168
fixed mindset, 76. *see also* attitude; growth mindset
Foundation. *see* Years F–2
foundational learning, 27, 54, 61
    evaluation, 65–66
    literacy, 5, 8
    maths skills, 63, 66, 69–70, 74, 84
    numeracy, 5, 8–9, 110, 169

G

general capabilities, 170
    assessment of, 101
    context, 10–12, 13
    definition, 5, 6–7
    financial literacy, *158*
    importance of, 27
    literacy, 9–10
    numeracy, 6–7, 27–28
    in teaching, 155
gifted and talented students, 79–80, 81, 82, 84
grading, 79, 80, 84, 99, *99–100*
growth mindset, 76, 78–79, 171. *see also* attitude

H

higher-order thinking, 8, 29, 81–82, 107
    assessment of, 92, 94–95
    need for, 170
    teaching, 54, 57–58, 141

I

improvement
    case study: Mundaring Christian College, 140–147
    celebration, 143–145
    goals and targets, 129, 141
    guiding questions, 113–114, 131
    planning, 136–140
    principles, 132–133
    process, 114, 169–170
    whole-school approach, 121–126, 131–140
innovation, 8
intervention, 67–74
    definition, 63, 74
    focus of, 123
    levels, 134–136
    one-on-one support, 75
    planning, 86
    school-level approach, 122–123, 134–136
    turbocharged intervention, 74–75, *134, 135*

K

knowledge base, 10–12, 31

L

LANTITE. *see* literacy and numeracy test for initial teacher education (LANTITE)

Index

learning. *see also* foundational learning
    big conceptual steps, 68–70
    equity, 82–85, 93, 123
    flexibility, 136
    goals, 26, 27
    maximising, 137
    outside classrooms, 46–47
    progression, 71, 74
    quality, 80–81, 84–85
lesson planning, 36, 82–85. *see also* pedagogy; teaching
    backward design, 83, 91
    concept-focused, 59
    curriculum alignment, 64–66
    gaps in student knowledge, 63–66
    numeracy demands, 38
    numeracy opportunities, 42
    problem-solving, 81
    review, 65–66
    use of assessment, 66, 90
lifelong learning, 27, 155, 170. *see also* continuous improvement
literacy
    as capability, 6–7, 9–10
    definition, 9
    dimensions of, *10*
    as foundational skill, 5, 8, 171
    relationship with numeracy, 9–12, 139–140, 154
literacy and numeracy test for initial teacher education (LANTITE), 150–154
lower-order thinking, 54, 56

M

mathematical fluency, 105
mathematical literacy, 6, *18*, 168
maths
    across school years, 13–16, 61–62
    application of, 14–15, 21–22, 34, 46, 57
    assessment, 93–96
    deep understanding, 55–56
    distinct from numeracy, 8, 16–17
    foundations, 63, 66, 69–70, 74, 84
    in learning, 33–34
    learning outcomes, 61–62
    need for, 5, 11, 13–14, 22, 33–34, 50, 62
    non-maths areas, 33–34, 38–45
    progressive, 65–66, 69–70
    relationship with numeracy, 29–32
    surface-level understanding, 55–56
    teaching maths well, 49–50
    in unfamiliar contexts, 104, 154
memorisation, 54
mindset, 76, 78–79, 171. *see also* attitude; school culture
modelling
    improvement, 142
    numeracy skills, 4, 16
    outside learning contexts, 46–47
    problem-solving, 24–25, 38
motivation, 124–125
Mundaring Christian College, 140–147

N

NAPLAN (National Assessment Program – Literacy and Numeracy), 49
    and Australian Curriculum, 102
    as data source, 105–106, 116–118, *119*, 143–145, 146–147
    numeracy assessment, 8, 98, 102–104
    numeracy testing format, *103*, *104*–105, *109*
    preparation for, 106–110
National numeracy review report, 18, 46, 171
NNLP (national numeracy learning progression), 14, 32–33, 70–74
    and Australian Curriculum, 71, *72*
numeracy
    across school years, 13–16, 28–33, 61–62, 173–192
    as attitude, 6, 163
    as capability, 6–7, 27–28
    context-specific numeracy, 13, 15
    critical numeracy, 12–13, 17, 22–23
    definition, 1, 5–6, 17, 32
    difficulties in assessing, 97–98, 101–102, 110
    dimensions of, 11, 16
    distinct from maths, 8, 16–17
    error tolerance, 13, 15, 21, 97, 158
    financial literacy, 157–159
    as foundational skill, 5, 8–9, 110, 169, 171
    importance of, 1, 8–9, 169
    levels in Australia, 14, 49, 168, 171
    literacy and numeracy test for initial teacher education (LANTITE), 150–154
    non-learning contexts, 46–47
    numeracy demands across curriculum, 28, 33–34, 38–41, 71, 173–192
    numeracy opportunities across curriculum, 28, 34, 42–45, 48
    planning, 136–140
    relationship with literacy, 9–12, 139–140, 154
    relationship with maths, 29–32
    school-level assessment, 97–101
    teaching, 16–17, 32, 156–157
    and text, 18–19
Numeracy across the curriculum, 36–38, 50, 171
numeracy moments, 35–38, 48

O

OECD (Organisation for Economic Co-operation and Development), 8, 49. *see also* PISA (Programme for International Student Assessment)
open-ended questions, 95–96

P

pedagogy. *see also* extension; intervention
    Bloom's taxonomy, 54, 55–57, *81*, 142
    content-focused *versus* concept-focused teaching, 51–55, 57–59, 169
    curriculum alignment, 64–66
    differentiation, 64, 66, 67–68, 80, 36

pedagogical style, 38
research-based, 68, 71
SOLO (Structure of the Observed Learning
    Outcomes) model, 54, 57
PIAAC (Programme for International Assessment of
    Adult Competencies), 150
PISA (Programme for International Student
    Assessment), 6, 17–18, 49
PLCs (professional learning communities)
    definition, 113–114
    guiding questions, 113–114, 167–168
PLTs (professional learning teams)
    celebrating achievements, 125, 143–145
    collaborative data assessment, 119–121,
        131–132, 136–137
    collective problem-solving, 123
    definition, 114–115
    improving learning, 114, 131–133, 139–140
    numeracy planning, 137
policy, 149–150, 154, 170, 172
principals, 126–129, 167–168
problem-solving
    assessing, 91, 98–99, 101
    designing curriculums, 81
    dimension of numeracy, 11–13, 17–19
    five-step model, 19–25
    framework, 19–25, 170
    levels in Australia, 169
    literacy in, 10
    modelling, 24–25
    teaching, 19–25, 107–110
    tool for deep learning, 53
    tool for increasing numeracy, 23, 170
    whole-school approach, 124, 125, 132, 137
professional learning communities. *see* PLCs
    (professional learning communities)
professional learning teams. *see* PLTs (professional
    learning teams)
Programme for International Assessment of
    Adult Competencies. *see* PIAAC
    (Programme for International
    Assessment of Adult Competencies)
Programme for International Student Assessment. *see*
    PISA (Programme for International
    Student Assessment)
psychology. *see also* confidence
    can-do attitude, 50
    cultural mindset, 171
    growth mindset, 76, 78–79, 171
    motivation, 124–125
    praise, 78–79, 125
    role of expectations, 77–78
    self-efficacy, 125
    students, 75–79, 141

Q
quality assessment, 90–93

R
reasoning
    justification skills, 22, 107–110
    students' use of, 24, 54
    teaching, 141, 169
role model. *see* modelling
rote learning, 54

S
school community, 113, 126, 130
school culture, 77–78, 114, 119, 121–122, 124–125,
    127, 128
school leaders
    capacity building, 122
    collaborative culture, 119
    commitment to improvement, 113–115,
        170
    decision-making, 129
    guiding questions, 167–168
    planning, 140
    role in school improvement, 129–130, 148
schools
    capacity building, 121–122
    as community, 113, 126, 130
    continuous improvement, 128, 133
    culture, 77–78, 114, 119, 121–122, 124–125,
        127, 128
    improvement, 117, 121–126, 128, 133,
        140–148, 170
    intervention, 122–123, 134–136
    leadership, 128–129
    low expectations, 77, 123
    numeracy outcomes, 130–131
    numeracy planning, 136–140
    resources, 127
    role of principals, 126–129
    role of school leaders, 129–130
    support for teachers, 123–126, 128–129
    teamwork, 124, 126, 128
    whole-school perspective, 139–140
shared problem-solving, 124
SOLO (Structure of the Observed Learning
    Outcomes) model, 54, 57
standards
    APST (Australian Professional Standards
        for Teachers), 115, 143,
        150–154, 155–157
    improvement, 141, 143
    literacy and numeracy test for initial teacher
        education (LANTITE),
        150–154
    numeracy in students, 49, 170
    numeracy in teachers, 154
student development, 14–15, 71
students
    backgrounds, 60, 75, 123
    community members, 27
    expectations of, 77–78, 79, 81, 123
    gaps in knowledge, 63–64, 67, 70–71
    gifted and talented, 79–80, 81, 82, 84
    psychology, 75–79, 141
    range of abilities, 64, 85

response to intervention, 136
self-conception, 76
standards, 31–32, 75, 143, 170
student development, 14–15, 71
superficial learning, 32, 50, 52
support for teachers, 124–125, 128–129, 130

T

teachers, 34–38. *see also* school leaders
- APST (Australian Professional Standards for Teachers), 115, 143, 150–154, 155–157
- attitudes, 75–76, 89–90, 136
- career levels, 155, 156–157
- commitment to improvement, 113–115, 130, 131–133
- data literacy, 115, 136, 141, 166
- education of, 57, 149–154
- expectations of students, 77–78, 79, 81, 123
- guiding questions, 167–168
- increased expectations of, 52, 149
- knowledge of students, 60–62
- literacy and numeracy test for initial teacher education (LANTITE), 150–154
- low expectations, 77, 123
- moral imperative, 123
- motivation, 124–125
- numeracy of, 1–2, 16, 36, 50, 149, 150–154, 166
- one-on-one support, 75
- professional development, 132, 155
- self-evaluation, 133, 157, 159–162, 163–165
- standards, 142, 149–150, 155–157
- support for, 124–125, 128–129, 130
- testing of, 149–154

teaching. *see also* concept-focused teaching; content-focused teaching; intervention; lesson planning; pedagogy
- acceleration, 79–80, 82
- adapting to students, 64–66
- challenging all students, 82–85
- content-focused *versus* concept-focused, 51–55, 57–59, 169
- content knowledge, 69, 80
- data-driven, 86, 105–106, 116–121
- emphasis on effort, 79
- emphasis on grades, 78
- extension, 63, 79–82, *85*
- flexibility in, 65
- inquiry-based approach, 38, 58
- learning goals, 64–66, 82, 91
- numeracy moments, 35–38, 48
- pedagogical moments, 66
- rubrics, 82, 83, 85, *99–100*, 99–101
- scaffolding, 67, 69, 82, 84
- strategies, 20, 66, 68–75, 107, 122, 156–157
- strategy examples, 37–38, 77–78, 84, 107–110, 139–140
- teaching for understanding, 83–84
- using NAPLAN tests, 107

teaching maths well, 49–62

TIMSS (Trends in International Mathematics and Science Study), 49
twenty-first century competencies, 8, 9, 159, 170

W

whole-school improvement, 121–126
- benefits, 125–126
- capacity building, 121–122
- case study: Mundaring Christian College, 140–147
- celebration, 125, 143–145
- culture, 77–78, 114, 119, 121–122, 124–125, 127, 128
- data over time, 116–119, 147
- effects on numeracy, 143, 146–147
- focus on numeracy, 130–133, 136–140
- intervention, 122–124, 134–136
- principals, 126–129
- school as community, 113, 126, 130
- school leaders, 129–130
- support for teachers, 124–125
- teachers, 130

Y

Years F–2
- Australian Curriculum, 61, *69, 72,* 173–192
- intervention, *85*
- maths skills, 14
- numeracy, *16, 30, 39–41, 43–45*

Years 3–6
- Australian Curriculum, 61–62, *69, 72,* 173–192
- intervention, *85*
- maths skills, 14
- numeracy, *16, 30, 39–41, 43–45*

Years 7–10
- maths skills, 14–15
- numeracy, *16, 30*

Years 11–12
- maths skills, 15
- numeracy, *16*

www.ingramcontent.com/pod-product-compliance
Lightning Source LLC
Chambersburg PA
CBHW051310110526
44590CB00031B/4362